ORE

SMALL BOAT TO NORTHERN GERMANY

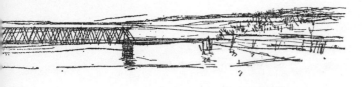

SMALL BOAT TO
NORTHERN GERMANY

BY

ROGER PILKINGTON

Illustrated by David Knight

MACMILLAN
London · Melbourne · Toronto
ST MARTIN'S PRESS
New York

© Roger Pilkington 1969

First published in 1969 by
MACMILLAN AND CO LTD
Little Essex Street London WC2
and also at Bombay Calcutta and Madras
Macmillan South Africa (Publishers) Pty Ltd Johannesburg
The Macmillan Company of Australia Pty Ltd Melbourne
The Macmillan Company of Canada Ltd Toronto
St Martin's Press Inc New York
Gill and Macmillan Ltd Dublin

Library of Congress catalog card no. 78–97941

Printed in Great Britain by
ROBERT MACLEHOSE AND CO LTD
The University Press Glasgow

Du bist der Mann Herr Jesu Christ
Dem Wind und Meer gehorsam ist.
Drum halt in Gnaden deine Hand
Auch über unserm Schifferstand.
Vor Sturm, vor Räuber und Gefahr
Herr, unsere Seefahrt stets bewahr.

Lass die Gesellschaft und Gemein
Der Schiffer Dir empfohlen sein.
Gib Frieden, Freund und Einigkeit,
Bewahr dies Haus vor allem Leid,
Dein Segen sich hei uns vermehr,
Dir sei, o Gott, allein die Ehr.

> Verses over the door of the Schiffergesellschaft
> or Shipmen's Guild, in Lübeck

Thou art the man, Lord Jesus Christ,
The man whom storm and sea obey.
Extend thy saving hand we pray
In blessing o'er our shipmen's trade,
From storm and piracy and harm
Protect, O Lord our voyaging.

May this our shippers company
Be all acceptable to thee.
Give peace and love and unity,
Protect this house from every ill.
Thy blessings on us multiply.
The glory be, O God, to thee.

Kein guter Boots- und Steuermann
Ohn' Beten und Singen fahren kann.

> – Old North German saying

No boatman good and steersman strong
Can voyage without prayer and song.

MAPS

The course of the *Thames Commodore* from the Schlei
to the Mittelland Canal   *page* 4
From Schleimünde to Haddeby   24–5
From Geesthacht to Lübeck   88

FOREWORD

FOR the *Thames Commodore* all voyages begin on the Thames. That is only right and proper, for she was built at Teddington, within the first two hundred yards of the tidal Thames, that river which ebbs and flows beneath London's bridges and carries on its broad bosom lighters, dead fish, some rather dirty swans, the cutters of the Metropolitan Police and a surprising amount of driftwood; and probably once a year the *Thames Commodore* herself, outward bound for another voyage of inland exploration or inward homing with Christmas shopping accomplished and a reasonable quantity of French and German wine stowed under the floorboards and duly declared and excised at Ramsgate.

Yet the actual narrative of this, the fifteenth volume of voyaging, cannot start at Teddington or Limehouse, and that for a good reason. Ten years ago I wrote *Small Boat to the Skagerrak*, which wove a tale all the way from Holland across part of Germany and up through the Danish isles to thread the hundred miles of Sweden's skerry coast and end at last in Norway, but as time goes on and life loses much of its unnecessary haste the journeying itself seems mysteriously to become expanded and the mileage per page decreases. This, I think is all to the good, but it poses problems for me as a writer. I may plan to write a book about a voyage on the Moselle, but once the spirit of that river has established herself on my table, swinging her legs over the edge and smiling at me the while in her diaphanous and watery gown whilst reminiscing about Ausonius, the Electors, the vintners and the fair maidens of long ago, I have to make it two volumes and not one, just to please her. And so it has been with the northern lands also.

The *Thames Commodore* sailed from Limehouse one night in March, locking out from the Regent's Canal Dock at high water and turning her nose toward the Isle of Dogs, the Nore and the Baltic. I believed that her voyage would be interesting, and that during the winter evenings I could rake over the stock of my memories and maybe write another book of inland and coastal discovery. Yet once again a weird being visited me, and this time it was Ekke Nekkepen the merman king who flopped into my study, curled his wet tail beneath him in my armchair, and told me that this would never do. The Isles of Denmark could not be dismissed in a score or two of pages. I must not skimp them as I did last time, he said.

So I obeyed. And when I had written as much as any reader could wish to carry home or Macmillans could manage to squeeze into the costing sheet I had to stop. And there we were, at Elsinore, with Hamlet's ghost whiffling over the ramparts. It would need another whole book to bring us home again, particularly if we were to explore the Schlei, visit Europe's oldest canal, and bump the bows against the Iron Curtain at the entrance to Germany's Eastern Zone.

That is why this book starts in so curious a place as Latitude 54° 46′ North and exactly 10 degrees of Longitude East of Greenwich – or, to put it in such a way that one may visualise it more clearly, some 750 miles due east of Durham cathedral. The position is in fact in the sea, in the comparatively shallow water off the low cliffs of Schleswig Holstein. The time is about one hour after noon on a clear August day of light breeze following a traditional Baltic storm, and the *Thames Commodore* has been on the way since three o'clock in the morning, when she disturbed the yachtsmen sleeping in the harbour of Faaborg on the Danish island of Fyn by starting up her engines and disappearing into the night. Threading her way through the shoals and turning one winking buoy after another she headed for the Aabenraa fjord three hours away, turned down to the sound of Als and stopped in Sønderborg to have breakfast, buy fuel and lay in a final stock of delicious Danish pickled herring before aiming southeastward to cross the imaginary frontier line and chug out of Denmark's waters into those of the Bundesrepublik.

It is twenty minutes since the red-and-white *Dannebrog* of the Danes was hauled down from the yard-arm and the black-red-gold of Western Germany run up to take its place as courtesy flag.

Looking astern we can still see Danish Als, and just visible as a smudge on the horizon to port the Isle of Aerø. We are just about to enter the Kieler Bucht, and those stowing away for the next 200 pages will do well to heed the warning in vol. 1 of the *Baltic Pilot*, that 'firing, mining, boom, submarine and similar practices must always be expected in the Kieler Bucht'. There is also an ammunition dumping ground in which presumably ammunition is dumped, but this is something of which any peaceable person will approve. It is one of the economic dilemmas of Western Europe that every country makes great quantities of shot and shell, but as they nevermore fire a shot in anger these must all be dumped in the sea. A politician once explained to me that this was the only possible solution, for if production were reduced what would become of the thousands of mine-stuffers, torpedo-aligners, shell-founders, cordite growers and diggers of villainous saltpetre? Poured into the sea the stuff could do little harm, and it probably provided a good home for conger eels.

All the same, the thought of stranding on a pile of hand grenades is not a pleasant one, and voyagers will be relieved to know that we shall only have to endure the navigational terrors of the Kieler Bucht for a few minutes more. Ahead lies a buoy – which we can already just make out through the binoculars – and there we shall turn and head up through the gap in the coastline to take refuge in the Schlei from the mines, torpedoes and guns which otherwise might be fired at us. In the Schlei all will be safe and reassuring – until we turn up the page in the *Baltic Pilot* and discover that 'vessels should exercise the utmost caution with regard to the buoyage when using this channel, because the buoys are frequently rammed by vessels and damaged or carried away'. This is frightening indeed, but at least it is reassuring to note that the swing bridge at Kappeln cannot be opened when a train is passing over it.

But we must not run too far ahead. Let us turn the buoy and aim just to the left of the lighthouse which stands on the tip of the mole half a mile in front of us, and enter a waterway which one thousand years ago was among the busiest in all the world.

Highgate, 1969 ROGER PILKINGTON

The Schlei

I

Into the Schlei – Schleimünde and Maasholm – Kappeln,
port of Anglia – home of the English – the ship of Skeaf –
the wind-maker of Sieseby – Ulsnis and Rieseby – the night
of the Star of Darkness – King Abel rides again

I HAD passed the mouth of the Schlei eleven years earlier. It was
on a day of Baltic blue, when the midsummer sun blazed astern
to throw a train of golden sparkle from our wake. The water was so
still that our own wash made the only disturbance in the wide surface of the sea, for although there were other craft on our course

I

they were all sailing yachts from Kiel which had hopefully left on the breeze of dawn and now lay quite motionless, the little wind-ribbons from their mastheads dangling downwards as though tired of holding up their arms to feel for a breath of wind where none existed. The sea was as transparent as only the Baltic can be, and through the azure of the upper layer the jellyfish in which this Eastern Sea abounds tolled their leisurely and silent bells as we passed.

We ran up the coast about half a mile offshore, but we did not turn in by the Schleimünde lighthouse. Looking back, I think this was partly because of the name of the inlet itself. Hundreds of boatmen must have been deterred from exploring one of the finest rivers of Europe because it is called the Meuse – or, which is even worse – the Maas. It is not just the recollection of the First World War, now grown dim, but the grey, cold, fog-bound name itself which somehow works upon the imagination, yet does so quite wrongly. It is the same with the Schlei. Chill, muddy, perhaps with a trace of slyness about it, the name is enough to make any boatman set course for the Danish isles further ahead. Besides, if the boat happens to be British the steersman will almost certainly have read *The Riddle of the Sands* by Erskine Childers.

It is difficult for a boatman to sail those waters without wondering at the stupidity of politicians who could have the author hanged for becoming involved in the 'troublous times' of that poor country of Ireland, and impossible to forget the hue and cry over the sands and watts and among the siels as the *Dulcibella* followed the trail of the crafty Dollman in the smart yacht *Medusa*. And it was at Schleimünde that the *Dulcibella* waited in the fog beside the barge *Johannes*, and the mystified Carruthers sat on his bunk while Davies told him of Dollman's curious attempt to wreck him on the sands outside the Elbe. Apart from the few sailing-barges or trading schooners lying at anchor close inside the entrance 'the only sign of life was a solitary white house – the pilot's house, the chart told us – close to the northern point of the entrance'. It was just the right setting for the careful relation of the background to one of the greatest spy stories ever written, and even now a reader can feel the chill fog drifting over the marshy flats of the Schleswig coast.

That book was written more than sixty years ago, but I doubt if Schleimünde has changed. The barges still trade to Kappeln, though nowadays they have motors, but Schleimünde itself is still a desolate place consisting of the same solitary white pilot-house, a stage for a customs cutter, and a scatter of huts concerned with the lighthouse and signal station. Otherwise there is nothing on this bar of dune, which runs down to groynes on its outer side and trails off into brackish marsh on the inner. In fact it is an island, separated by muddy watts and swamp from the mainland of Angeln to the north, that Anglia from which came some of our fore-fathers long ago. To the south is the Schlei mouth itself, then more marsh and dunes before the bare moles of the harbour of Olpcnitz – a private harbour belonging to the navy and therefore extremely *verboten*. Schleimünde must be a lonely place to carry on the trade of a pilot, and no doubt it is a pleasant relief to take a cargo ship up to the commercial wharf at Schleswig and do the wife's shopping before homing in the little private railway of the one-time State of Schleswig.

The channel which runs in by the lighthouse is a new one. The older Schleimünde lay a mile or two further north, and it was a place of busy trading and shipment. Attacked by Vikings and plundered by raiders, its position was always in danger, and in the fifteenth century the Dukes of Holstein dealt it a different kind of blow when they sunk a dozen ships in the channel, laden with stones. This certainly protected the Schlei from hostile vessels, but it also caused such sanding that an exit could hardly be kept open at all. Eventually there came a great storm, and in a single night the faded and decaying settlement was wiped away by the waves. Mynnaesby it was called – Mouthpoint town one might say – and from that night Mynnaesby was no more. Not even its position is known for certain.

Further up the Schlei there were several communities of shippers and fishermen who needed a much better channel than the old silted entrance past the vanished village, and in the eighteenth century they joined together to buy a piece of land and cut a broad new shipway through it, a channel which has served ever since. At the time of its construction the Schlei was Danish,

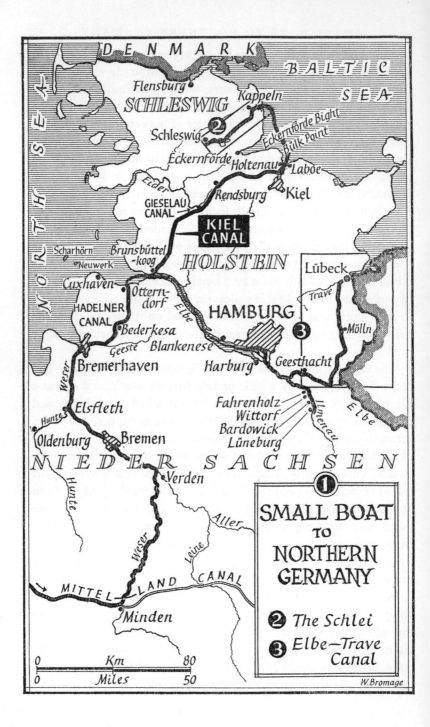

DENMARK

NORTH SEA

BALTIC SEA

Flensburg

SCHLESWIG

Kappeln

② Schleswig

Eckernförde Bight

Bülk Point

Eckernförde

Holtenau

Laboe

Eider

Rendsburg

Kiel

GIESELAU
CANAL

KIEL
CANAL

Scharhörn

Brunsbüttel
-koog

HOLSTEIN

Lübeck

Neuwerk

Trave

Cuxhaven

Ottern-
dorf

Elbe

HAMBURG

Mölln

HADELNER
CANAL

Bederkesa

③

Geeste

Blankenese

Harburg

Geesthacht

Bremerhaven

Elbe

Elsfleth

Fahrenholz
Wittorf
Bardowick
Lüneburg

Ilmenau

Hunte

Oldenburg

Bremen

NIEDER SACHSEN

Hunte

Verden

①

SMALL BOAT
TO
NORTHERN
GERMANY

Weser

Aller

Leine

② *The Schlei*

③ *Elbe–Trave*
Canal

MITTEL LAND CANAL

Minden

| 0 | Km | 80 |
| 0 | Miles | 50 |

W. Bromage

and during the regrettable trouble with Nelson and his pestilential ships the Danes wisely closed the Schlei with a chain to prevent English ships from running in and bombarding the places along its shores.

Schleimünde, or its forerunner of Mynnaesby, once flourished on the trade in cod. If today a cod is occasionally caught in the broad water inside the dunes this can only be because the poor fish has lost its way and taken the wrong turning, for the Schlei is closed to cod. These fish, people say, stay away from the inlet because they were told to. Once they brought great riches to the Angles, and they were so common that even the serving wenches grew tired of eating them. Remembering my own schooldays I can understand this, for my recollection is of cod, cod, cod, and kedgeree. Even then we had less of it than the Mynnaesbyers and their neighbours, and it is not astonishing that one brave girl at last revolted. Snatching a large cod from the catch she pushed a skewer through one eye and out at the other, and flung the poor creature out into the waves of the Kieler Bucht.

'Depart,' she screamed. 'Go! Happy swimmings, but never may a cod find the way to the Schlei again.'

The girl must have been delighted when the codfish failed to return in their swarms. The diet on the farms was probably changed to venison, and even if one day she began to feel surfeited with stag too, for a while the change must have been pleasant. But the fishermen and curers were angry, and altogether I think the girl was lucky not to have been strangled – or, if she was under age, merely buried alive with her mouth stuffed full of clay, which was the specially considerate treatment reserved for those regarded as too young to be broken on the wheel or pinched to death with red-hot tongs.

We ran straight past the customs jetty, for I have always believed that if there is any real need to be certificated and cleared the officers will leap into their powerful cutter and come chasing up behind. They did not do so, but merely gave us a friendly wave as we passed through into a wide mere where the water stretched away for a mile either side of the buoyed course across it. There were eider ducks and mallard and gulls on the water, and terns twisting

Maasholm

and calling over our stern. Hundreds or perhaps thousands of swans sat mirrored on the rather yellowish expanse, and when swans sit in flocks on the sea it means only one thing – that the bottom is so close beneath their downy keels that they have only to bend their necks to pluck another beakful of shloopy grass-weed from the sea floor. This outer part of the Schlei is in fact extremely shallow, much of it being no more than two feet deep. In places it must have been less, for the waves of our wake would run out to break on hidden sand bars and send foamy after-ripples to wash the knees of gulls standing in the shallow sea.

Across the first widening of the water Maasholm lay to our right, a little village on the tip of a flat peninsula, a street and a half of houses with its own harbour packed so tight with sturdy white fishing boats that a few had had to drop anchor outside or moor to piles off the shore. Eel boats lay drawn up half out of the water along the beach, and if we did not put in there it was because there did not seem to be any place where the forty-five feet of the *Thames Commodore*'s length could easily find a berth. Passing only a few hundred yards from the harbour we could see that Maasholm was a fishing village and no more, and somehow it reminded us of Marken and Urk in the Ijsselmeer.

In fact Maasholm, like those two Dutch villages, is really an island which has been linked to the landward world by land reclamation and a dike which carries a road, and it shares with them a certain stand-offishness. When in the nineteenth century, E. F. Knight sailed up the Schlei in his yacht *Falcon* he noted that the people would not marry with the mainlanders and would only speak Danish. There were, he said, no more than four or five surnames among them, and as the number of Christian names was limited the individuals had often to be distinguished by nicknames or attributes. For example, there were in the village thirty men named Peter Mass, and he saw a letter for one of them addressed on the envelope to 'The elder of the two Peter Mass's with red hair'. In fact the Maasholmers were truly something of a race apart, and they are believed to have come there by several removes from the old Schlei-mouth village of Mynnaesby when it was overwhelmed, its houses demolished by the sea and its foundations covered by the driven sand. The men and women first founded a new home north of the Schlei entrance, but in the seventeenth century this also was overcome, and in the eighteenth its successor was in turn swept away in a storm. Maasholm was their fourth habitat since Viking days, and it has remained above water, a village for fishermen only.

Twenty minutes from Schleimünde (almost three miles, that is, at the *Thames Commodore*'s cruising speed) we were already beyond buoy N of an alphabet which had begun at the dredged channel in the sea outside. The banks had now closed in, wooded and very beautiful, the Schlei curving away to port like an inland river. Soon Kappeln came into view, at first some chimneys and then a dreamy town of towers and spires, nearly all of which proved to be waterworks or factory buildings but which in the distance gave a curious illusion such as one may have when looking down the lake of London's St James's Park on a hazy evening and seeing at its further end the whole mystery of Byzantium – which in fact is nothing but Scotland Yard, a few government offices, and some particularly unsightly blocks of flats. Kappeln is better than that, for when the town itself opens up it is very charming indeed. There is a long curve of quayside with a dozen fish cutters, some schooners and a couple of rusty old German tramps alongside. Behind, the ground rises so steeply that a flight of age-worn cobbled steps leads up to the baroque church with its elegant tower and the thin tapered spire which has a hint more of Russia than of Denmark or Germany. The station of the Schleswig railway has a pair of baroque gables just to help the view, and very pleasant they look. Behind there is a winding main street and a market-place, and just such a pair of good inns as one would expect to find in any little German town.

Yet Kappeln smelled different from many, for added to the usual aroma of woodsmoke seasoned with a trace of manure we could sniff the strong ingredients of herrings, and chaff or grain dust. This was not surprising, for Kappeln is a place where the fishing craft deliver their catches to the smokeries, and grain is continually pouring down from the tall silos to the tramps and schooners at the wharf. When we drew in, the tractors were waiting in line as far down as the bridge, each pulling one or more carts of grain from the threshers. There were trucks, too, and all this traffic was awaiting its turn to run up to a large round hole in the road. A load would pass over the weighbridge to be checked, and was then moved up so that the cart or truck ran its starboard wheels up a portable wooden ramp and the vehicle came to lie at what looked a precarious angle, its body tilted to port like a ship aground. The bolt would be knocked from that side of the wagon, the flap would fall, and out poured the rich grain with its delicious scent. The wheat cascaded into the roadway and the tilt of the cart made it a matter only of moments to sweep the whole load up to the pile which already was pouring through the open manhole as though disappearing down a drain. Four men with brooms shovelled the grain toward the opening, and with a slight admixture of road dust another ton or two of wheat was soon safely gathered in and carried by elevator belts up into the storage floors of the silos. In at one end, out at the other, for the pipe-lines were continually filling the ships so fast that I wondered the ship's boys who were superintending the outflow into the holds were not buried alive.

At Kappeln we stepped ashore in a land which was curiously related to our own England. We were in fact walking the quay of the capital of Anglia, our ancestral home. It was nothing less than the decline and fall of the Roman Empire which had led the Anglians to leave the Schlei for the land across the North Sea.

In the year 407 the Romans, hard pressed at home by the hordes of Franks, Alemanni, Goths and other vigorous invaders of German origin, were forced to withdraw their occupation troops from outlying parts of their dominions and bring them home to defend the tottering Empire. The cold northern islands of Britain were evacuated and the Celts left to look after themselves.

As soon as news came to Jutland that the holding troops had disappeared southward the Saxons renewed their attempts to conquer the isles of opportunity and mist, and this time they sought allies among the Jutes and the Frisians, but also in their immediate neighbours to the north. These people lived along the narrows (or *Enge*) of the Schlei inlet, and were to be known as Angles. The Anglo-Saxon ships sailed out from the rivers of the German Bight and the coast north of it, and they conquered the islands. They brought over their wives and children, their pots and pans and whatever they could load aboard ship. And they never went back. The name of their land beside the Schlei came to be applied instead to the new country of the Angles across the North Sea. So one may say that the narrow inlet of the Schlei is in fact the Eng- in England.

One of the Anglian boats has been preserved. It was found a century ago, buried in a bog close to the Sound of Als, in what is now southern Denmark. Today it is perhaps the most striking of all the exhibits in the Gottorp Castle Museum at Schleswig, a 75-footer with a beam of 11 feet and seats for about twenty-eight oarsmen. It could have carried some forty-five people with their provisions and weapons, which were placed down the centre of the boat between the two rows of oarsmen. Clinker-built, it was strengthened by ribs secured with thongs to wooden blocks mounted on the planking, and of course it had a large steering oar at one side of the thin stern. There was no keel, only a strengthened keel plank, but the ship is even now a masterpiece of craftsmanship and good design.

At Kappeln the Schlei is crossed by one of its two bridges. With the mast lowered we nosed cautiously up against the current but found that the windshield was two or three inches too high for the closed bridge. However, it was just on opening time – for the span was swung whenever the clock struck the hour – so we were able to lie off and look at the elaborate wooden ice-deflectors which protected the buttresses, and wonder even more at the curious maze of stakes and faggots in the water to port. They had the appearance of a complicated watery maze put there to trap any evil spirit who might dare to enter the Schlei. In fact the fencing was not put there to catch sprites but to trap herrings, and what we were looking at proved to be the last surviving herring trap in Europe. Dozens of such mazes used to exist in the Schlei, for if the heartless maiden with her skewer had driven away the cod their place was quickly taken by the herring which swarmed into the Schlei until they, too, preferred a change of scene. Not that they have all gone, but the Baltic has lost many of its herrings, which no longer drive in through the Sound and the Belts in quite their former millions.

Kappeln's herring trap involves hundreds of yards of paling fence, and it comes into use at Easter when the old fish stream inward to spawn, and at Whitsun when the younger herrings come down from Schleswig, to be followed by the third wave in late autumn when the older fish decide that the time has come to put to sea again. Ashore, the smokeries wait hopefully, knowing that from the trap and the fishboats a good catch can be expected. Then the tang of woody smoke will drift even more strongly through the streets of the little town.

Kappeln – the name obviously tells of a chapel. Presumably it was an early foundation of monks, and the chapel itself was certainly the forerunner of the baroque church which soars above the houses and over its own cluster of churchyard trees. This church is dedicated to St Christopher, but the original chapel to St Nicholas, and as the one is the patron of ferrymen and the other of sailors they give between them a fair indication of why Kappeln is there at all. It was the port for the trade of Anglia, and it was also set at the first narrows where the Schlei could conveniently be crossed.

Above Kappeln and also below the town we found not only swans sitting in groups on the water, but herons standing in the shallows. One does not associate herons with salt water, but if the Schlei is so well stocked with fish any enterprising heron may find it a sensible idea to take up his post somewhere along the flats. Besides, he may be a local bird, for in the trees beside the inlet behind Maasholm are the nests which make up the largest heronry for a very long way, a colony which is said even now to be the largest in all Germany. All up the Schlei these beautiful birds would stand pensively to watch us pass, usually balancing on one foot until the moment our wavelets came to test their acrobatic ability. Then they would fly off, flopping with heavy wing-beats to circle over the fields and marshes before alighting further ahead to watch us again out of the sides of their heads.

Just as the first alphabet is running to its end at black buoy Z the Schlei closes in to a narrow strait where the ferry crosses between Sundsacker on the port side and Arnis, a famous little town of shipbuilding. If at first the houses of Arnis seem unnaturally cramped together this is because it was once an island. Not originally, but after the landowner had decided that it would be an admirable place for a fortification to defend the waterway, and even better if the defences were not built at the tip of a peninsula but were protected by water on every side. So he cut Arnis adrift, and it was not until a century ago that a new causeway was laid to it. Then the marshes to the side of the roadway were little by little reclaimed, so that now Arnis is as much a part of the mainland of Anglia as is Kappeln lower down.

The slipways of Arnis were busy with yachts and fishing-boats as we sailed past, anxious not to tip on our wash some of the new craft lying at the wharf. Then the channel turned a little to starboard to open up one of the most splendid views of all the Schlei, with the water stretching six miles ahead to the next narrows at Lindaunis. To either side of the channel the fishing nets ranged between stakes came almost down to the buoys. These were eel nets, for the Schlei is a wonderful water for eels, but here and there men were also netting from small boats, red or green and black, the traditional boats of the Holm fishermen from the inner end of the waterway. We eased off for these little craft just as we did for the scullers we sometimes met in their coxed fours, and now and again we were close enough to see the fishermen haul in a catch of flounders – for the reach above Arnis is a splendid catchment area for these small flatfish. Indeed, with herrings and eels and flounders the Schlei has everything that most people would want.

We were not the first British ship to enter the Schlei – that honour probably belonged to Mr Knight's *Falcon* a hundred years earlier – but the Red Ensign was a rare enough sight for the fishers afloat and the farm-workers ashore to pause and watch the curious vessel as it passed them. Some fifteen centuries ahead of the *Thames Commodore* another unusual ship had sailed up the Schlei, a craft without sail or oars or rudder. Without crew or pilot it forged up the inlet until at last it drew in to the shore and the people who lived near the bank of the river at what is now Schleswig hurried to the beach to draw the craft up to the land. Lying in the bottom of the boat they found a new-born baby boy, his head on a sheaf of straw. Strewn around him were sword and shield, dagger and helmet, jewellery and riches.

As none knew whence this mysterious infant had come, why the boat was filled with such treasures, or how it had successfully entered the Schlei and navigated all the narrows against wind and current, the people rightly regarded the arrival as a wonder sent by the gods. They called the boy Skeaf (or Sheaf, after the pillow he had lain upon) and as he grew so strong and fair they made him the first king of our forefathers the Angles.

Skeaf's son was named Skild (or Shield) and he became a dearly loved king who for long remained childless. At last in his old age a son was born to Skild, that same Beowulf who was to wrestle with the dragon Grendel and its horrible hag-like water-spirit mother. Once his son and heir was grown into a man Skild's life drew to an end, and his sorrowing people laid his body in the bottom of a boat more richly decorated than any that had ever been seen. Around the corpse they strewed gold and jewels, weapons and trophies until it was filled with treasures as costly as those of the craft in which his father Skeaf had made his unaided landfall on the Schleswig shore. Then they pushed out the boat, wailing as the wind drove it away down the Grosse Breite (the Great Broad, below Schleswig) toward the distant sea. Skild vanished, just as Skeaf had come, disappearing into the distance of wide wave-swept 'Codan' – or the Baltic Sea.

At least, that is the way they like to tell the tale along the shores of the Schlei. In other versions Beowulf was not the offspring of Skild, nor was Skeaf the first King of the Angles. But that matters little. The legend of the boat without a steersman and the infant surrounded by riches is just such a tale as would grow up naturally around the romantic waters of the Schlei. If all history were truly historical, northern Europe might be as arid in its ancestry as a planned new town of modern Britain.

Four miles up from Arnis, the church of Sieseby lay half hidden in its cluster of limes to port, sited on the spot where the legend says that a large space remained clear and bare in the winter snow-fall, leaving an area which was shaped like a cross and so could only be taken as a hint that the monks should build a church on that piece of ground – which they dutifully did. But Sieseby was also known for another curious incident of more special interest to mariners, and especially to sailing men.

With our Perkinses humming happily beneath the saloon floor we were independent of the wind, but for sailing ships certain narrow stretches of the Schlei must always have been difficult indeed if the wind were contrary. However, there used to be a sorceress at Sieseby who was very willing to help where she could, and she often assisted the fishermen of Holm in one way or another. There was not much that she could not fix in return for a dish of fresh fish, of which she was inordinately fond. Maybe she had a number of cats to feed.

One day when the wind was blowing straight down the Schlei some fishermen who wished to return up the inlet to Holm landed at Sieseby and asked the good woman to back the wind through half a circle. This she promised to do in return for the miscellany of fish they could offer her, and she produced from her stock a piece of cloth with three knots in it. The first two they were to untie, one at a time, but the third was not to be touched until their boats were back at Holm.

So the men went aboard, hoisted sail, and immediately began to drive down towards Kappeln because the wind was blowing from the west. When clear of the shore the oldest member of the Guild of Holm Fishers ceremoniously untied the first knot. Instantly the strong westerly ceased, the boats stopped driving seaward, and a fair and moderate easterly breeze sprang up. As the little ships began to make progress toward Schleswig the chief fisherman opened the second knot. At once the easterly increased to force 8, so the little ships flew along with filled sails, surging up the inlet with the wind astern and the waves rolling up usefully behind the boats to give them an extra push on their way.

The fleet quickly made up to Holm and the keels grated on the beach. Then out of curiosity the men urged the Father of the guild to see what might be hidden in the third knot. He untied it, and instantly the gale from the east was replaced by a full hurricane from the west, the waves breaking over the shallows and so lashing the little port that the men had all to leap into the water to draw their ships up to safety.

At Lindaunis the only bridge above Kappeln crosses the water, carrying road and railway together on its span. Much of this girder bridge once served to carry the railway tracks over the Kiel Canal at Rendsburg, but when the original swing bridge had to be replaced by a high-level structure which would not continually hold up the shipping the old one was taken up and the more suitable pieces of it put out to grass on the less busy railway track from Flensburg to Kiel. As we approached it the lifting span glowed bright in its new orange underwear where the painters were giving it a periodic overhaul, and if the road and railway tilted on their heels as though to salute us this was really only because a tall-masted yacht was coming the other way at that moment and the span had to be raised to pass her.

Sieseby, Krieseby and Rieseby, these were only a few of the

by-villages dotted along the course of the Schlei or lying a mile or
two back from the shore as a reminder that the Vikings had once
settled this area, but Rieseby could hardly bear the name of
Giant-town without its being surrounded by a suitable tale. Often
(as in the area of the Flensburg fjord only a few miles further
north) the giants were figures who opposed the idea of putting up
a church and flung stones at it – even firing from as far away as
Fyn, whence a female giant let fly a huge rock which she slung
with her elastic suspender belt. The giants of the Schlei seem to
have been more pious, even if they suffered from the sin of envy
and were rather ill-tempered.

One of these giants lived in Ulsnis (once perhaps Ollenaes, or
Old Man's Ness, the giant himself being the old man). His son
was even more gigantic, and in adolescence he began to revolt
against his father, this tendency being a disease which afflicted
old-time giants as much as it does modern humans, even if there
seems no record of one of the 'little people' ever having left home
in a huff. After one of those familiar scenes about the older genera-
tion being mentally out-of-date the son stormed out of his father's
abode at Ulsnis and waded across the Schlei to the further shore.
As the maximum depth at this point is about two fathoms one can
calculate that he need not necessarily have been an outsize giant to
have done so.

Some way inland the headstrong youth established himself, and
across the water father and son would often shout abuse at each
other. Soon they took to flinging glacial boulders across the sound,
some of which can still be seen lying about the fields. Then the
elder giant began to build a church in Ulsnis, and as the son hated
to be in any way outshone by his father he began another in
Rieseby. Each giant worked furiously to build a higher steeple
than the other, but at last they abandoned all self-control and
started hurling rocks as never before. Soon both steeples had been
knocked off, and as each builder strove to revenge himself he
seized the largest boulder he could find and flung it with all his
might. The result of this domestic quarrel was that both giants
were struck and felled at the same instant. At last the local people
could live in comparative peace, each village being left with a

pleasantly built church to which they had only to add a small spire to support the bell.

A few miles beyond the bridge at Lindaunis the Schlei begins gradually to narrow. To port the dark, tree-clad mound of the Königsburg conceals what appears to be a Bronze Age settlement, but is in fact all that remains of a fortress built five-and-a-half centuries ago to defend the southern shore from the wicked Danes. Somewhere behind it there once stood a place with the rightly sinister name of Finsternstern (or Star of Darkness), but no trace is left of the pilgrimage chapel to which people came from far and near. A few bricks and pieces of charred timber have been turned up in the marshy land behind the deserted fortress in the trees, but that is all. Yet the chapel was once well known, and it was watched over by a monk who cared for the pilgrims and did whatever was necessary. And on one occasion this included a very unusual assignment connected with a notable murder, and it is said that the name Finsternstern was in fact given to the locality after the body was washed ashore there. But that is to jump too quickly to the end of a tale which is perhaps embroidered by the passage of time but which is founded upon a historic quarrel between two brothers.

The tale carries us back to the violent times of the early Danish kings, for at that time the Schlei was within the area of Danish rule. King Valdemar II – Valdemar the Victorious, to whom the Danish flag dropped miraculously from the sky when he was slaughtering the Estonians – had two queens. The first was the fair and generous Dragomir from Bohemia, who so endeared herself to the people that they converted her name to Dagmar (the Maiden of Day, or Bringer of Light) and remembered her across the centuries in some of the most beautiful of all the Scandinavian ballads. But after only two years Dagmar died, and she was replaced by Berengaria, a dark-eyed and dark-hearted beauty from Portugal who made herself as heartily detested as her predecessor had been loved by her subjects. She bore the king two sons, and one of them inherited all the worst characteristics of his mother's nature.

When King Valdemar died, the crown for some reason did not pass to either of Dagmar's sons but to Erik, the better-natured of

the two sons of Berengaria. This Erik is remembered mostly for the
original and unpopular tax he introduced in the form of a levy on
every field-gate through which a plough could pass, and as Erik
Plough-Penny he has become a misty but slightly comic figure in
school history books. His ill-disposed brother Abel had been
fobbed off with the Duchy of Schleswig, an unwise gift because it
put him in a particularly good position to incite the Jutish nobles
and the Duke of Holstein and other German lords against his
brother. He lost no time in doing so, and for years Denmark was
rent by revolt and war until at last King Erik got the upper hand
and forced his brother to swear allegiance. Schleswig should still
be Abel's, but only as a dominion under the Danish crown.

It was perhaps a pity that Erik did not hand over his own
brother to the executioner, but he seems to have been too mild a
man to take such revenge. Indeed, when Abel was again established
in his somewhat restricted ducal authority Erik decided to visit
him in his palace at Schleswig. His friends and advisers besought
him not to be so foolhardy, but Erik was sure that his brother would
forgive and forget, and he insisted upon going to see him.

Duke Abel received the king and treated him to a banquet at
which the food was not even poisoned. After dinner Erik settled
down to a game of chess with one of the nobles, and Abel stood
watching him. A combination perhaps of hot-headedness, anger
and a heavy draught of wine worked upon him until he could no
longer bear the sight of his brother sitting there, calmly playing
chess without the least sign of fear. Suddenly he swept the board
away and overturned the game. Towering over the king he asked
him if he had forgotten the time when he had attacked Schleswig
itself and Abel's own daughter had had to flee barefoot through the
streets like a peasant girl to save herself from Erik's soldiery.

Erik sought as usual to turn aside wrath by a soft answer.
'Patience, my dear brother,' he said. 'If she went barefoot I have
plenty with which to buy her a fine new pair of shoes, now that the
kingdom is mine.'

But he was not to have the chance. The mere mention of his
victory was more than Abel could stand. 'Never shall you do so,'
he shouted, and he ordered his men to seize Erik. Together with

his own chamberlain the king was swiftly carried to the shore of the small island where the castle stood, and bundled into a boat. As it disappeared into the darkness over the water of the Kleine Breite (or Small Broad) Abel quickly sent a messenger to fetch a certain man of violence named Lauge Gudmundsen. Soon this man and his servants were also under way, rowing swiftly down the Schlei to overtake the other boat.

Just where the two craft came together is naturally not known, but it is believed to have been several miles below Schleswig and not very far from the narrows at Missunde, a mile or two upstream of where the pilgrims' chapel lay on the right bank of the Schlei. But, as the second boat began to loom in the darkness and the beat of oars drew close, Erik asked who it might be that was rowing to overhaul them on the water.

'It is Lauge Gudmundsen,' was the reply.

'Then my end has come,' said Erik, for Gudmundsen was one of his bitterest enemies. And he asked his captors just the one favour that he might be allowed to confess his sins and accept the last sacrament from a priest. Then he would die in peace and with a clear conscience.

It was about midnight on that 7 August 1250 that the good monk who kept the chapel heard a knocking at his door. A messenger was there, a servant of Lauge Gudmundsen, and as the monk wrapped his cloak around him the man said that he was to come quickly to confess a man who had been taken dangerously ill on board a ship in the Schlei. The monk hurried down to the shore and the man rowed him out into the narrows and up the Schlei to where a large row-boat floated on the water. Probably there was no light aboard, for the deed which was to be done there was a particularly dark and evil one.

The chronicle tells that the heart of the monk was heavy when he discovered the identity of the alleged sick man in the boat and stepped across to perform the last rites. It must indeed have been an eerie scene, with the oarsmen resting silent, King Erik seated in the boat and listening to the drone of the monk's voice as he recited the office in Latin, while behind him Lauge Gudmundsen stood waiting, his axe raised above his shoulder.

'Amen.' The priest came to the end, and instantly Lauge's mighty axe struck off King Erik's head.

It had of course occurred to Abel that when Erik failed to return from his visit to Schleswig people might naturally become suspicious. He swiftly assembled a number of men who were prepared to swear to the same story, that the king's boat had unfortunately been overset on the way back from the feast, and King Erik himself had most regrettably been drowned. Quite as important was to dispose of the body, and this was taken care of immediately after the beheading. The murderers must have known that if they merely dropped the corpse overboard it would eventually rise and float, so they had set out with the necessary means to dispose of it more permanently. They wound the body in a heavy chain and weighted it with stones before they stealthily slipped it over the gunwale near the Missunde narrows. What became of the monk is not related, but perhaps he was merely threatened with a fearful death if he should say what had happened out on the water.

Missunde is a place where fishermen have sometimes been known to feel a sense of horror, and to see unearthly blue lights dancing upon the water. This strange haunting is connected with the murder of King Erik, and with his reappearance, for in spite of the chain and stones the corpse had no wish to be concealed and before long it rose, weights and all, and drifted to land. The people took the body of their beloved monarch to Schleswig, and as the bier approached the city all the bells began of their own accord to ring. In fact King Erik's grave is still there in the cathedral, and a piece of the sinister chain also hangs upon the wall.

As for Abel, his victory was not to last for long. He took the kingdom which by right had belonged to his brother Erik, but soon he became embroiled in battle with the Frisians. When the fortunes of the fight went against him he was obliged to flee along the dike, and in so doing he had to pass over a siel, a navigable lode which went under the causeway. Unknown to him, a wheelwright named Wessel Hummer was purposely hiding there, his largest trade hammer in his hand.

Hummer did not approve of Erik's murder, and that was why he was lying in wait. As the king passed over the lode he leapt out, scrambled up the bank, and running up behind the king he smashed in his skull with a mighty blow of his hammer.

But Wessel Hummer in turn went to his doom. Some time later he had taken passage on a ship, when a terrible storm arose. One may suppose the sailors to have known something of the Book of Jonah, for at once they suspected that Hummer must be a wicked man. He admitted that he had murdered King Abel, so the crew seized him, bound him, and threw him overboard. At which the storm suddenly ceased.

Abel having been Duke of Schleswig it was natural that his body should be carried there for burial in the same church where his murdered brother already lay. This time the bells did not peal of their own accord. On the contrary, the very first night after the burial the cathedral was so filled with creakings and groanings and polterings that the dean and chapter could not even sing their psalms through to the end. Every night the disturbance continued until the authorities decided that the consecrated precincts of the cathedral themselves so rebelled against housing the remains of the murderous Abel that the king must be exhumed and buried in a marsh, with a stake driven through him to hold him down. This apparently restored peace to the cathedral, but the marsh became a centre of unearthly commotion, and sometimes one might hear Abel rising to blow his horn for his nightly hunt. Those who actually saw him described him as being entirely black about his face and body – in keeping, no doubt, with the blackness of his character. He had three great hunting dogs with him, real hell-hounds, red-hot from snout to tail.

One of those who said that he actually saw Abel was a certain villager who happened to be driving home in his cart one night, somewhat unsteady from liquor. Like others he knew that King Abel had long hunted by night over the Haddeby woods across the Schlei from the town, not from choice but out of restless damnation, and that one might still hear the baying of the hounds, the gallop of a horse and the cry of the king's own voice, although Abel and his mount and dogs were not usually to be seen. On this particular night the man was lurching homeward when he heard King Abel and his pack most clearly, and as the sounds were very close to him he shouted boastfully to the king that he would like to hunt along with him. To his surprise Abel stopped and invited him to come along. Leaving his cart in the road he set off through the night air, clutching the powder-horn and flintlock which one of the royal servants gave to him – for King Abel's hunt was unusual in that it always kept abreast of contemporary weapons.

King and villager together shot plenty of hares, and only when the first trace of light appeared in the east did they draw rein. Before taking his leave the man asked King Abel to spare him some game to take home to his wife and family.

'With pleasure,' exclaimed the monarch. 'Here is your reward, a haunch of venison which will provide a roast too fine by far for the table of a mere peasant.' So saying, King Abel flung a haunch into the cart and vanished.

By dawn the man had reached home, and in reply to the familiar question he assured his wife that he had not spent the night carousing, or lying in a drunken stupor as she supposed. King Abel himself had invited him to go hunting. She did not believe him? Then let her stop being so smug and just step down to the yard and see what he had brought home for the larder.

That was just what she intended to do, the wife assured him. She dropped the tailboard of the cart, and there was the meat right enough. But instead of being a haunch of venison it was the rotting hind leg of a horse which had been dead a very long time indeed.

II

The Schlei broads – unnatural gulls of Schleswig – secret of
the yellow flower – the Holm fishermen – Black Margaret on
the Schlei – the head of John the Baptist – Haddeby and
Haithabu – the vanished port of portage – milestones and
wine – a Russian hat for the visitor

THE history of Erik and Abel has already taken us up to Schleswig, carrying us there on its curious carpet woven of fact and fiction. But to reach the city from the Königsburg and the vanished Finsternstern where the monk received his midnight summons we still have an hour's run ahead of us. Buoy S of the second alphabet lies off the Königsburg hill, and we shall not dock at Schleswig until we have reached W in the third alphabet.

Only a few minutes up from the monk's port of embarkation the channel twists and doubles to disappear round a headland to where the ferry at Missunde crosses what might be a river of southern England, its gentle course curling past moorings and by summer cottages set on the slopes of the cliffs, then doubling back beside a pinewood above which the hawks circle in the safe knowledge that this is a nature sanctuary and nobody will be imprudent enough to shoot at even the most predatory of birds.

Another kink, and across a low promontory of pasture where a pair of fat Frisian milkers were cropping the grass the spire of Schleswig rose up in the strange light of a thundery haze, like some spectral sunken cathedral beckoning us from afar. In fact it was still six miles distant across the long steel-grey water of the Grosse Breite and the Kleine Breite, two broads of astonishing beauty, their low shores fading away into a monochrome of overcast fields and trees and shy manors. We turned the flat point, rounded the cows, and as we did so the western sun peered above the heavy layer of cloud to pour shafts of silvery light through crevices in the greyness so that the cathedral seemed to lie in the centre of a Shekinah specially designed for it by a master of the baroque who disapproved of its being so unashamedly ancient and gothic.

Beyond the cows and a mile away on the port beam we could make out the hamlet of Weseby, huddled on the shore of the Grosse Breite. This place was said to be on the site of a strong castle in which there once lived a violent and marauding knight named Weser, who would sally out by land or on the Schlei itself to raid and sack any place within reach. He had a virtuous sister, whose name is not recorded but who continually warned him – as virtuous sisters will – that he was heading for disaster. She was right, for the other lords eventually banded together and raised a force to attack Burg Weser and sack it.

Weser himself happened to be out on some aquatic venture of plunder when the news reached him, and he at once turned about and sailed swiftly home, just in time to jump ashore and be struck down by his opponents. They bound him, but promised him his life if he would hand over the castle. Having no choice, he agreed. However, Weser's own men-at-arms and retainers had no wish to be handed over so cheaply, and fired with the courage of desperate men they surged out of the castle and smote their enemies so effectively that they drove them off and managed to free Weser and carry him back to his fortress.

The enemy retired, but not for long. They came in even greater force and invested the castle by land, blockading also the escape by the Grosse Breite. Yet by then the defenders had amassed within the walls a good supply of provisions, and everything seemed set for a long and costly siege. But the attackers had no wish to be tied down for months or years, and one day when a fierce wind was blowing they shot burning materials into the castle until they had it well alight and burning furiously, the wind driving the flames through its rooms and galleries.

Weser now realised that he was defeated, but rather than be taken alive again and hanged or imprisoned in the dark and dank dungeon of an enemy castle he climbed to the top of one of the towers, leading his virtuous sister by the hand. Together they leapt into the burning debris below. The moral of this tale of medieval

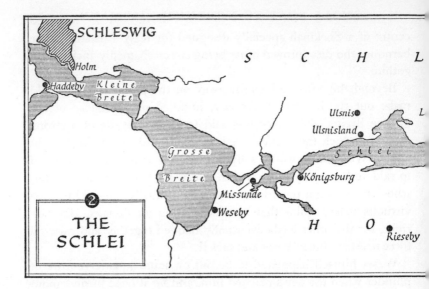

adventure is presumably that if a girl is virtuous she may be heading for a violent death just the same unless some gallant knight aflame with pure love can rescue her in time. And at Weseby it seems there was no such hero on that particular occasion.

I had actually steered up the Schlei before, only a few weeks earlier, and on that occasion I had been quite alone. My wife and I had left the *Thames Commodore* at Kiel, and I had promised to have her away from the Olympiahafen before the beginning of Kiel Week, when every inch of quay and jetty would be needed for the sailing craft gathering there for the greatest yachting event of Europe. In the grandparent years meetings and committees seem to proliferate rather than die away, and Miriam was unable to get away in time to keep our promise to the harbour-master of Kiel, and that was why I returned alone. I expected a Baltic of idyllic calm such as I had known eleven years before, but somebody must have been untying knots in witches' handkerchiefs, for although this was the last week of May there was a ferocious wind driving waves all the way from Estonia, and it was only at the second attempt that the *Thames Commodore* and I managed to force our way out of the Kiel fjord at all. We did so by going to bed late and pretending that we were settling down in Laboe for

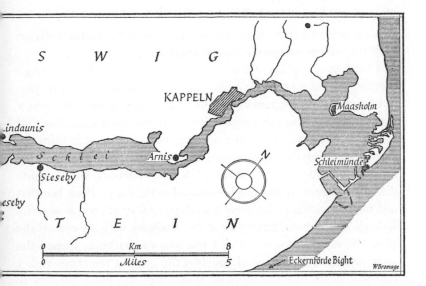

days on end. Then, very stealthily, we stole out before four o'clock in the morning and set out at full speed for Sønderborg in Denmark.

We were already up to the Eckernförde Bight before the wind awoke, yawned, discovered that we had deceived it, and got up steam to race after us with as much fury as if wicked King Abel himself were in command. Soon the combers were breaking on the open sea, and only the powerful push of our Perkinses kept us from being pooped. I could hear that the furniture and stores down below did not like the motion. So much crockery and hardware was being flung about below decks that I decided to run for the shelter of the Schlei, and after rolling in through the entrance past a lighthouse almost invisible in the sheets of spray flung up by the impact of the waves on the mole the boat suddenly emerged into the unbelievably calm water behind Schleimünde. She shook herself and ran on at a more gentle speed to draw in at Kappeln so that I could quell the mutiny in the stores, dispose of broken glasses, mop up the jar of red cabbage which had sprung open and emptied itself down the bulkhead, and collect the hundreds of sticks of spaghetti which lay everywhere from beside the galley stove to inside the shower tray of the forward toilet. Being

Mediterranean and volatile by nature spaghetti always behaves badly in a storm, and so do paper bags of flour.

That first few miles of the lure of the Schlei impelled me to go further, and three hours up from Kappeln I was bearing down upon Schleswig itself. A channel led off to the right to the jetties of a sugar factory where two cargo ships lay to load, but I decided that that was no suitable place for me because it was too far from the town. Searching the shore ahead very carefully with the glasses I eventually made out the shape of a small harbour with a quite distinct entrance. It was not mentioned in the *Baltic Pilot*, but that did not surprise me, for their lordships' information was sketchy indeed. Steering cautiously over the shallows with an eye on the pink line of the echo sounder I ran into the harbour, turned the ship, and brought her neatly against the quay at the inner end. I had just made fast and noticed that I had the place entirely to myself when two soldiers walked down to look at the ship. They said their Good Mornings in rather awkward and stand-offish fashion, I thought, and then they walked away. A moment later they returned with an officer resplendent in silver oak leaves and other insignia.

'Good morning,' I said.

He disregarded the greeting, except that he gave a sort of grunt. Then, 'Who gave you permission to come into the harbour?'

The *Thames Commodore* has never been a boot-licker, and I could feel that she was offended.

'Nobody,' I said briefly.

'And why are you here?'

Really, I thought, this was too much. 'You guess,' I said a trifle haughtily. 'See if you can think why any ship might possibly draw into the harbour.'

He brushed this comment aside. 'You did not ask permission,' he said.

'It is not the habit of myself, or of any other ship's captain known to me, to drop anchor outside a harbour, row in, and grovel before the harbour-master for permission to enter,' I said. 'If that is what is expected at Schleswig, then I have no wish to be here at all.'

The officer looked at the stern and eyed the flag. He also read the name and port of registration. 'Englishman,' I could see he was thinking. 'Mad as a hatter. These animals are dangerous.' He cautiously raised a hand as though to smooth my ruffled fur. 'This is not Schleswig,' he said. 'This is the Bundeswehr's private port at Freiheit. It is military territory. That is why permission is needed to enter.'

I apologised for my error, and the officer seemed relieved. There was not going to be an international incident after all. He advised me to sail straight for the gap between buoys R and Q, as there were patches less than three feet deep to either side. Then I should continue as far as the red buoy marked Haddeby and fork right, aiming straight for the cathedral. That would take me to the town quay

This second time we ran straight for the quay, still used by ships which occasionally came to lie below the conveyors of a grain store to load wheat. Our only companion alongside was the sturdy police boat, and after spending a while on board her I could not help thinking that of all the watery beats a pair of kindly and gentle policemen might have, this must be one of the best. I doubt if there can have been much crime on the Schlei since the night of the murder in August 1250, and there must be plenty of jetties and villages where a reasonable excuse can be found for pulling in and checking that nothing has come to disturb the peace of the inns of this long, quiet and beautiful inlet. In the summer there will be regattas to be watched, capsized dinghy sailors to pull out of the water, objects lost overboard to be retrieved, and perhaps occasionally a deep-keeled craft to be pulled off a mudbank. And just once or twice in a lifetime a glass of rum aboard the craft of some eccentric Englishman. Not an unpleasant life, I thought.

Ahead of the quay and lying out in the shallow water of the inner end of the Schlei is an island, the Möweninsel or Isle of Gulls. On that morning in May it was teeming with birds which I very naturally took to be ordinary common or herring gulls. It was only the following morning that the old woman in the bakery behind the cathedral explained to me that this was not so, for not only had Abel been sentenced to ride the night skies for ever in expiation of his crime, but the twenty-four perjured noblemen and all those who assisted the Duke of Schleswig in the murder of his brother came to a variety of dreadful ends and were to know no peace in their graves. Each year around the feast of St Gregory, the gulls still came flying in from the Baltic in their thousands to nest upon the Isle of Gulls hard by the Schleswig shore, and if in flight they appeared to be quite like other birds every honest Schleswiger knew that these gulls were the wicked men of Duke Abel, and their descendants, none of whom might ever rest.

I thought they were unusual shades or ghosts if they actually went so far as to reproduce and lay eggs, for this they certainly did. These black-headed gulls are said to come from Africa to nest on that island alone, and the city used to appoint a 'King of the Gulls', a fisherman whose duty it was to protect the birds until they had finished breeding and it was time to initiate the shooting, when the men of Schleswig would row out to the island and blaze away until they had slain as many as possible. Originally this was the privilege of the aristocracy, but later all the people of the city would row over to massacre the gulls in one great jollification, and the pictures of the island crowded with dogs, children, and men blazing away at the wheeling and diving gulls make one wonder that the human casualties were not heavier. All the same, one can only suppose that in spite of appearances the birds cannot really have been killed. If they were indeed Abel's men and their families condemned to fly for ever as seagulls, would they not have been invulnerable?

For more than a century the island has been a bird protection reserve and the gulls no longer face a barrage of gunfire at the end of their breeding, but the King of the Gulls still exists. It is he who rents the island, and his modern duty is confined to collecting the eggs from 20 April to the beginning of June. They are one of Schleswig's specialities, and on my first visit in May I noticed they were on sale in the butchers and poulterers shops all through the town. Olive green and blotched with black, they certainly looked appetising but I declined them just the same. After all, they were the shelled descendants of Schleswig noblemen, and I for one did not approve of cannibalism.

Strongly entrenched in Schleswig's tradition is the story of the yellow flower which blooms only once in a hundred years. To say that the flower is a cowslip conceals much of its mystery and power; but in German the common cowslip bears the name of Schlüsselblume or key-flower, and one may reasonably expect it to be the key to open secrets or reveal riches, to unlock doors or even hearts.

It is generally thought that the castle of Abel, murderer of Erik, once stood on the Isle of Gulls which has so curiously remained unbuilt upon at the very edge of the city. Under the rough grass stamped down by the sea birds foundations of walls certainly exist. It would have been a good site for a castle, defended as it was on every side by the water, and there is no reason to doubt that here was Abel's residence. In past centuries weird flickers and glows were often reported over the isle, and treasure-seekers would sometimes row over by day to scratch unsuccessfully for the treasure which they believed these signs to indicate. But the only one to see the riches of Abel's palace is the man that takes the centennial cowslip in his hand.

The last recorded appearance of the yellow flower is undated – which is unfortunate, as otherwise I would myself try to be there an exact number of hundreds of years later to venture my luck and load the *Thames Commodore* with gold. On that occasion a man was walking along the shore one night when he saw the whole Isle of Gulls aglow. Even stranger was the fact that the water solidified as he stepped upon it, so that he was able without difficulty to reach on foot the island, where he came upon a great castle which had certainly not been there that same afternoon. In the courtyard was growing the mysterious yellow cowslip, shining so brilliantly that he soon realised that this was in fact the source of all the illumination which floodlighted the building. Unafraid, he picked the flower and walked round the outside of the palace to examine it by the bright light of the little bloom.

Trying the doors he found them all locked, but when he held the key-flower against them they invariably opened. Thus it was that he passed through passages and ante-rooms until he at last came to a hall where a magnificent meal was laid. Being apparently a very practical man he sat down and made an extremely good dinner. He was just about to leave when a voice called to him.

B2

'Don't forget to take the best!'

He had already eaten all he could, so he wandered round the room to inspect all the plate of silver and gold. He came to the conclusion that a particular goblet of silver must certainly be the finest piece of all, so he took it up. Once more the voice called to him out of the air, urging him not to forget the most valuable of all, so he looked over the furnishings once again. But no, there was nothing to equal the silver cup, so he left the dining-hall with the voice ringing a third time in his ears.

The man had no difficulty in reaching the land again, and he still had the cup – which is said eventually to have come into the possession of the Dukes of Gottorp. But immediately he had crossed the water the castle sank from view. He should of course have realised that the 'best' which the voice had encouraged him to remember was neither a piece of plate nor an item of jewellery, but just the golden cowslip which would have given him the key to all the fabulous treasure in the castle and perhaps to many other things besides. However, he had had his chance. Perhaps, they say, another will one day see the same rare glow and recall the error that his predecessor made. If that should happen I have no doubt that the government will find some good reason to relieve him of all but a token of the wealth which might have been his.

Schleswig is without a doubt one of the most interesting cities of the north. It is also one that is not much heard of. The main Europa-road from Scandinavia to Lisbon carries the traffic streaking past within only a few hundred yards of both Haddeby and Holm, yet I have never met any traveller who had bothered to spare a few minutes to visit either of these curiosities. And each in its way is very curious indeed.

The older quarter of the city runs down to the shore east of the silo quay and then suddenly stops. Across the road is Holm, a community entirely distinct from Schleswig itself. Once it was an island, and although the creek which divided it from the city was eventually filled in it remained a place on its own, as much of a fisher village as Maasholm but much more picturesque. As far back as the twelfth century the fishers of Holm had their own privileges and catching rights which extended all the way to

Schleswig Holm

Schleimünde. Today their descendants are still there, living in their delightful cottages which form a ring round the burial ground, very much in the style of some early community in New England.

The Holm houses with their standard roses at either side of the door are designed for neighbourliness and gossip. The front doors open in two halves, so that a woman may lean comfortably on the lower section and gossip with any who pass by. The same surname difficulty which Knight noted at Maasholm applies here also, and the little plates on the doors carry instead the nicknames by which the men are known – names such as Ningelnangel and Rummelpott giving a curious Grimm Brothers atmosphere to the gay little houses of the ellipse.

The parlours project into the street, their squared bay windows giving the opportunity to see one's neighbours – for nothing that may happen in Holm is hid under a bushel. Holm is a village built for the women to gossip while the men are about their work. Or, of course, gossiping among themselves, though as far as the men are concerned this chit-chat does not occur in the doorways, but on the beach. For Holm has a tiny shore of its own, tucked away down an alley between the fisherhouses, and there the boats are drawn up on the sand. Others lie moored to stakes in the water, each stake topped with a gull – a real bird, I think, and not a reincarnated nobleman of medieval Schleswig or Holstein. At the top of the beach there is a seat by the wall, and a huge tree to give just the proper amount of shade for fishermen's yarns and boatmen's tales. There the old men sit, and with them such friends as the water-policeman in his white cap. They sit, and talk, and watch as a kayak-shaped little craft is pulled up from the water and a lid unlocked in the middle of its top.

This is not really a canoe but a live-box, so shaped for easy towing from the lower reaches. It will contain eels, hundreds of them, and as soon as it is open the boys are sitting astride it to delve inside with fingers dipped in sand, grabbing an eel, and throwing it into one box or another according to its size. Then the catch is weighed, a few pounds of eels being scooped into a pan and carefully balanced by an official of the guild, probably the headman or an old fisherman appointed as weighmaster. Another wriggle and slither, and the creatures are on their way to the shops or the wholesalers.

The summer months are the time when the Holm fishers take

most of their catch. But there is also a winter fishery, and the Guild of Holm Fishers is probably unique in that a portion of the winter earnings of every fisherman is pooled to provide for the old, the widows, and others of the community who may be in need. This custom is a relic – and a very practical one – from the plague years, when several such guilds of mutual help were founded, and the Beliebung – literally Beloving – has been the centre of the life of Holm's community for more than three centuries.

Two Holm fishermen once had a curious adventure which involved that weird character 'Black Margaret', widow of King Christopher I of Denmark who succeeded Abel on the throne. She was black, not in her complexion but in her thoughts and deeds, and perhaps also in the dress she wore as a widow. A tough queen, she had all the characteristics which would ensure her fame in the rough Scandinavian world, and she quickly became a legend, the woman who built the Dannevirke wall outside Schleswig, the cunning leader who deceived and beheaded a chivalrous Duke of Holstein, tried to dam the river Stör to drown the people of Itzehoe, ruined the port of Flensburg by laying chains across the entrance and had a pact of mutual trust with the devil, with the result that her shade could never rest. This redoubtable woman would often appear to the fishermen of Holm, especially on a misty night when they had need to ply the bottle to keep themselves warm, and on one fateful night two of the men were fishing in their little boat, somewhere in the Kleine Breite, when they saw gliding to them across the water from the direction of Haddeby the queenly figure dressed entirely in black but majestic in pearls and diamonds, her jewels sparkling in the faint glimmer of moonlight which filtered through the mist. The men, who had caught nothing, were naturally frightened as the apparition of the ghostly virago of the Schlei came whiffling towards their craft, but she quickly put them at their ease. They were to cast the net again, she said, her instruction curiously reminiscent of the New Testament. She only demanded, she added, that the best specimen was to be thrown back.

Not daring to disobey her the men laid out the net and slowly hauled it in. The catch was so rich that there was scarcely room for all the flopping and floundering fishes which they lifted over the gunwale into their small boat. One of the fish, they noted, was unusual in that instead of ordinary scales it had overlapping plates of gold, and in place of eyes and snout emeralds and pearls.

This, one fisherman said, was obviously the best fish, the prize specimen they had to put back. But his partner grabbed it and stuffed it away under the rest of the fish so that Black Margaret would not see it; then he snatched up the oars and rowed swiftly toward the shore.

He was a foolish man to think that Black Margaret could be deceived so simply. As he rowed, the whole heap of fishes began to shimmer and shine, turning to pure gold under the infectious influence of the rare specimen buried at the bottom. Had the fishermen been close inshore this might have made their fortune, but they were not. And as gold is one of the heaviest of elements the weight quickly took the craft below the surface so that it sank, taking into the depth the load of golden fish and the greedy fisherman also. The other just managed to struggle free, and almost exhausted he succeeded in making the shore. He ran to the village to tell the other fishermen what had happened out on the waters of the Schlei, and there is no mention of any of them having doubted his tale for an instant.

Holm has another curiosity. There was in the twelfth century a religious institution in Schleswig which contained both monks and nuns. A mixed residential foundation was no easier to run then than it is now, and within fifty years the bishop had to descend upon the place to wind it up. The monks must have transgressed the bounds very gravely, for they were expelled from Schleswig; but the ten women were given a new home on the island of Holm. There their successors were eventually overtaken by the Reformation, when the abbey underwent a very curious change.

It happened that the Benedictine sisters came mostly from noble Holstein families, and the Abbey of St John the Baptist was so well connected that the aristocracy succeeded in having the place preserved along with the three other convents in their land as a sort of communal home for their unmarried and noble daughters. And thus it has remained to this day, a conventual institution for

Schleswig Holm – St John's

protestant women, who must be Schleswig-Holsteiners and also of
noble birth. I believe there were originally ten women, and
actually to be accepted as a member of such an exclusive society
became the goal which any aristocratic woman would wish for her
daughter. Even nowadays a baby girl will be placed on the waiting
list the moment she is born, but she may only enter when a death

or a marriage leaves a vacancy. Until that time she is known as an
'Expectant Maiden'.

Very beautiful are the quiet, aged buildings nestling under the
limes at the edge of the Schlei with no neighbours but the fishermen of Holm. The cloisters are a little overgrown and here and
there some paint is needed, for the aristocracy cannot nowadays
afford to endow its daughters as richly as it did when the girls had
their private boxes in the chapel, where each would sit with her
serving maids. The heraldic plaques of those who occupied these
stalls in former centuries remind one of the Garter stalls at
Windsor, but if the chapel and the abbey buildings themselves are
in surprisingly good repair this is because the Bundeswehr has
stepped in as benefactor where the Dukes and Counts have been
unable. The chapel is now used for the garrison.

The sisters still exist, and there is a waiting list. But they no
longer reside there all the while – though two elderly and titled
ladies still had their homes in the quiet and mellowed cloisters
when we visited the abbey. Times have changed, women are
emancipated, and a titled girl will no longer be a fading conventual
flower but a doctor, a business-woman, a lawyer or teacher, living
a full life in the world outside. She will have a home of her own,
perhaps a city flat far away beyond the borders of Schleswig-
Holstein, and yet she will return to Holm for some special occasion
– driving up from Hamburg or Frankfurt in her Mercedes to slip
softly into the chapel to celebrate the Festival of St John. She has a
life of her own and yet will always remain a member of this very
exclusive sisterhood unless she should marry.

Marriage is a bar for all except the abbess herself, and many a
titled young heiress may have wept into her pillow whilst weighing
up the advantages of being in love or remaining a member of a very
highly sought-after clan. As for the abbess, she not only may marry
but she *must* do so, and her wedding is a very extraordinary affair.
She has to marry John the Baptist.

The widow who showed us round the convent produced a large
round wooden plate, the 'charger' of the New Testament. Upon it
lay the carved head of the decapitated John, its eyes closed after it
had been struck from his body to please the mother of the cabaret

dancer, the beard falling down in handsome, oaken, fourteenth-century curls and just a trace of blood round the edges of the severed neck. This gruesome object would be produced when a new abbess was to be installed, and wearing a full wedding dress of black she would undergo an otherwise regular 'Solemnisation of Holy Matrimony' with it, the service being performed as any other wedding might be by the chaplain (now the army chaplain of the soldiery to whom belonged the Freiheit harbour). Before her sisters of the order the abbess would promise to take the said John to be her lawful wedded husband, to have and to hold, love and cherish, until death should part them.

This marriage was not a mock wedding but carried all the authority of law behind it. If the unthinkable should happen and an abbess should become prey to more ordinary marital desires, then to take a human husband would – according to the woman who showed us the much-married platter – be bigamy true and proper. More than that, the fact that the abbess had a husband was recognised in the community. Whenever a matter was discussed and put to the vote the abbess had a second vote – that of her decapitated conjugal partner whose effigy lay on the dish beside her. The whole arrangement gave me a curious prickling sensation over the scalp as the woman described it to us, and one seemed to be in contact with something which smelt more of the weird rites of the Nordic mythology or even of Oriental magic than of a Christian community. Yet I have no doubt that the abbesses were very worthy women in every way. And certainly they must have made ideal wives, for if there was no doubt about who gave the orders in the household it was indisputable that husband and wife had ever lived in harmony and had never been known to take opposite sides in any dispute, however mild.

The *Thames Commodore* lay at the quay only a few minutes' walk from the Holm fisher-beach and even nearer to the quiet close which surrounds the great cathedral begun in the eleventh century and slowly extended, a building of brick, tufa-stone, granite, and black bands of hard material as shiny as lava but also an early form of brick. By Scandinavian standards the cathedral city would rank as a very ancient one indeed, and Schleswig in fact was the key position in the spread of Christianity to the northern lands. Yet the earliest church was certainly on the further shore of the Schlei, in the great trading centre which once existed behind where the Haddeby buoy now marks the edge of the navigation channel.

It was to the site of that earlier Schleswig that we were bound when we moved out from the silo quay to run across to the Haddeby buoy and then turn cautiously toward the ferry jetty in front of the hamlet lying among the trees. When the depth had fallen to one fathom we dropped the anchor and lowered the dinghy – though as it was such a warm afternoon of summer sunshine I myself found it even more pleasant to drop over the side and swim to the small beach beside the jetty. Up the path from this ferry landing stood an inn, the Gasthaus Haddeby, on the wall of which was painted a Viking ship under sail – a reminder that the Schlei had carried trading vessels more than one thousand years before the *Thames Commodore* thrust her inquisitive nose into its innermost recesses. Beyond this inn and across the road stood the village church of Haddeby, one of the oldest in this part of Germany.

Haddeby is no place at all. That is, there is the church and an inn, and a single house in the trees which is presumably the parsonage. All the other houses and the school and stores are at the neighbouring village of Busdorf. But Haddeby possesses one thing of great value – its name, which is nothing more nor less than the relic of the long-vanished Haithabu, one of the greatest trading centres of the early medieval world.

Haithabu – the name might surely be that of some romantic isle of the Pacific, a place of grass-skirted maidens and giant turtles, and perhaps of skulls hung up to decorate the walls of the men's parlour. In fact Haithabu might equally well have been written Heide-by (Heath-town), not so very different from the name of the tiny hamlet still existing near the site of the vanished town. Haithabu was the name by which the Scandinavians knew it, whereas the Saxons called it Sliesthorp and then Sliaswich – which eventually was transmuted to Schleswig (or Schlei Market). We can now escape from the intricacies of language and return to the roadside by Haddeby church, having only strayed into semantics to show that Schleswig on the northern shore is really the same place as ancient Haithabu on the south, having merely crossed the short stretch of water after the disaster of 1066, when Haithabu went up in the smoke of its final sacking at the hands of its rivals.

As the Dark Ages drew slowly to an end and the first glimmer of a medieval dawn appeared, the narrowest point of the Jutland peninsula became the scene of what today would be called international transit trade. Ships plied between Birka, the Viking port on a small island in the Mälar lake west of modern Stockholm, and such places as Novgorod and Kiev. By means of land portages they even traded with Byzantium and Baghdad. Other ships sailed to the ports where Lübeck and Danzig later developed, or up through the Kattegat to the coast of Norway and into the Arctic. All these voyages were based on ports east of Jutland; but to the west lay the Rhineland, the marshy Netherlands and even the strange isles of Britain to which the Saxons and Angles had sailed away long before. Between these two areas lay the Jutland peninsula, with its nightcap tip of Skagen, the Skaw.

Skagen has always been a place of such danger that one might well wonder why captains did not give it a wide berth and sail past in safety. But there is more to Skagen than that. From miles away one may hear the seas breaking where they fling themselves to attack each other, the opposing armies of steep rollers driving up from the Kattegat and in from the North Sea. And if in comparatively modern times this corner still proved so dangerous that at last the Kiel Canal was built to bypass it, one can imagine that the earlier men of the sea would have found the Skaw a formidable obstacle to their trading, and that they, too, preferred to establish a link across the base of the Jutland peninsula. Besides, it was not just a matter of keeping clear of the Skaw itself, for the whole of the west coast of Jutland was always most inhospitable, and the storm-waves surging in from the Atlantic and round the north of Scotland would scoop the sand into a series of dangerous banks extending for miles offshore. On these the waves themselves would break in a roar of surfy fury to form a sea so dangerous that in modern times the pilot books would warn sailing ships never to pass up the coast unless the wind was blowing offshore, and when they saw a lighthouse to regard it as a warning that they were imprudently close to land. In Viking days the passage round Jutland must have been extremely unpleasant. If the wind turned to the north-west it would always blow with great vigour, just as it does today, and the ships were inevitably driven upon a shore entirely without natural inlets into which to flee before the waves and wind. Right up to the opening of the Kiel Canal vessels were being lost round the Skaw at the rate of two hundred a year, and there must have been considerable relief at Lloyds when at last the corner was cut by the great new waterway.

The inner end of the Schlei is less than eight miles distant from the middle reaches of the river Treene, a stream which joins the Eider shortly before that river opens out to the North Sea. It was here, where the land gap was at its narrowest, that the early traders set up their portage route and established at either end of it a transit harbour. Rhineland goods and cloth from Friesland and the Low Countries were unloaded at Hollingstedt on the Treene and carried overland to Haithabu, there to be loaded into other ships. From at least the beginning of the eighth century this short cut across the narrows of the Jutland peninsula was used by the men who traded between east and west.

There were of course other means of reaching the Baltic. For example, small ships could run up the Eider to within a very few miles of the Kiel fjord, but this route involved tolls and the per-mission of the riparian owners in the upper reaches. The way by the Treene and the Schlei was undeveloped, a route of free trade. It was shorter, too, and the flat countryside between the two rivers made it possible eventually to think even of moving ships from one sea to the other on rollers – not so much to prevent transhipment as to meet any demand for more coastal ships on one side than were needed on the other.

The first settlers, the founders of Haithabu, were certainly Frisians, cloth merchants and traders who used this short land crossing between the two seas and after portaging their goods from the Treene river would fit out again on the banks of the Schlei and stay there awhile before setting out on the second part of their

journey to the rich settlements of the southern Baltic. But
Haithabu became transformed when, in the year 808, the Danish
King Gottrik fell upon the city of Reric in the Wismar Bight, until
then a flourishing place of transhipment and international trade.
Instead of slaughtering the merchants and artificers he shipped
them all to his own lands and settled them in Haithabu, thus taking
advantage of their wide trading contacts and their experience in
commerce. It was Gottrik also who built the first of the defences
which were eventually to become the Dannevirke, the rampart
which crossed the peninsula between the Schlei and Treene and
for long kept the German peoples at a safe distance – even forming
a defence in the Danish-Prussian wars of the nineteenth century.

It would be pleasant to relate that Haithabu still exists in at
least such recognisable detail as the destroyed city of Pompeii, but
unfortunately it does not. Stone was not used for the buildings,
and as its houses were built entirely of wood there is little that
sacking, fire, rot and the ploughs of centuries of farming have not
removed. However, excavations have been going on for some time
and much has been discovered and taken to the museum in
Gottorp castle. Otherwise Haithabu has to be imagined rather than
seen, for even the site is kept clear of visitors by barbed wire. The
reason for this is, I think, a particularly unfortunate one. The site
is closed just because the excavation is being done by civil
prisoners.

When the Stratford-upon-Avon Canal was restored by enthusiasts they had the energetic help of volunteers from prisons. This
was a particularly happy idea because the prisoners caught the
enthusiasm of the others and worked alongside them with only the
most nominal guard or watch. For once they were in contact with
others and were not fenced away like creatures in the more old-
fashioned type of zoo, and the result was that they soon began to
feel accepted and to lose the apartness which prison bars must
necessarily induce. But when we came through the 1000-year-old
gateway and approached the site of Haithabu itself we found a
fence and notices warning that visitors must on no account enter,
or attempt to speak to the prisoners carefully excavating the floors
of the houses. If one had binoculars one might watch them from

afar off, just as though they were rare mammals digging in the African bush. A great chance of exercising sense and humanity had, I thought, been missed. Surely it would have been much better to admit anyone who *would* speak to the prisoners or work alongside them.

With the site closed, we could still see the position of the vanished town and visit its surroundings. Behind the Haddeby church a path climbed to a plateau hidden in the trees, and the trace of a wall and ditch which once had surrounded it. As for the few dozen simple burial mounds which used to be there, these had been so flattened by the ages that one could detect only the slightest undulations in the turf, and of the Hochburg itself there was nothing else to be seen. Certainly this was some kind of a fort, and it is believed originally to have been a defensive mound to which the population of earliest Haithabu might flee from raiders. That, of course, would have been before Haithabu was itself developed as a fortified town, and probably in the eighth century A.D., before the days of King Gottrik. Certainly there were never any buildings on the Hochburg, and if it was a hill of refuge it must have been used as such in the years before the semicircular wall and ditch were established to defend Haithabu on the landward side, and only quite temporarily whenever danger seemed to threaten from outside.

Haithabu itself lay down by the shore of the Haddeby Noor, a side inlet leading off the inner end of the Schlei. Its site is surrounded by a half ring of immense rampart on which today a copse of alder and birch and bramble stands in place of the ancient palisade where the guards watched for raiders. A chestnut horse was cropping the short grass at the northern end and he paused only briefly to look up as we passed him, just one more group of these foolish humans who had no idea of the fine taste of the green and well-drained slope but hurried by as though the Wends were after them.

The vast bank surrounding the town was begun about the year 900, by the Swedish Vikings who had then possessed themselves of Haithabu. It was made higher and more impregnable on half-a-dozen later occasions, for as the city grew richer so did it also become the more worth attacking. Without security, traders could not be expected to come to Haithabu, but once the ring-wall was erected they came in such numbers that Haithabu could not provide all the goods they demanded, and artisans and craftsmen were drawn from the Rhineland to settle in these more favourable surroundings where their work would be bought from them as fast as they could produce it. Instead of merely importing cloth, pottery and jewellery, Haithabu manufactured it.

So, if the depots of Haithabu and Hollingstedt both began as mere terminals of a portage route, the more easterly of them was quickly to develop into one of the largest and most important trading towns of northern Europe. Settlers flocked to the banks of the Schlei, and in the ninth and tenth centuries Haithabu was a manufacturing centre for luxury goods, the raw materials being imported mostly from the north and east. From Norway came skins and walrus tusks, dried fish and eiderdown, from the shores of the southern Baltic the ships brought cereals and flax, skins and amber, honey and silks and staghorn – an article much used in the Haithabu workshops. From the Netherlands came rolls of cloth, from the New Anglia across the North Sea jewellery, and the manufactured products shipped from the Rhineland included jewellery, glass and pottery, and of course wine. Among the heavier imports were millstones, which came all the way from quarries of volcanic rock in the Eifel hills west of the Rhine. Sometimes they were shipped in a finished condition, but the large hole for the grain-feed in the upper stone made it particularly fragile and eventually the stones were imported to Haithabu in a semi-fabricated condition, the hole-cutting and general finishing being left to local craftsmen who must have been experienced in such work. Probably they had emigrated thither to set up workshops for just that purpose.

As for the wine, it was mostly imported not in barrels but in pottery jars made in the Cologne area, and there was no such thing as a traffic in returned empties. The used wine vessels were in great demand by the women of Haithabu for use in the larder and kitchen, and the remains of enormous numbers of them have been found in the remnants of houses already excavated.

The wine was probably loaded at Dorestad, a trading centre on the lower reaches of the Rhine near the site of the modern city of Utrecht. It was brought to that place by ships from far upstream in Alsace, the Rheingau, and probably the Moselle also. Shipped via Jutland, it found its way right up to Birka, the trading city in the Mälar lake. Because of its use in the eucharist it has always been a fact of geographical economics that wine follows the church.

The church at Birka (as at Haithabu) was founded by Ansgar, the courageous monk from the abbey of Corvey on the Weser, and in his biography written by his successor Rimbert there is an account of how at Birka there was a wealthy widow named Friedeburg (obviously not a Viking woman) who remained true to her faith in spite of the repression of the Birka church. When she thought her last days were approaching she began to long for the sacrament to be administered to her on her death-bed, and as there was no priest – Gauzbert had been forced to leave the settlement – she told her daughter Catla to buy some wine and lay it in a special jug so that when her last hour came some of it might be poured into her mouth as a promise of the grace of God, in lack of a proper sacrament. This wine she kept by her for three years.

In an age when we are accustomed to think of Burgundy with steak, Hock with the halibut and a glass of a treasured Moselle Spätlese sipped by the fireside with only the closest of friends, it is difficult to realise that wine was also once something very different. It is doubtful that any northerner would have preferred it to a good mead, and if the shops in Birka and Haithabu stocked it this must have been partly for use by Christians. As for the 'special jug' used by Friedeburg, this may well explain the jugs excavated in both Haithabu and Birka which have a particular design that includes a large cross down towards the bottom. These earthenware vessels have only been found along the trail of the Christian missions, and they must have been made and marketed – probably by the Frisians – for sacramental use, even if non-Christians found them useful to purchase for ordinary use in the kitchen and about the home.

As trade increased, so the ships from the Schlei ranged ever further, and Haithabu merchants dealt with others in Poland,

Russia and Bohemia. Their trading was not based on a barter system, but goods were bought and sold on a silver standard, and the many little balances and weights dug up in the remains of the town show that first and foremost it was bar silver that was used for payment, although a mint was later established which copied the Netherlands coins of Charlemagne.

From the remains of the houses unearthed the detectives of archaeology have been able to deduce many facts about life in Haithabu – for instance that local hazel nuts were much used for food, but walnuts were sometimes imported. Apples and cherries were grown, and plums also. There was a brewery in the town and also a small glassworks. Pigs were common, and many of the houses had sties behind; dogs and cats were commonly kept. Altogether the town with its streets and shops of traders and artisans was not so very different from a medieval one elsewhere; but of course one of its greatest features was the harbour, with a narrow entrance protected by stakes which left a gap only one ship wide.

The port of Haithabu was not one with silos and warehouses, cranes and elevators and storage depots. The ships which used it were of relatively shallow draught, and their cargoes were either light enough to be lifted out and carried ashore by men wading, or if the goods were livestock they could disembark on their own legs. All that was needed was the gently sloping shore of the inlet of the Haddeby Noor, on which the ships could be hauled up by the sheer pulling of their crews. In fact some lighterage seems to have been used for the larger craft, and the remains of mooring piles and dolphins have also come to light.

One ship, a 50-footer badly damaged by fire, has already been retrieved from the mud of Haithabu's vanished port, a typical shallow-draught vessel which could have navigated the Baltic creeks and rivers without running aground. Another – perhaps one no longer seaworthy – was installed as a memorial, covering two burial chambers, each of which held the graves of two or three individuals who were important enough to be accompanied by rich and valuable gifts. A wrought sword, a glass beaker and a bronze dish, shields and spears and jewellery were found there when the site was excavated, and also the skeletons of three horses. Of the ship only the rivets remained, but these were enough to show that it was about fifty feet in length with a beam of some ten feet, a Baltic as opposed to a North Sea or Atlantic merchant vessel.

It must have been a splendid sight when the ships with their striped square sails and the proud dragons rearing up fore and aft came driving over the water of the Grosse Breite before an east wind, just like the craft painted on the side of the Gasthaus Haddeby today. Usually they would have been Baltic craft of moderate size, flat bottomed and of comparatively little draught, for they had to trade far up the rivers and reach other trading centres than Haithabu itself. These boats could stand up to the conditions of the Baltic, but for the North Sea and Atlantic voyages much sturdier craft were necessary, the famous 'long-ships' of deeper draught which could withstand the storms of the open sea. Such craft also sometimes came to Haithabu, and one such visit is described in detail in *Nial's Saga*.

Gunnar – the hero of the story, who lived in Iceland – came sailing down from the Eastern Baltic with his fleet of ten ships and he ran up the Schlei to Haithabu, where he found King Harald Bluetooth in temporary residence. The king invited Gunnar to visit him, and the Icelander stayed for two weeks, his men competing with the entourage of Harald in friendly sports – though none could beat Gunnar in any of them. Harald offered him a wife and a high position if he would agree to stay, but Gunnar was determined to sail on to Iceland. At the parting he gave the king a good long-ship, and many presents. In return Harald presented him with a lord's robe, a pair of gold-embroidered gloves, a head band with golden knots, and a Russian hat – gifts which show very clearly the far reach of Haithabu's trading at that romantic period of medieval history.

III

*Ships roll overland – slavery on the Schlei – Rimbert and the
captive nun – an Arab visits Haithabu – Erik the steersman
– the end of Haithabu – to sea by night – the* Theodor
Heuss *– the naval memorial – digging in at Laboe*

I HAVE never been overland in a ship. The nearest was the night
when the *Commodore* ran down a Dutch Island in the dark and
almost collided with a cow. Yet this was at least unintentional, a
slight error of navigation, whereas at various times in history men
have deliberately hauled ships out of the water and dragged them
across country. The Greeks did it at the isthmus of Corinth. The
Americans developed a canal boat which could be taken apart, put
on wheels, and pulled over the Alleghenies behind a railway locomotive with the passengers still in their seats. Halfway in history
between the two come the men of the Schlei.

It is almost inconceivable that the ocean-going long-ships of the
Vikings could have been rolled overland, but it is more or less
certain that the smaller Baltic boats were actually transported
across the isthmus of Haithabu, just as they were in later medieval
times. And if the sight of the Icelander's flotilla surging across
the Grosse Breite towards the narrow entrance of the Haddeby
Noor must have thrilled the sailor-traders of this early Schleswig,
so one can also imagine the children running out of the houses to
watch in amazement 'as a vessel came slowly bumping up the
street and passed through the gap in the ring of rampart to
edge its way slowly over the heath from which Heath-town took its
name.

A causeway had been laid and levelled, and with furled sail the
ship would roll forward over the smooth rounded logs, a pair of
hefty horses harnessed to the keel plank in front, and the men
walking on either side to keep the hull upright and see that it did
not run on stones or snags. A yard or two, then one man would

lift up the roller which had come clear of the stern and run forward to drop it behind the hoofs of the horses. The ship would move over it, and another roller from aft would be carried forward. And so on, for all the eight miles of the haulage way to Holling-stedt and the creek which led to the Eider and the sea beyond. It might just be that an extra craft was needed at the western port to shift the goods accumulating for export to the Rhineland, or sometimes a ship would cross the peninsula in the course of a single long haul from Birka to the Netherlands. It was one of the most enterprising transport arrangements of the early medieval world; but Haithabu's men were energetic and imaginative in their trading and communications.

Some of those who came as traders or craftsmen to Haithabu would certainly have been Christians, for the town also drew settlers from the Holy Roman Empire, which began at the Dannevirke wall. So it is natural that when Ansgar, the courageous monk from Corvey on the Weser, offered to take the gospel to Scandinavia he came on his first missionary journey to Haithabu and tried to establish there his mission school for boys. Not that Ansgar was the first missionary ever to penetrate into the northern lands. Willibrord, himself an Anglo-Saxon, left England to estab-lish the church among the very hard-headed and obstinate Frisians, and it was while he was there that he journeyed by the already well-established trading route into Denmark, probably passing by the Schlei on his way.

The Danish King Horich the Elder gave Ansgar permission to found a church in Haithabu, and himself set aside a house for the priest in charge. Five years later (in 854) the monarch died, and Horich the Younger proved less well-disposed towards the Chris-tian community. Some of the nobles, led by Hovi who occupied a position which was something like that of mayor and magistrate, petitioned the king to close the church and expel the Christians from Haithabu or at least proscribe the religion. Certainly the church was closed and the community suffered a period of repression.

Ansgar had already left on his mission to Birka, and the Christians were defenceless. Whether the men of such a cosmopolitan community as Haithabu would really have seized their fellows and associates and sold them into slavery seems doubtful, but there is no doubt that slaving was one of the trades of Haithabu. In general the slaves came from the Eastern Baltic, where they were occasionally rounded up in organised drives, or from Britain – though by this time the British Isles were no longer such a good source of slaves such as had earlier delighted the eye of Pope Gregory. The Church at that time regarded slavery as quite normal – just as in our own time some of the most degrading practices in production-belt industry are accepted as quite reasonable. What the ecclesiastical authorities abhorred was the sale of Christian slaves to non-Christian and particularly to Moslem destinations, but they took no particular exception to heathens being sold to heathens or Christians to other Christians. Some of the Baltic slaves passing through Haithabu were probably bought by Frisian traders who sold them up the Rhine and Meuse and perhaps over the divide toward the Mediterranean, where the caliphs ran through a surprising number of women.

Verdun, one of the earlier episcopal sees in that part of Europe, was a notable distribution centre and market for slaves, many of whom must have passed through Haithabu on their way south. It was there that the male slaves destined for the caliphates were castrated to swell the numbers of eunuchs who served the Moslem rulers.

The slaving at Haithabu – as natural then as the Smithfield market in our day – is shown very clearly in an incident in the life of Ansgar's successor Rimbert, as set down by his own biographer. It may be the same occasion that was retold by Pontoppidan, but here it has a ring of much greater truth. About the year 870 Rimbert was travelling to Haithabu 'where he had recently established a church for the newly-founded Christian community' when he saw a number of Christians going about in chains. Among them was a nun, who in order to attract his attention bowed her knee repeatedly and began to sing psalms at the top of her voice.

Rimbert, his biographer related, 'prayed in tears to God to help her, and as a result of his praying the chain around her neck broke

open of its own accord'. However, the slave-minders did not let her
go, and the bishop 'moved by fear and love for her began to offer
various articles of value in exchange for her'. The slavers would
accept none of the things he put forward, but they offered to
barter her for the bishop's horse. Rimbert at once slid from his
saddle, handed over his steed and harness, and bought the nun.
Then he immediately gave her her freedom – a clear indication
that he could have kept her himself – and let her go wheresoever
she wished.

This story certainly shows that slaves were a natural commodity
which could be bought and sold like any other, and no moral
stigma was attached to the trade, even in the eyes of the bishop.
He was sorry for the nun, and bought her free, and that was the
end of the business. But the tale also sheds an interesting light on
the traffic, which must have been in both directions; for this
particular consignment of slaves, which included a nun, cannot
conceivably have come from the northern regions or Estonia, where
there were neither churches nor convents. These captives can only
have been brought from the west, from Britain or France,
captured by raiding Vikings and shipped up the Treene to the
divide which led to Haithabu. Whither they were to be consigned
one can only guess, but it was presumably to Sweden or Russia.
Yet they were presumably not an import order, otherwise Rimbert
would not have found it so easy to buy the nun at a reasonable
price. Vikings had merely rounded them up and sold them to
middlemen, just as English traders did with Africans two centuries
ago and some Africans do with their neighbours today.

Learning of these events as I lay in my bunk hoping in vain that
the Northern Lights would visit the *Thames Commodore* just as
they had flashed an electronic welcome to her predecessor ten
years earlier, I could not help thinking that there were three
characters whose paths always seemed to cross or converge with
our own. The first was Charlemagne, who trotted most of the
globe known to him and left his trace on half the river navigations
of Europe. Next was Bayard, the magical steed of Reynaud,
leaping the Ardennes crags, swimming the Meuse, beating his
competitors at Paris, grazing in the Languedoc, vaulting the river

Main in Bavaria, leaving his hoofmark even upon the watery city of Amsterdam. And last, Ansgar, the man from the Somme who must certainly have fished and bathed in the Upper Weser near where the river board has built its harbour of Corvey, the man who voyaged the seas swept by raiders and who hacked his way through the Swedish forests until he came to the great Mälar lake and was ferried out to that strangely beautiful isle of Birka where once we also had dropped anchor and rowed ashore, our eyes streaming with the heady perfume of the lily-of-the-valley carried to us on the gentle breeze of a Swedish summer's day. Bayard would have been a nuisance aboard the *Thames Commodore*, and the restless Charlemagne would have been itching to up anchor and away; but Ansgar, I thought, would have felt at home aboard her, for he was a practical man and an incorrigible inland voyager.

I had to convince myself that eleven centuries had passed since Ansgar was there, on the Schlei, and his successor Rimbert had his curious encounter with the captive nun. Yet it was not difficult to picture the shiploads of captives tramping across the isthmus on their way to their new owners. As the trading station where north and east made contact with the south and west, the town at the head of the Schlei must have seen many such consignments pass through the port, and the flourishing slave trade may well have been the reason why the Arab trader Ibrahim ibn Ahmed from Tortosa travelled up to Haithabu about the year 965. He described the early Schleswig as 'a very large town at the uttermost extreme of the seas'. There was a small church and a Christian community, but most of the people worshipped Sirius and had a religious festival at which they ate and drank. From the details it seems that Ibrahim ibn Ahmed attended the city dinner of a merchant guild and himself mistook it for something as improbable as an act of worship to the dog star. He also described how eye-shadow make-up was in fashion at Haithabu, and made the considered judgement that it improved the natural beauty and never detracted from it.

It is only from the excavations and such references as those of the Arab trader that we have any picture at all of life in the once busy town at the very head of the Schlei, for Haithabu flourished too early to have a monastery with learned monks recording the events for later generations to read. Yet here and there in the literature of the period Haithabu and its trade are mentioned. We know that a trader named Wulfstan went there from England to negotiate business on the German shore of the Baltic, and there is also the report written for Alfred the Great by a Norwegian skipper-merchant named Ohthere, who was despatched to sail round the North Cape to the lands that lay beyond. On his return he put into the Oslo fjord, and then sailed due south for five days to reach the harbour of Haithabu, having Sweden on the port side and for three days a broad sea (the Kattegat) to starboard. For the last two days to the Schlei Ohthere had Jutland to starboard, and many islands to port. Then he came to the parts 'where the Angles lived before they came over to our own land [England]'.

If Haithabu grew to an extent where it has left cemeteries with thousands of graves, this was because its site was ideal for development as an international market. Not only did it lie on the portage route, but the great north–south road between Viborg and the Elbe passed only just outside the settlement. More than that, it was a frontier post in the sense that the territories of four peoples met in the neighbourhood. Not that these people had precisely demarcated boundaries in the modern nationalistic sense, but to the north and east lay the Danish territories, whilst the isles off the west coast of Jutland were at that time inhabited by the energetic Frisians. To the south lay the lands of the Saxons, and eastwards the Wends were no further away than the Kiel fjord. Rimbert remarked that once the church had been established the merchants of Hamburg and Dorestad could travel there without difficulty, and he also recorded that before the Haithabu church was founded many of the traders from that place had been baptised at Dorestad or Hamburg when travelling on business.

As the years passed, Haithabu attracted more and more settlers from among the Swedish Vikings, and there must have been many young men at Birka and elsewhere who decided to abandon the rather harsh living of their northern settlements and move instead to this civilised town with its international trade and wealth. Yet the peaceful atmosphere of prosperous trading was not to last for ever. At first the voyages of the merchant ships had only been threatened by storm and natural disaster, but in the ninth century there came the new menace of the robber bands of Vikings, who attacked the traders on the sea. Rimbert's life of Ansgar contains a vivid account of how Ansgar and Witmar set out with a party of merchants to sail for Sweden. This was about the year 829, and already the ships sailed in convoy for safety. In the Øresund the traders' vessels found a party of raiders bearing down upon them, and at the first attack they managed to beat off the pirates. However, the onslaught was repeated, and in this second engagement the merchants were overcome and lost everything. This was the occasion when the two monks only saved their lives by diving overboard and swimming to the shore, their precious collection of forty books and the imperial gifts for the church all being lost.

When Ansgar himself made a second visit to Sweden in 852 and the question of adopting Christianity was raised in the *thing* of Birka, one of the old men stood up and made a speech which contained the significant statement that 'whereas some of us used to go to Dorestad to accept the religion for ourselves, the voyage thither is now made extremely dangerous by the attacks of pirates'.

Because of the pirates, the merchants had to be armed, and that is why the sword and shield and spear are found along with the weighing scales and coinage in their graves. The ring-wall of Haithabu itself was reconstructed and made more formidable on more than one occasion. Yet in spite of the new dangers the transhipment centre flourished and the silversmiths and ship-wrights, the glass-workers and craftsmen, farmers and cloth merchants and slavers expanded their trade until, about the year 1000, a decline set in. Why it did has never been discovered, but excavations have shown that the entire area within the rampart was no longer fully settled, and that when a number of houses were burned down they were not rebuilt. Perhaps the place and its lines of communication were even more threatened now that the German and Slav tribes were becoming so bellicose and bringing unrest into the Baltic lands.

Then in the year 1050 the Norwegian King Harald the Hard

c

descended upon the town and burned it. From end to end the rows of houses stood in flames, and the smoke drifted over the water of the Haddeby Noor as the defenders fought upon the wall and on the beach. Some must have escaped, for the town was partly rebuilt – though in an even smaller compass than before.

Yet the end of Haithabu was not long delayed. In the same year that William of Normandy defeated England's King Harold, a fleet of the Wends forced its way up the Schlei to put their once powerful trading rivals out of commission. The port was destroyed, the town so thoroughly sacked that the dead lay unburied in the stream where they fell, to await the coming of the archaeologists nine hundred years later. It was nearly a century before the new town of Schleswig, clustered round its cathedral on the opposite side of the inlet, could try to establish the Schlei once again as a trading centre between east and west, but by then it was too late. The Wends were in the ascendant, and the future belonged to Lübeck. It was for that great city of the Hansa merchants that the *Thames Commodore* was bound when in the late afternoon we turned our backs upon the memories of Haithabu and ran down the slope of the huge defensive earthwork to swim out to the ship and haul up the anchor, just as other visitors from Britain had done a thousand years before us.

The wide expanse of the Grosse Breite lay still under a breathless sky crossed only by the thread of a vapour trail five miles overhead. The low banks and even the cows stood on their heads in the water until the ripples of our wake swept across to wipe the slate clean. Slowly Schleswig faded astern, the cathedral and sugar factory competing to see which could see us furthest on our way. By Missunde and lost Finsternstern we forged down this most lovely of waterways on which once King Erik had sat in the boat and waited for his enemy to strike off his head. Here and there a child was out in a dinghy, a sailing-boat lay waiting for the first breath of evening, or a pair of Holm boats were laying out a net.

I thought we might just catch the eight o'clock bridge opening at Kappeln, but we did not hurry. Except to escape from a storm or the bows of a Rhine tanker speed is out of place on inland waters where there is so much to be seen, and lived. Besides, speed always involved bad manners, and it was only reasonable to ease right off for the skiffs and pairs, for fishermen drawing a net, and for craft moored at the landings. We were still a mile or two short of Kappeln when we heard eight strike in the village belfry of Arnis, and at that same moment the sun began to drop behind the land on the port side, flooding the swans with a weird purple-pink where they snabbled in the shallows close on our beam. It was so fair an evening that we did not resent the prospect of drifting for nearly an hour to wait for the bridge, but as we hovered in the stream above the herring trap there came a loud hoot from down-stream. A cargo ship was coming up the Schlei, laden with Swedish timber. The bridge swung open to let her pass, and ourselves also. We drew in at Kappeln quay and climbed the cobbled steps below the church to find our dinner in one of the old inns of fisher-men and shippers.

I had at first intended to spend the night at Kappeln and run for Kiel early in the morning, but somehow the exhilaration of the evening's voyage had worked upon the crew so that they all received with enthusiasm my suggestion that we should set off late that same night instead. The crew consisted of four young friends whom we had invited not for their usefulness – for my wife and I could in fact run the boat better unaided – but just because it seemed a pity that no others should share the sheer fun of the voyaging as well as the delight of exploring such places as Schleswig. We nearly always had company on our travels and we could have had more if we had wanted it, for people occasionally wrote to me offering to cook or scrub or do anything I might suggest if only I would take them along. It seemed heartless to refuse, for I am sure they would always have been the most pleasant of companions, but my wife and I both thought it would be rash to take people we did not know when we were already well supplied with friends and relations who were continually dropping hints about how difficult it was to think of anything for their summer holidays.

We liked every summer to take young people with us, but if the young like to have older people present to take the responsibility of the voyage they do not necessarily want to spend the whole time with their elders. Now that we had for some years been in the grandparent class it seemed reasonable to think that those of student age might prefer to explore places on their own, so we had a crew of four of them at once. The *Thames Commodore* could easily accommodate them and the girls could each have a single cabin whilst the males had a toilet and shower all to themselves – a useful provision, not because they were particularly in need of cleaning up but for the reason that young ladies can take a very surprising time over their own toiletry. Even at the time when Ibrahim ibn Ahmed visited Haithabu, eye-shadow was probably not put on in a matter of seconds.

Of the crew which had sailed with us from Råå in Sweden to wind through the Danish isles and visit Schleswig *en route* for Lübeck, Juliet Maguinness was an old hand from our voyage on the Moselle a year earlier, and worked in research in classics on a subject so abstruse that I could never remember what it was. Joanna Ide was also a Moselle sailor from the previous year, and was a few rungs up the tricky ladder of medical training. These girls each had their own cabins, and the young men shared the two-berth guest cabin in the bow, an excellent place to experience curious dreams in a rough sea. Both these male members were new, as the two nephews who had served as hands on the Moselle had been overtaken by the urgency of life, one of them being far too occupied with his medical finals to come boating and the other having gone to Guyana as a missionary. Of our first-year deck-hands John Cooper was half-way up the creek of theology at Oxford. He had never been on a boat before and all the way from Sweden to Lübeck he would hopefully fish off the wharf, never downcast by complete failure to find a fish stupid enough to think the metal spinner was anything but a metal spinner. With him was one of my own innumerable cousins, Indrei Ratiu, who had just finished his Modern Languages Tripos at St John's, Cambridge.

Indrei was an excellent crew member, because he had canals and locks in his blood. His mother had a boat, the *Lorelei*, on the canals in England, and as a family they had done some very enterprising voyages through such weed-strangled waterways as those of the Middle Level. Being used to boats Indrei knew there was always something that needed doing, and he would sand and varnish the superstructure as we went along. He was a good linguist, too, but it was a surprise to me to find that although the Cambridge Tripos could fill a man with information about Thomas Mann – which later in the voyage was to prove quite useful – it could turn out graduates who did not know the words for freeboard, stern, bollard or tide. However, one with a knack for languages can quickly pick up these things from the skipper, so Indrei's vocabulary soon came to include more useful words as well as academic ones. The only one of our crew to be able to speak German – though Juliet could talk better French than a Frenchwoman – Indrei could talk the hind leg off any lock-keeper we met on our way to Lübeck.

This crew had by now been with us for ten days, and was used to the irregular hours which voyaging imposes, but as young people have an inexhaustible capacity for sleeping it still came as a surprise to me that the company should all wish to make the voyage to Kiel at once and in the dark. Perhaps it was the excellent wine that did it, but only an hour before midnight we were flicking off the lines and pushing out from Kappeln's quayside to move past the grain coasters and the silent, sturdy fishing-boats on our way toward Schleimünde.

After twenty years of voyaging there are certain journeys which stand out in my memory with a vividness which nothing can dim. If I were a deep-sea sailor used to running over the parallels of latitude for weeks on end with nothing to look at but the sea and my own face in the shaving mirror the unforgettable moments would probably be those concerned with storms and hazards, with snapping booms and riven sails, but as I share with the *Thames Commodore* a belief that inland voyaging is really much more interesting the times I remember most clearly are those when the water or the landscape suddenly revealed itself to us in a beauty quite unexpected. The coast of Schleswig is by no means magnificent, and yet the run from the Schlei to the Kiel fjord was one of the most entrancing I have ever made.

There was just a reasonable cheese-rind of moon when we set out, but in the clear night the stars accounted for half of what little

light there was. Three pairs of leading lights held astern in turn
would see us right through the shallows to the entrance, but as
their lines of sight cut so close to the edge of the channel I sent
John to sit on the fore-deck and sweep the water ahead with the
searchlight, picking up each of the sixteen red spars in turn so that
we would not be one of those vessels alluded to in the *Baltic Pilot*
which battered the buoys or swept them away.

The buoys stood out well in the sharp ray, and so did the swans,
some of them awake and watchful and others with neck coiled like
a hose-pipe and head tucked under the edge of one wing so that they
resembled pillows floating on the water. Some would stir on the
waves of our wash, others remained sleeping, drifting slowly over
the shallows in the very slight flow of the Schlei current. Once the
beam picked up what appeared to be a stump until the orange glint
reflected from its eye showed it to be a heron standing and watching
us sideways. I wondered that he could fish in the dark, but
perhaps he was merely enjoying the calm night air as much as
ourselves.

As we bore down upon the kink of channel just short of the
lonely pilot station I wondered what we should find outside. I had
not forgotten putting out from Kiel in calm water to find such
rollers driving past the fjord that I had had to turn back. A calm
Schlei did not necessarily mean that the sea beyond the mole
would be as smooth as float glass, but in another few minutes we
should know. In fact the Baltic itself was lying as still as the inlet,
and heading out to give the shore a safe offing of a mile the *Thames
Commodore* cut her way over water which could not even faintly
rock her to assure her that this was really the sea again.

To starboard the line of the shore cut dark against a sky in which
the minute droplets of condensing dew glowed with just the faintest
tint of whitish orange, and as the thin moon tipped our wash the
scene was one of such rare beauty as can never be experienced with
quite the same intensity on land. I would not have been greatly
surprised if a mermaid had popped up to see what we were doing
in her private waters, for we were not sending down a rain of
dumped explosives, as was the custom in this area marked by four
yellow buoys.

A curious stillness hung over sea and shore alike. It was not that menacing quiet which precedes a storm but just a complete absence of motion, of sound, and even of light outside the sphere of our own little ship. It was as though we were in some strangely peaceful space-craft, coursing through outer space remote from any bustle of the distant earth.

The Schleswig coast can hardly have been uninhabited, especially in mid-August. Its cliff-tops and tideless beaches must have been strewn with tents and caravans, and even if the villages lay prudently back from the edge of the soft boulder-clay the line of land which made a dark streak between sky and water cannot have been entirely devoid of buildings. And yet as we voyaged southward shortly after midnight there was only the fading light of Schleimünde far behind us and otherwise not a glimmer to be seen on the landward side. If there were houses, their lights had already been extinguished and the families had gone to bed – which perhaps at such an hour was not unreasonable. Only a tiny flash from a yellow buoy at one corner of the ammunition dumping ground came and went regularly on our port bow. Beyond it lay a vast expanse of blankness, and only because we knew the geography of the Baltic could we imagine that not so very far away over the horizon the lights of the Danish isles would be blinking to the ships.

It was two hours before the light of Bülk Point broke through the faint mist on the right. On our left there soon appeared a curious affair with windows ablaze with lights. This could not possibly be a ship, I decided. It was more like a city office block delivered to the wrong address and dumped down in the Baltic with all the main services connected. The building appeared to be very much where the Kiel lightship should have been, and as there was no trace of the light vessel to be seen I concluded correctly that it had been removed and replaced by a light-tower. Another mile or two and we entered the main shipping lane from the Kiel Canal to the north and east, and soon there were ships coming and going on both sides of us – timber carriers, tankers, tramps and fishing-boats, craft large and small hurrying in or out of the fjord, throwing up their curling bow-waves to sparkle in the starlight.

Very faint against the dark sky a black finger pointed upward on the further shore, the great column of the Naval Memorial at Laboe. We turned to starboard to run past Bülk at a distance which should keep us clear of its half-mile or more of offshore boulders, then aimed down the safe sector of the Friedrichsort light in the neck of the inlet. To our left Laboe itself lay in complete darkness, the thousands of holiday visitors very properly asleep at half-past-two in the morning. Between them and us there was a great sand fixed, but already the flasher at its inner end was in sight, winking to us cheerfully to cross over between the ships, turn into the harbour at the foot of Laboe Hill, and draw in ahead of a pair of grain ships lying against the quay.

Laboe's harbour is a pleasant one with fishing-boats, a few motor barges unloading Scandinavian timber or filling their holds with grain, and a score or two of small sailing yachts. Berthed just inside the entrance are a powerful pilot cutter festooned with old motor tyres, a customs boat, and the bright yellow *Theodor Heuss*, ready to dash out at a moment's notice to rescue the shipwrecked along the Baltic coast. This ship is one of the busiest of all the fleet of the D.G.R.S., the German Lifeboat Society, and if it makes more sorties and saves more lives in the easy summer months than it does in the winter gales this is because the pattern of seamanship has changed. There are few brigantines or under-powered old tramps to be swept ashore these days, and the merchant ships are not only more powerful but better equipped for knowing where they are. Radar, radio-fixing and echo-sounder have made it much less likely that a ship will get into serious trouble. On the other hand the summer brings out the thousands of yachtsmen, many of them hopelessly inept and quite unwilling to take weather forecasts or sky portents seriously. Add to these the bathers blown out to sea asleep on rubber mattresses, and visitors who have rented a pedalo for the day, and there are sure to be plenty of customers floundering in the summer sea until – if they are fortunate – the *Theodor Heuss* arrives in time to save them from drowning.

Just now the Baltic lay as still as a painted sea, but it was not necessarily so motionless in the summer. In fact it was on an

August day that the wind decided to spread itself for a frolic, and soon a large German yacht was seen to be driving towards the shore. The lifeboat went out to fetch her out of danger, arriving back at Laboe just in time to make another sortie to save a second expensive sailing yacht from being smashed to pieces by the surf. Soon afterwards the coastguard reported the distress signal flying from the top of the brand new and magnificent *Minka III*, a Dutch yacht which was driving helplessly before the storm. Aboard were the owner and his wife, two young children and a pair of guests, and with not a single sail left intact and the motor out of commission this craft was driving on to the ammunition dumping ground where a heaving swell was pounding and breaking. The *Theodor Heuss* got a line aboard and towed this ship also to Laboe; but there was to be no rest, for now it was the English yacht *Zoom* which was reported driving down the Baltic coast before the ferocious sea with all its sails hanging in shreds like those of a Sadler's Wells Flying Dutchman. One man and two women were aboard this one, and they were lucky that the lifeboat could reach them in time and fire a line across, for the ship was already holding plenty of water and rolling wildly at each fresh attack of the waves.

Because of its position at the centre of the German yachting coast and close to beaches visited by many thousands of holiday-makers the *Theodor Heuss* could expect to have plenty to do during the summer months. So could the others, and during the year before we arrived at Laboe they had together saved 814 people from drowning, nearly half of them along the Baltic shore. No less than 399 were yachtsmen, and 72 were bathers or people swept out to sea in rubber dinghies and other craft hardly suited for facing a Baltic or a North Sea storm.

Since my wife happened to be chairman of a branch of the R.N.L.I. we silently saluted the *Theodor Heuss* as we ran slowly past her, but there was no one aboard to see our greeting. On such a night as this the lifeboat could lie idly at her berth just inside the jetty, reasonably confident that not even the most irresponsible dinghy-sailor could get into trouble. There was not so much as a cat on the prowl in Laboe, and the only creature awake was a rather sleepy black-backed gull which was standing dreamily on a post by the ferry landing and opened one eye to watch us pass his roost. We stilled the motors and turned in until the morning, which lay just over the eastern horizon behind the hill.

Laboe is best known for its huge monument which faces out across the Baltic Sea. I am not one who finds war memorials necessarily attractive or even emotionally moving, but there are two which for sheer grandeur and imagination seem to me to be as worthy as anything can be of the hundreds of thousands of men whose death they commemorate. One is the United States Air Force memorial at Madingley, and the other the Marine-Ehrenmal at Laboe, the same tall finger which guided us in the starlight to the fairway of the Kiel fjord. Curiously enough the German government did nothing to provide a naval memorial after the First World War, and it remained for the mate of one of the ships to campaign among his own comrades to raise the money. Admiral Scheer became patron of the scheme, but it was nearly seven years after the armistice before a site was acquired. The choice was a brilliant one, a disused and dynamited fort which stood on a slight rise commanding the entrance to the fjord in which lay the Kiel naval base.

The underground bunker was converted into a Hall of the Dead so impressive that even today many people who know little about either of the two successive mass slaughterings find themselves standing silently weeping. The light is dim, almost ultra-violet, and a faint glimmer falls through the central roof lens upon the space round which the individual memorials and flags are clustered, their legends in sombre Gothic script. A long gallery slopes up toward the court above, and at the edge of this is the great tower itself, its outer side falling a sheer 250 feet to the Baltic shore, its inner face curving down like a hyperbola graph-line to the court-yard. At the foot of the curve is the bell of the cruiser *Seydlitz*, one of those sunk at Scapa Flow, and inside the base of the tower a hall with a plain greyish expanse of wall on which are cut the outlines of every unit of the German navy lost in either of two costly wars.

It is this silent fleet which to me makes the Laboe memorial something unforgettable. 210 merchant ships, 122 minesweepers,

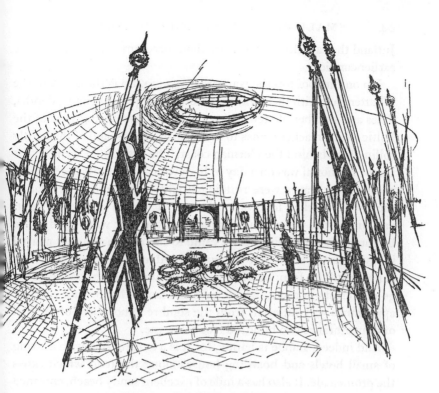

Laboe – The Hall of the Dead

211 U-boats, 46 Zeppelins, squadrons of destroyers and naval aircraft, cruisers and torpedo-boats, corvettes and battleships, each individual ship is there on the cold grey sea to recall the 35 thousand men of the navy who by 1918 were never to come back. One can hardly believe that this vast mass of engineering and invention could have been sent to the bottom of the sea as only one part of the fantastic slaughter which followed a fanatical murder in the Balkans, but it was. And as one turns toward the other wall where the losses of the Second World War are similarly carved, one notices at once that the ships are packed more thickly on their background. Hitler's Germany had few large naval ships, but the losses of smaller ones were staggering. Not many survived who served in that navy. More than 800 German U-boats were destroyed in the second of the world-wide wars over the oceans, and although there were no engagements on the scale of the Battle of

Jutland the casualties were more than three times as great as in the earlier conflict.

Up on the roof top the wars are forgotten. So is the drone of the lift attendant with the familiar useless catalogue of heights, depths, dates and number of steps. Instead there is a sweeping view of the Baltic which reaches across to the Danish islands, and of the lightly rolling land behind the German coast. The first time I went up the Laboe memorial was on a day of high wind, and across the fields of charlock the waves were running bright yellow and as regular as their white-flecked fellows on the sea. It was an intriguing sight, and timing the watery and vegetable waves over what I judged to be roughly similar distances I came to the conclusion that a swell in charlock travels at just the same speed as a swell in water. The sun was still far from overhead and it gleamed in the tossing of the golden crests in a way which gave the land a happy and carefree appearance very different from the sombre atmosphere of the hall of remembrance two hundred feet below me.

And indeed, Laboe is happy, for it is a small resort with a string of small hotels and boarding houses along the road which skirts the promenade. It also has a mile of excellent sandy beach, entrance to which is absolutely *verboten* until one has paid one mark. Just why I should object to paying to go on the sand I do not know; perhaps it is merely the Lancastrian in me that refuses to pay for something which I feel should be public property. I will pay to enter a park or garden, or to see over some crumbling castle keep, but the idea of paying merely to sit or walk on the bare sand is one that I cannot bring myself to accept. Illogically, I expect the beach to be open, and kept clean by the local council without any special charge to its users.

Perhaps the payment is the cause of the extraordinary activity of the German families entrenched along the Laboe shore. Having won a place at the cost of several good marks for a season ticket they will dig themselves in. A biologist might see in the Laboe beach a demonstration of the territory-claiming habit found in so many very different creatures, and perhaps a psychologist would interpret the scene in terms of curious Freudian concepts, but maybe it is just that a strong wind will often blow across the Baltic shores, making it difficult to snooze in the sun unless one has taken certain precautions. This was the simple explanation given to me by a yachtsman in Laboe, but it does not account for the fact that the Danes do things differently. In the Flensburg fjord, Danish Sønderborg and German Glücksburg both have good sandy beaches. On the Danish shore people merely lie in the sun – just like cats or humans. On the German beach the thing is done regally. Merely to place the torso on a beach formed by nature would be impossible.

Central to the German family holiday at the seaside is the two-seater cuddle-seat, something without which a holiday at a German seaside resort would be unthinkable, and at Laboe as at Glücksburg we found the beach well supplied with them. The throne is designed to take the ampler figure – two of them, in fact – and beneath it are drawers and lockers for all the equipment one must have if intending just to sit in pleasing side-by-side idleness or to flop down and recover from the sheer exertion of digging. Walking along the Laboe promenade I thought there was a fortune awaiting the man who could market a miniature bulldozer for sea-shore use, its tracks guaranteed safe for infant fingers; but perhaps it would be unnecessary, for when the German family begins to dig it can shift more sand than a gang of Irish navvies, working tire-lessly to surround the seat at a reasonable distance with a bank as impressive in its way as a Bronze Age fort, a miniature ring-wall of Haithabu with a single narrow entrance.

This rampart is no rough bank – or is only so in the case of what must clearly be problem families. Geometrically accurate, its precisely graded faces and top are smoothed so that the edge is as sharply cut as that of a wall. The family has brought with it from the Ruhr not only the necessary digging tools but also a rake to smooth the outfield and remove the footsteps of strangers, and a water-can with a rose. This last is essential, for if there is the least breeze the exactness of the contours may be destroyed unless the bank is watered the moment a piece has been shaped. Tirelessly father runs down to the edge of the sea for another can of water while the rest of the family shovel and shape with man-sized spades. So vital is the watering, that the first people astir in Laboe the morning we arrived there were the fathers sent out before breakfast to wet their fortifications after a dry night.

Some families had turned their entrenchments into real works of art. Shells were not common on the Laboe beach, nor were cobbles, and the youngsters must have ranged the shores for days or miles to collect the materials for the life-sized two-tone shark laid out in pebbles, or the giant octopus entirely constructed of cockles. After so much work I am sure I could not easily have been torn away at the end of the fortnight by the sea. I would have wanted to squat there in my wicker shelter till frozen out by the pack ice of a hard winter, or until my encampment were sacked by marauding Norwegians or destroyed by a force of fiery Wends.

IV

Canal of the Kaiser – Rendsburg and the ghost train – Offa,
champion of the Angles – fog on the canal – Brunsbüttelkoog
– murder on the dike – portents of flooding – the waterways
of Hamburg – fashions from London – the humility of Duke
Adolf

'BY Jove, we want a man like this Kaiser, who doesn't wait to
be kicked, but works like a nigger for his country and sees
ahead.'

That was the opinion of Davies as he steered the *Dulcibella*
down the Kiel Canal, revealing some of the admiration which
Erskine Childers himself had for the great work of iron-age
Hohenzollern competence, this 'mighty waterway that is the
strategic link between the seas of Germany', as he called it. 'Broad
and straight, massively embanked, lit by electricity at night till it
is lighter than many a great London street; traversed by great war
vessels, rich merchantmen and humble coasters alike, it is a
symbol of the new and mighty force which, controlled by the
genius of statesmen and engineers, is thrusting the Empire
irresistibly forward to the goal of maritime greatness.'

The Riddle of the Sands was written more than half a century
before the *Thames Commodore* came galloping by moonlight into
the Kiel fjord, but the impression of power and purpose is still
there, from one end of the great waterway to the other, and no
boatman can run through the Nord–Ostsee Kanal, or Kiel Canal,
without feeling something of wonder and awe. So huge are the
locks at either end that one may walk a quarter of a mile to round
the end of the pen, pay the dues and receive clearance from the
lock-keeper, and on the main locks each actual moving gate is
larger than an entire lock on the river Thames. One feels small, and
unless the ship is at least a two-thousand tonner one is small. Yet
the canal is not only vast. It is a waterway of real majesty, and each

time I have been through it I have vaguely hoped that if in Paradise
there should be any canals running from the Glassy Sea to other
oceans of delight, then at least one of them may be modelled on
that splendid Prussian waterway. Even before entering between
the pierheads which lead to the giant locks one is overawed by the
light-towers, the radio masts, and the signal arms waving their
giant ping-pong bats in welcome or as a sign to wait. In the
roadsteads ships of every size and nationality are steaming slowly
around to wait for an open gate, and no doubt some of the skippers
must be wondering whether they will be refused admission under
Article 7, section (a), subsection 3, which provides that a vessel may
be turned back if, because of misgivings caused by the nature of its
crew, a doubt has arisen in the minds of the canal staff that the
ship can indeed succeed in passing safely through the canal. I was
not sure how such misgivings might be caused. Would the canal
men think our young companions looked irresponsible? Was it
necessary to appear very serious-minded and not risk anything
which might be interpreted as the sign of a frivolous mind? I did
not know – and I was still pondering the matter as we made across
from Laboe toward one of the 1082-foot Holtenau locks behind
such a collection of vessels as would have filled a fair-sized port to
overflowing.

A mere fifty yards ahead of us a big freighter was steaming
slowly towards the gates, her thick black smoke drifting overhead
and making the gulls dodge to the windward side. She was black
and ochre, a typical Russian with all the works screwed to the
outside like a French locomotive. Derricks and booms, capstans
and davits, cable bins and masts and ventilators, she was a fine
collection of chandlery and looked as though she cared more for
business than smooth looks. I could not read her lengthy name but
managed to decipher her home port as Riga. She took the port side
of the lock and the *Thames Commodore* the starboard, and across
the intervening space we exchanged smiles and nods, and skyward
gestures which conveyed that it was a glorious day of late summer
sun. And this willingness to exchange even such commonplace
courtesies came as something of a surprise to me, for I remembered
passing through the canal a decade earlier aboard the *Commodore*

and finding that if we waved or smiled at the Russians they would look past us or over us with expressions of stolid blankness as though anything originating beyond the barbed-wire fence which separated the eastern and western worlds was either dangerous or contaminating. Ten years had worked a great change, and as I walked round the lock with the papers and passed their ship some of the hands – typical ship's lads who could as easily have been Scots or Londoners as Russians – tried a few remarks in English. One of them said the *Thames Commodore* was a good ship, another wished us a good voyage and asked how many days I reckoned to take to reach London. And all through the canal it was to be the same, for we met a number of Russian ships and in every case the old-time surliness bred of insecurity seemed to have vanished.

When another twenty thousand tons of shipping had come in behind us the bells rang and the gate began to close. As it did so I realised that once again we were turning our backs on that clear, beautiful, friendly and inhospitable, blue or grey, calm or ferocious sea, the Baltic. Its myriad jellyfish were now being left behind, slowly and thoughtlessly tolling their silent bells of translucent violet and trailing their tentacles to strain from the water the incautious fry of fish. I felt strangely sad, for the Baltic is a curiously romantic stretch of sea, and it was so distant from London that I knew it would be years before the *Thames Commodore* would see it again – if ever she should. I hoped that she would, and that one day she might even chug up the approaches to Leningrad; but now she was bound for Hamburg, Lübeck and then home. I was still thinking of the strange lure of the smaller Danish islands when the bell rang to announce that the inner gate was opening to let the *Thames Commodore* thrust out and lead the field toward the first high bridge, with the Rigan hot in pursuit and a long line of ships astern.

From Holtenau to Rendsburg was a run of only two hours and a half, bucking pleasantly over the washes of each fresh fleet of oncoming traffic. Looking up the log I found that there were only twenty-four more locks between us and the Regent's Canal Dock in London, but in fact we were going to double this number by the diversion to Lübeck. There being no lock in the whole length of the Kiel Canal we might have thrust ahead and passed through in seven hours, but I decided that once again we would turn off at the Audorfersee and run down to the centre of Rendsburg, where there was a convenient quay close to the shops. The town had the advantage of lying at the end of a dead arm of the river Eider, and one could lie there peacefully without being washed up to the roadway by the rollers set up by passing giants.

I had always had a particular affection for Rendsburg since the night eleven years earlier when we had first taken the *Commodore* to the quayside by the grain silos. Our friend Fred Doerflinger had given Rendsburg as a mail pick-up point, and although it was just after midnight when we walked up to the post office a clerk was on duty. We rang the bell and he came to converse with us through a sort of speak-easy grating. There were no letters, he said.

Fred decided to leave a forwarding address, and started to feel in his pocket for a pencil, but at that moment a pen on the end of a small chain popped out of a hole in the door. Fred took it, but he had no time even to start producing a piece of paper before a single sheet came gliding out of a slit. He said something about the wonderful service of the German post office, and thanking the clerk he took up the paper. Holding it against the door he began to write on it.

'One moment,' said the clerk, speaking through the visor. There was a curious clanking sound, and a table materialised from a flap in the side of the door.

If there was one disappointment it was that there seemed no mechanism to drop an office chair from a hoist, and Fred actually had to stand while writing his message. He handed it in, and with a flip the pen vanished into the post office, the table was hexed away through the solid door, and the speaking-flap shut with a pleasant '*Gute Nacht*'.

Rendsburg is now a place of busy shipyards, but it has laid out the banks of the canal with flowerbeds and seats, and pleasant tree-edged walks for the hundreds of visitors who come there on Sundays just to watch the ships go by. Its swing bridge had been

Rendsburg Transporter Bridge

replaced by a tunnel since our last visit, but the tea-tray transporter was still clattering across the canal, hanging from the underside of the high-level railway bridge and reminding me of the similar tray at Runcorn on which I had so often travelled as a child. Alas, that wonderful bridge over the Mersey was not even to be preserved as a monument of great engineering, but had merely been scrapped as out of date. The Rendsburg transporter was just as old-fashioned, but its future seemed more secure. The carrier-bridge itself was needed for the railway, which then descended to earth again by doubling back through its own legs into Rendsburg station, and the tray was established to fulfil a statutory obligation to the particularly obstinate villagers of Osterrönfeld on the opposite side, who had rightly objected to being sundered by the new waterway from their friends and relations, and from the grocers and butchers and drapers of Rendsburg, where they were accustomed to do their shopping.

The high bridge of Rendsburg is connected with that same faculty of certain Holsteiners which enables them to know what unusual phenomena may portend. Or rather, with a curious kind of second sight which extends itself even to providing a preview of various works of engineering. That old Mars Sievers saw the Kaiser's yacht sailing across the fields some years before the canal was built is well known. Nor was he the only one, for some of those returning at night from Rendsburg's hospitable inns caught glimpses of the most surprising things. Among these weird sights were rows of dots of lights moving high in the air over the edge of Rendsburg, a manifestation which was puzzling enough at the time but was easily identified when the railway bridge was built and the trains had to soar up into the night sky to clear the mast-heads of the ships, and the dotted lines of their carriage windows crept high above the pale surface of the Kaiser Wilhelm canal.

Rendsburg is more than a shipyard town. It is an ancient place, set on what was once an island in the river Eider, the same eyot which was the scene of the great fight when the crippled Offa saved the Angles from the tyrannical demands of the Duke of Holstein. Wermund the Wise was then the King of the Angles, those same people who lived in the land around Kappeln and beyond the winding inlet of the Schlei, but besides being old and wise he was blind. His only son, the child of his old age, was Offa, who had also been blind to his seventh year, and even now in his earliest years of adolescence was still dumb and hopelessly deformed and crippled. The Duke of Holstein was well aware of this, and it was just because old Wermund and his only son were such a weak and helpless pair that he sent his envoys with a peremptory note demanding money and the surrender of Anglia, or satisfaction in combat between his own sons and any that Wermund might have.

Despair came upon Wermund and his attendants when they heard the insolent demand, but it so happened that Offa was present in the audience chamber. Suddenly his tongue was loosed, his limbs were straightened, and though only thirteen years old he took up the challenge. He would take on the Holsteiners, he declared, and show them where they belonged.

The king and his counsellors were astounded to hear the boy speak, and old Wermund groped for him and felt his sturdy new limbs. He called for armourers to bring breastplate and mail, but the boy Offa had only to take a breath and the metal burst. Finally Wermund's own youthful armour was brought, cut open down its full length and extended with riveted plates. This suit held, and Offa declared himself satisfied with it.

Next he had to have a weapon. Every conceivable kind of sword was brought forward, but each of them only broke to shivers when Offa merely shook it in his young hand. Finally Wermund's own ancient trusty blade was tried. It had long been buried in a hillock by the Eider, but the men were sent to dig it out, and as soon as he took it in his hand Offa insisted that only that one sword would serve him.

It was Offa who chose the duelling place in the Eider, and soon there came the day when he stepped out before the ranks of the Angles and left them on the northern shore of the river as he advanced to the neutral ground in midstream. However, the crafty Duke of Holstein had decided to make short work of him by sending his own two sons to fight him together. Had he not issued a challenge to 'any of Wermund's sons'?

When Wermund heard that these two redoubtable toughs were to fight his own young boy he stood trembling at the bridge parapet, ready to fling himself in when Offa fell. And indeed he nearly cast himself over, for at first Offa merely received the blows of both his attackers upon his shield and the sound of his sword was not heard at all – for he had not yet used it. But when he judged the time had come he taunted the elder son so that in his fury the fellow lunged at him. Offa side-stepped, and brought the trusty old sword down with such force that he split the young Holsteiner right from the crown of his head to his rump, armour and all, leaving him much in the condition of two sides of bacon. He then taunted the second son to hurry up and avenge his dissected brother's death; and when the incautious young man rushed in upon him he treated him in similar fashion.

Old Wermund wept tears of joy from his blind and aged eyes. The Angles were saved, and their land is still there to this day.

It was evening before we left Rendsburg quay and doubled back to the main canal, chugging up the course of the Upper Eider with its sandy beaches, and its pine-woods, and the children running to paddle in the shallows and let the waves of our wash surge right up to their knees. Little by little the western sun began to fall toward the horizon, casting a golden glow upon the water ruffled by the continual passing of the big ships. Ahead of us was a Danish coaster, slowly overhauling a humble barge of the East Frisian peat moors. Astern another Russian giant towered up, the fading light flickering on the hammer and sickle of her streamlined smoke-stack. The first patches of a light mist were coming to lie faintly over the pastures and creep round the ankles of the cows. When darkness fell we still continued on our way – for stopping in the canal except for urgent navigational reasons was prohibited – but I remembered that there was a small canal leading off on the northern side to link the main waterway with the Lower Eider. This would be a good refuge for the night, and we could sleep there without fear of being run down.

Half a mile or more along this canal we came to a small lock which was closed for the night. There were some piles, and a German sailing boat was already moored there until morning. There was a lock-house but no village, not even a farm. Some peewits called in the dark and I heard a coot in the layer of mist on the water, but otherwise the only sound was the faint background of ship engines, dim in the distance. The sky above was very clear, the stars shining with a brilliance which in southern England would have seemed almost frightening.

When the morning light stole pale and grey into our cabin I looked out of the stern hatch into a mist so blank and yet so solid that the further side of the Gieselau canal was only faintly visible as a darkening in the pale greyness of all around, but as the time was already past five o'clock I decided that we must be off. If we kept the bank within sight we should be able to feel our way back to the main waterway, I thought, and there we could proceed in the same fashion. There was no throb of motors carrying to us through the mist but only the distant tolling of bells on ships made fast to the dolphins of the next lay-by, a sound curiously eerie and reminiscent of ghostly monks summoning to prime in an abbey engulfed in the waves as retribution for some unspeakable sin.

The crew were roused, and turning the ship we set off. Now and then a tree would break the line of the bank but otherwise only the faint, damp thicket of reeds lay close on the starboard side. The visibility was no more than twenty yards, so when we turned the angle into the Kiel Canal itself I sounded the first of the occasional long blasts on the hooter as laid down in the *Rules for Prevention of Collisions*. It so happened that the builders of the ship had at my request fitted a particularly powerful hooter so that on waterways such as the Rhine its note would penetrate the closed wheelhouse of an oncoming barge and break clean through the noise of transistor radios and machinery to let the skipper know our intentions. So, although of only 20 tons net register, the *Thames Commodore* had a hooter which in a fog suggested a ship a hundred times as large. The effect of using it in the Kiel Canal was impressive indeed. Hearing such a mighty blast within a few yards of them, the look-outs of the cargo vessels lying at the piles to wait for a clear view were galvanised into activity. Whistles blew, orders were bellowed through loud-hailers, and the occasional tolling of the ghostly brethren was replaced by such frenzied ringing as one might find in an Indian temple as the men clanged and hammered on the bells to avert what they thought was an impending run-down by a sizeable vessel.

We ran so close to the sides of the big ships that sometimes we could have leaned over and touched them, and as their hulls were often undercut we might see faces looking down on us as the men leaned over the rail to see what curious craft was creeping past their flank. One ship, a Panamanian, was so huge that its side rose above us like an office block with row upon row of small round windows.

'Cor,' said a Cockney voice, looking down upon our deck, 'you didn't 'arf give the mate a fright. Thought you was the *Queen Mary* coming straight for us.'

There was a curious unreality about the dim shapes, the clanging bells, the voices speaking in German and Swedish, in Polish and French and Japanese, all half swallowed in the fog. Beyond the moorings there was silence, then suddenly a sound improbable and unexpected, the lowing of a cow. A mile or two of silvery quiet, and then a blast from our own hooter would release another chorus of dinner bells of every conceivable pitch. Again a quiet broken only by our own engines running at dead slow. We proceeded in this way for almost two hours and during that time we met only one ship, a fine modern coaster clipping along at a fair speed with the radar scanner twirling aloft. Astern the sun at last began to show a silver and moonlike disc through the vapour and then within only a few minutes all trace of fog had vanished and the waterway stretched ahead under a clear blue sky. Two hours more, and we were at Brunsbüttelkoog, the town at the western end of the canal, a place of chandlers, customs officers, shipping agents and pilots.

Brunsbüttelkoog is not a town the landsman would ever visit but it is a wonderful resort for any man who loves ships. Right beside the inner gates of the locks is a little harbour put there just for yachts, with excellent mooring and staging in a position so exciting that one cannot easily sleep at all. For the four alternative locks are busy all through the night, and several times each hour another batch of ships will come streaming out of one of the pens to disappear down the long reach towards the first bridge at Hochdonn. The night is lit by the dockside lamps, the moving rows of porthole lights, the green and red of starboard and port lamps, and the floodlit funnels as the great cargo-liners go gliding by, sending a cradle-rock of ripple into the yacht harbour. There are bells and toots and sirens, and occasionally the long wheezing and hissing as some giant gets up his steamy breath to send a loud bellowing hoot to float away as a white cloud across the trees on the sea-dike beside the locks. Voices call orders over amplifiers, shouting to the winch-hands in Russian and Spanish, American and Scots and Japanese. Several times as many ships, large and small, use the Kiel Canal as go through Panama and Suez combined, and if there are boatmen who can casually turn in and stretch out on a bunk when such a cavalcade of romance is flitting past the portholes, I am not one of them. At Brunsbüttel I must always jump down to the jetty and walk just once more across the gates of the four locks in turn to see who is coming or going, and sometimes to pick out the name of a ship I have seen in the Thames, or lying at the dolphins in the Rotterdam fairway.

It was a little after low water when the giant gates of Brunsbüttel-koog opened to let out another cageful of ships. With a flick of her lines the *Thames Commodore* was swiftly away, surging into the wide estuary to follow the course taken by the fleet of the Emperor Tiberius, which sailed up the Elbe in the year A.D. 5 and reached Hamburg, perhaps even Lauenburg further upstream. The tide was beginning to push powerfully, and for several hours we sped up the river beneath a sky dabbed with the white clouds of late summer. To either side there was little to be seen, for the land lay prudently behind the high banks which would keep at bay the storm floods, and even the village churches had to stand on tiptoe to peep over the massive dikes. Fifteen miles up from the canal I searched in vain the line of land to port for the oak-tree below Glückstadt, but either I failed to pick it out or wind, storm, lightning and flood had removed it. Conceivably it might have died or decayed, for the last reference to it which I had aboard the ship was in a book printed in Schleswig fifty-one years earlier, a volume which even then was only quoting what Professor Müllenhoff of Kiel had written in 1845. Between the eras of Müllenhoff and *Thames Commodore* anything might have happened, even to such a hardy and long-lived species of tree as an oak.

According to Professor Müllenhoff, two labourers sat down together to eat their midday meal and drink their ale in the shadow of a clump of bushes upon the dike-top, and then settled down to snooze away the rest of their lunch-hour in contentment. When they awoke they were surprised to hear the clink of coins, and they realised that another was now taking his rest on the further side of the same bushes. Their curiosity aroused, they stole round from behind and came upon a travelling merchant who had lain down his pack and was counting his takings. The sight of the money was too much for the men. They flung themselves upon the unfortunate traveller, seized his silver and gold, and beat him to death.

Just before their victim expired a flight of ducks swept over the bank, and raising one arm to the sky he called upon them to be witnesses of his fate. The ducks merely flew on their way, as ducks usually will, and the labourers prudently destroyed the evidence by throwing the trader's pack into the tide. However, they must have thought that the body could be washed ashore, for they dug a shallow grave under the bushes and buried it.

From that time onward a blood-red weed appeared and grew over the place of the murder, becoming such a well-known feature that the bend of the dike at that point was soon given the name of Red Patch. Yet this name had no sinister significance for any except the two murderers, and even they eventually forgot the incident of their lunch-hour robbery. The one married, the other became a servant on a farm in the neighbourhood. Neither thought any more about the fate of the traveller.

Forty years had already passed when the married man was walking out with his greyed and ageing wife. It so happened that they strolled in the evening sunshine along the dike by Red Patch, and at the same moment the farm servant came up, on his way to bring in the horse which had been put out to graze. The couple nodded a casual greeting and just at that moment a flight of ducks flew screaming over the top of the dike. Both men started, but they quickly recovered themselves and went on their separate ways, the one for his leisurely walk, the other to round up the horse. On their return they again met close to the bush, and once more the ducks came twisting and crying over the bank. The two men went pale, and the wife was surprised to hear her usually sober and upright husband mutter a terrible curse.

When the couple reached home the wife began to ask her husband the cause of his strange behaviour, but he would tell her nothing. Instead he became morose and downcast. His usual cheerfulness left him and he began to stay at home, avoiding his former friends and preferring to be left alone. At last the wife became so worried for his health that she asked the advice of the neighbour who in turn told her own husband about the curious affair of the ducks and their effect upon the worthy fellow who lived nearby. Something in the account aroused his suspicions, and that same evening he went off to report to the magistrate all that he had heard. The magistrate took some men with him to the river bank, and digging under the turf by the bushes they soon unearthed a skeleton.

Both the evil-doers were arrested, both admitted the murder and revealed that the victim had been a wandering merchant whom they had slain for his money forty years earlier. They were executed at Glückstadt, and to mark the place of the crime a solitary oak was planted, the same tree for which I searched in vain as the *Thames Commodore* surged up the tideway toward the distant city of Hamburg.

It was such a pleasant afternoon of sun and breeze and fleeting cloud that I had not listened to the weather forecast. Certain prognoses were given over the air in a variety of languages, for we were in easy reach of carrier-waves undulating in Dutch, Danish, Swedish, Polish, and a few other languages I could not identify. But we were also in the area where East and West Germans shouted each other down round the whole wave-band, belching out rival news bulletins. In fact the West German ones struck me as showing the moderation which comes from self-confidence, whereas the East Germans smelled so precisely of the Goebbels era that I had only to close my eyes and find myself back in my student days of 1933, with the snarky voices of the 'Ministry for Propaganda and Explaining-away-to-the-People' angling out of the old-fashioned radio of Frau Geheimrat Axenfeld while we all sat round and laughed – except the young Prussian with the blond and bristling hair, who had just enrolled in the S.S. and later went, I presume, to a glorious death at Stalingrad.

The East German radio left nothing to the imagination. It always spoke of the 'criminal Americans' and had a selection of endearment-adjectives for the Russians and Ghanaians, with special titles of honour for Egypt's President Nasser, opponent of those international criminals the Israelis. It was amusing at first, then disgusting, and finally so boring that we could not bear to have the torrent of hatred spilling into the *Thames Commodore*'s cheerful saloon, and we only tuned in to the music programmes. For the weather I relied upon my eyes, and the portents.

North-western Germany is a great place for portents, and particularly of such storms as may cause floods. In the Elbe estuary, as everywhere in the German Bight, floods have often wrought havoc. Ploughed land overwhelmed in the fourteenth century was swept bare six hundred years later, to show the furrows still standing. Naturally the survivors always saw in the disaster a blow of divine punishment falling upon their wicked neighbours, and occasionally some strange phenomenon would underline the way in which nature was turned upside down – as in the December flood of 1287, when fifty thousand are said to have perished though many drifted ashore alive, borne on hay-ricks, beams or uprooted trees. It was on this occasion that a chronicler reported a large balk of timber coming ashore, bearing a man, a dog, a wolf and a hare, all companions in distress.

Each great flooding has been alleged, though only by hindsight, to have been preceded by strange portents. There are tales of bread being turned to stone and beer into blood as a celestial hint that something out of the ordinary was afoot, and both were reported just before the inundation which formed the Bosom of Jade in the Juliana flood of 17 February 1164. Similar curiosities were reported from other localities swept by the same storm. Indeed, beer turning to blood was always one of the commonest gale-warnings in the days before radio, and sometimes live eels would emerge from the glowing charcoal of the bake-oven, or hams hanging from the ceiling would begin to move of their own accord. Airborne armies appeared, battling in the night sky, and sometimes spirits would shriek and groan in the branches. A few of these had actually squeaked and gibbered through our halyards in the Baltic.

Before we left Brunsbüttel my wife had already assured me there were no live eels creeping out of the blower-box of the galley stove, and so far as I knew none of those aboard had relieved themselves of small fish while urinating, a particularly certain sign of impending storm among the Holsteiners. I had not liked to raise the matter directly, but I remembered that just before the *Commodore* became stormbound in Cuxhaven for two days we had a small eel in the toilet bowl, and before a rough run over the Ijsselmeer I had removed a fish from the filter of the engine cooling intake. These had certainly been portents – for normally such creatures never entered the plumbing, and the lavatory bowl fauna was usually limited to small snails, leeches, and freshwater shrimps.

If on this particular day there were no dreadful auguries, that was perhaps because the water was almost smooth, its surface ruffled by only the smallest of waves except where the ocean ships threw it into heaving folds to relieve the monotony. But in fact the Elbe estuary can be an exceedingly unpleasant place when gale and tide combine to drive the North Sea into the funnel of the German Bight and raise it to the top of dikes as massive as the ring-wall of Haithabu. Vast tracts of country are protected by these banks and for centuries their upkeep has been so vital that diking used to be regulated by rigid laws which regarded the matter as one of continual battle between the human defenders and the ferocious elements which ceaselessly lay in wait to launch an attack. Every man, whether master or servant, rich or poor, noble or farmer, was obliged to contribute to the cost of upkeep, and the sale of a piece of land carried with it the obligation to maintain a piece of dike frontage. The river banks thus came to be dotted with white marker posts which showed the limits of each owner's responsibility, and these were set up by the dike bailiffs whose business was to see that the defences were properly manned. If any man dared to obliterate the marks upon such a post or to pull a marker out of the ground he was liable upon summary conviction to a heavy fine, hard labour, or possibly to have his hand cut off. As late as 1743 the magistracy of Stade decreed that anyone convicted of wilfully causing a breach in a dike would be burned alive, so serious might be the effects of such frivolity.

In those days laws were certainly such as to deter all but the most foolhardy where the general safety was concerned, and equally rigorous discipline prevailed aboard ship. In these northern lands brawling was strongly discouraged, and any member of a ship's crew who drew his knife upon another would be nailed to the mast for one day by means of his own knife, which was driven through his left hand into the wood. This was an effective punishment and one which actually caused no permanent crippling.

Forty miles up from Brunsbüttel the low land gave way to the hills of Blankenese, with smart villas facing southward across the water, and small sailing craft crossing and recrossing the fairway. Then came the huge dry-docks to starboard and quickly we were in the world of great liners moored to buoys, of bustling tugs and harbour ferries and all the churning and heaving of a fairway second only to that of Rotterdam. To starboard the chimneys of the refinery area sent slender plumes of smoke to drift over the city, and to port Hamburg itself rose up with its green domes and its spires, and the Kaiserhöft, where punctually on the stroke of one o'clock (midday at Greenwich) the ball dropping from the mast used to be watched by the captains of scores of vessels anchored in the river, so that their chronometers could be set for the next voyage. Radio time signals have put an end to the value of Hamburg's time ball, as they have to its Greenwich counterpart which once announced the precise moment of noon to the skippers in the docks of the Isle of Dogs, but one o'clock is nevertheless the signal for work to begin again in the harbour after the lunch hour. From the St Pauli landing-stage and the jetties in the entrances to the canals of the city the tenders rush out to cross the water, the workers packed aboard them like cattle. Forging across the strong tide they add their stirring to a churning which never quite dies away, even on a Sunday morning.

Hamburg is famous for its Alster, half river and half lake, and for the sleazy sordid Reeperbahn (or Rope-walk) area, where women are exhibited in the shop-windows of their proprietors as though they were codfish. In this respect it is like many other world ports, but the city also has a considerable charm when visited by boat, for a reasonably determined boatman can force his way right into its stoutly beating heart by threading the courses of the medieval canals which link the Elbe on the one side with the Alster

Hamburg

on the other. These waterways are called *Fleete*, and perhaps there
is a parallel with the Fleet in London, now buried beneath
Farringdon Street and converted to a sewer.

Certainly in their hey-day the waterways of Hamburg must have
been very like that lost river of London. Nowadays they lie quiet
and still with hardly a boat upon them, but before the almost total
destruction of the old city in 1943 these same canals must have
given Hamburg an appearance of Dordrecht or Amsterdam. In
old prints one can see how the sailing barges and schooners and
small coasting vessels once used to lie all through the centre of the
city, ranged two or three abreast beneath the hoists. Visitors of the
Grand Tour period would often compare Hamburg with Venice,
not just because the canals were flanked by merchant houses of
great splendour but perhaps also on account of the thick effluvia
which rose from the channels into which the houses drained
directly. The fact that the tide ebbed and flowed in the canals made
this a less dangerous practice than one might imagine, although the

ebb would lay bare a decidely unpleasant mixture of mud and refuse. The practical-minded Hamburgers would carry out their commode-pots at night and empty them off the bridges, but the by-laws forbade the throwing in of dead dogs, stones, garbage and manure, and Fleet-watchers were appointed to see that the law was to some extent obeyed.

Like Gothenburg in Sweden, that Hamburg of a century ago had close trading connections with England and Scotland, and in the city on the Elbe anything English was extremely fashionable. Furniture, carpets and clocks were imported from London to give the better-class houses an authentic savour, and to speak or at least to swear or make love in English was the height of good breeding. Jermyn Street suits were worn by men who took five o'clock English tea in Wedgwood cups, poured from silver teapots of Mappin and Webb. *The Times* displayed its front page personal and agony columns on Hamburg stalls, the ladies reclined on English sofas from Maples and read Gray's Elegy or waded through three-deckers mercifully cut to shorter proportions for the German market. Their hair-dos had addenda fashioned by the most exclusive London hairdressers, and real Old English Lavender was the most exotic or at least the most aristocratic scent in all the world. Hunting prints looked down from the walls, plum pudding was served at dinner parties, ale and porter from Burton was thought far superior to the beers of Munich. Indeed there was a saying that when it rained in London the people of Hamburg put up their umbrellas.

This very Englishness of Hamburg's past gave the *Thames Commodore* a feeling of confidence as she poked her nose into the numerous creeks and openings to find just the kind of berth she liked at the very heart of things. Having no map of the *Fleete* – and indeed not even knowing of their existence – it was some time before we found an entrance which led into the centre of the city, but the exploring was in itself a delight for as we searched hither and thither we came upon some most attractive corners where a few old warehouses had miraculously survived along the sides of canals which formed the port in days gone by, in an age when the ships berthed in them were caravels and barques. The kinked course of the Zollkanal still had an austere beauty imparted by the brick warehouses above its deep gulley, and the fact that Hamburg is tidal gave the quays and steps and piles the same aged and water-worn appearance that is so characteristic of the wharves and jetties below Upper Thames Street in the fur-trading area of London.

I would have chosen the Zollkanal as a berth but for the fact that a heavily tidal area is not a good place to stop. There is always the worry of whether the lines have been left slack enough, or perhaps too loose, and what will happen if the boat is left waterless at the full ebb. But turning under the viaduct of the town railway we found a lock hidden away beneath a road bridge, and through this we came into a reasonably pleasant and quiet water-way, the Alsterfleet. A few bridges short of the Alster the head-room was too reduced for us to pass, but we found a pleasant and new-built quayside all to ourselves below the Graskellerbrücke. Two elderly Hamburgers were angling, but otherwise there was little life on the canal, which was the main route from Elbe to Alster for small sailing craft.

The Graskeller was formerly the site of the Mill Gate, and it must have been somewhere close to our mooring that an incident once happened which sheds a particularly pleasant light on the character of Adolf IV, the Duke of Holstein who at the battle of Bornhövede won a resounding victory over the Danes under King Valdemar, and so put an end for ever to Danish expansion into the European mainland. It is said that when all his men had fled, Valdemar was stumbling about the battlefield in the dark when he came upon a rider in armour and with his visor closed. Without revealing his identity Valdemar, whose own horse had been killed, offered the stranger a rich reward if he would convey him in safety to Kiel – which at that time was Danish. The knight agreed, and sweeping the unhappy king up to his saddle he galloped away, not drawing rein or even speaking until he had brought the fugitive into the courtyard of the royal castle.

At the royal command the money was brought, and Valdemar asked the knight to remove his visor and announce his identity. When the rescuer did so, the Danes were astonished to see that it was Duke Adolf himself, who had ridden fearlessly into the heart

D

of the palace of his own mortal enemy. Then Duke Adolf dropped his visor again, turned his horse, and galloped across the Danish territory to reach his own camp in safety.

That was in the year 1227. Twelve years later Duke Adolf decided that he was through with wars and government, tired of all pomp and ceremony, surfeited with the company of nobles and courtiers. He would go into a monastery. His dear wife seems to have been reconciled to the idea, and after bidding each other fare-well for ever the couple parted – he to his chosen monastery, she to a convent. They left behind them two grown sons, Johann I and Gerhard I, to whom the government of Holstein was entrusted. Duke Adolf entered the foundation of St Mary Magdalene of which he had been a great benefactor, and where his own brother was the highly esteemed provost.

Adolf – for he had now renounced his title also – was so modest that he did not wish to gain anything either by virtue of his own past life or by family connection, and so he insisted upon becoming the most menial of the brethren, a humble lay brother, a servant to the monks themselves. Daily he would go from door to door begging money for the poor, and he ran errands for the monks who worked in the kitchen. Thus it came about that one morning he was walking back from the Graskeller carrying a pail of milk when he saw riding towards him down the street his own two ducal sons, magnificently decked out and at the head of a smart retinue, accompanied by heralds with trumpets. Suddenly he felt ashamed, and perhaps fearful that his sons should see their father carrying anything so humble and practical as a milk-pail he quickly hid it under his cloak. However, his sons and their companions never even noticed the identity of the lay brother shrinking against the wall, and they passed gaily on their bustling way.

As they rode away along the street Adolf was again overcome with a sense of shame, but this time it was different. Mortified that he should actually have tried to conceal his menial occupation, he drew out the pail from under his gown, and to teach himself proper humility he inverted the bucketful over his head.

V

The Elbe and its hazards – the chain-ships – Geesthacht
barrage – the rail-ferry of Lauenburg – town of shippers –
salt for Scandinavia – the Palmschleuse – encounter by
night – where East meets West – tragedy of the frontier
fence

BELOW Hamburg the Elbe is a highway of international
shipping. Above the city it also carries the ships of other
countries, for just as the Rhine is the outlet to the sea for Switzer-
land and Luxembourg, so the Elbe carries the freight of Czecho-
slovakia and the 'People's Republic of Germany'. A few Polish
barges also find their way into the Elbe. Whilst the radio stations
of East and West were fighting wordy battles on the carrier-waves
pulsing overhead and competing for the aerial of our simple radio
set, the barges of the East were frothing up the course of the river
alongside their West German counterparts with as much natural
ease and friendliness as one would expect from men of the water
who are more interested in the position of the next sandbank than
in political theory, and as the *Thames Commodore* chugged up the
stream towards Geesthacht lock she was in the company of ships
of the national transport concerns of three Communist lands as
well as of West German privateers.

The Elbe is a tricky river. The tide carries to the Geesthacht
barrage twenty-five miles above Hamburg, and it ebbs and flows
with enough force to move the shoals a little at each spring tide,
and very considerably every time there is even a modest flood. For
this reason the chart has no soundings marked upon it and confines
itself to showing ferries, overhead cables and underwater groynes.
There are of course a few buoys, but only where they mark some
permanent and immovable obstacle such as a training wall at the
junction of two arms of the river – for the Elbe indulges in several
splittings and re-unitings on its way down to the city. But the

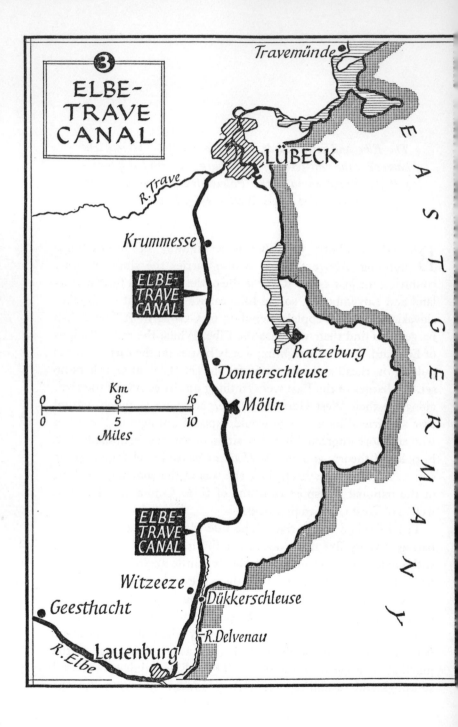

3

ELBE-
TRAVE
CANAL

Travemünde

LÜBECK

R. Trave

Krummesse

ELBE-
TRAVE
CANAL

Ratzeburg

Donnerschleuse

Km
0   8   16
0   5   10
Miles

Mölln

ELBE-
TRAVE
CANAL

Witzeeze

Geesthacht

Dükkerschleuse

R. Delvenau

Lauenburg

R. Elbe

EAST GERMANY

boatman is not without help in finding the channel, for some leading marks are provided in the form of diamond-shaped boards, half white and half red or black, standing on the bank. If the dividing line between the colours is horizontal, that means 'aim for this point'; if vertical the message is 'clear off and head for the other shore'. But the skipper is warned – if he happens to read the correct German publication – that these marks do not exist everywhere, and even where they are present they should only be regarded as 'generally' correct – a statement that is not very reassuring to the steersman.

The poor state of the Elbe channel goes back a long way in history. At the end of the Thirty Years War the river was in a lamentable condition, for the organisation of dike maintenance had gone and the river banks had had no attention for decades. Every flood brought new breaches, and entire hamlets were swept away. A single flood in 1672 put a quarter of the county of Altmark under water. So, over the years, the river spread and opened up new channels, the haulage-path vanished, acres of forest floated out to sea, sandbanks and stranded oak-trees barred the channel. Navigation was brought to a halt, at least until some effort could be made to clear a course and remove the obstructions. This, however, was not so easily achieved, for like the Rhine the Elbe flowed through the domains of a number of petty states which had little inclination to co-operate with each other. Indeed, many of them were convinced that any improvement they carried out in their own territory would inevitably benefit their own hereditary enemies and neighbours, and so they preferred to leave the river as it was, to the danger and hindrance of all. It was this attitude which produced the ramified course of the Elbe which still exists today, and apart from attempts by Frederick the Great to develop shipping on the river none of the riparian governments did anything more than patch and protect their own length of bank against further breaches.

But if governments have rarely liked to undertake works of river control which would benefit others, they have always been enthusiastic in setting up customs posts. Even now Europe is still provided with hundreds of thousands of customs officers at the imaginary boundary lines, men whose duty it is to levy as much toll as they reasonably can on any trade crossing the frontiers. On the river Meuse I have seen the officers of one Common Market country hold up a barge of another Common Market country for two days before letting it proceed along the river with its cargo – a load of river gravel. And if today we are still somewhat customs-ridden we can at least realise that earlier centuries were very much worse, and a ship travelling down the Elbe from Melnik to Hamburg had to stop for inspection and payment of tolls at no less than forty-eight points on the river. What with these and the added staple rights, transhipment tolls and lading dues, to send a consignment of goods by water was not a very profitable undertaking. It was better not to trade at all.

In 1798 the French used their mastery of Europe to put through at the Congress of Rastatt an enlightened measure which would abolish tolls on the Rhine and assure a towpath along all its length, but their effort to secure the same for the Elbe failed, the German states objecting on the grounds that if the tolls were removed there would be no money to keep the river in a navigable state at all. However, after the fall of Napoleon the Allied Powers managed to have nine articles included in the Treaty of Vienna which would ensure all the multi-owner rivers being brought into navigable condition and maintained. So the way was opened for the eventual coming of the first steamers, and in 1841 the old-fashioned bank-hauling by men and animals suffered a blow when six paddle-wheel tugs began a regular towage service up to Magdeburg. These in turn gave way to the *Kettenschiffe* or chain-ships which had the advantage that they had no paddle-wheels to be knocked off by shoals, sunken tree-trunks or groynes, and could operate even when the river level was far below normal. By the year 1874 a chain 410 miles in length had been laid in the river-bed, stretching from Hamburg to Aussig in Bohemia.

The chain-ship was a feature of many fast and shallow German rivers up to the 1920s, and on the Elbe they survived until 1938 – and on one stretch until 1945. At the bow there was a roller or dead-eye by which the chain came up over the deck to pass round a steam-capstan and be paid back into the water over the stern.

The chain-ship wound its way up the chain, towing behind it a string of barges, and it became such a feature of the German scene that up and down the country one can find river villages which have an inn named '*Zur Kette*' – The Chain. Within a few decades the origin of the name will probably be forgotten and visitors will naturally imagine that it refers to the fetters in which some unfortunate lover was doomed to die in a rat-ridden medieval dungeon, but in fact the name recalls the coming of the chain-tug tow-trains.

The chain-ship was certainly a curious vessel. It would puff and grind its way up the river well enough until the awkward moment when it came round a bend and met coming towards it another chain-ship, which was of course using the same chain. It is a strange reflection upon Prussian engineering genius that this problem was never satisfactorily solved, for the best that could be thought up was that the up-coming ship flung the chain overboard, drifted out of the channel and dropped anchor until its sister had passed. Then grapples were cast until the chain was hooked and hauled aboard again. In some cases the design of the ships with their high funnels made it impossible to drop the chain overboard without first severing it, and after the loose ends had both been recovered they had to be rejoined. For these occasions and the incidents when the chain merely broke of its own accord the ship carried a forge, some smiths, and a supply of spare links. This repair force was in any case necessary, as the chain sometimes parted under the sheer strain of use.

The chain-ships had long since vanished when the *Thames Commodore* began to forge her way up the river. So had the ancient steamers which carried passengers from Bohemia to Hamburg in three days, making the return journey in another nine. Even the great two-funnelled paddle tugs had nearly gone, and only one of them still remained in commission, flailing all the way up to Prague under the flag of the C.S.P.O., the Czechoslovak National River Transport Agency. Inevitably these splendid vessels were bound to give way to others, but nobody who has seen them threshing their way up the Elbe or the Rhine Gorge can fail to be sad at their passing. Still, the Czechs have a dozen stern-wheelers on the Hamburg run, and that in itself is something out of the ordinary.

The lower reaches of the Elbe are not spectacular. Oil tanks and pylons give way to a more rural scene with poplars and cows and banks of golden sand, but most of the hamlets lie hidden behind the high dikes, fearful that once again the river may overflow when storm-wind and spring tide combine to battle against a flood coming down from the lands upstream. If Hamburg is imprudent enough to flaunt herself along the river front, then she may do so; but she must take the consequences – as in the flood night of 1962, when more than three hundred people were drowned in their beds or frozen to death in the trees which they had climbed for safety, and twenty thousand motor-cars were given a ducking in the streets where they stood. Other, smaller places will prefer to be more prudent.

With the landscape thus hidden we could give our full attention to the extraordinary variations in depth shown by the echo-sounder. Crossing the river from side to side as instructed by the marker-boards the *Thames Commodore* sometimes had thirty-five feet of water beneath her, and a few seconds later less than three feet under her shallow keel. This made the voyage all the more exciting – for nothing causes suspense so effectively as a continual waiting for the slithering bump which announces that one is on the bottom. However, the tide was still making and much larger ships than ours were moving along the river, if somewhat cautiously, and after three hours we came in sight of Geesthacht lock without actually having grounded at all.

Geesthacht has a harbour. It also sets out to be something of a resort, but who could ever wish to escape to such a place I do not know. It is without exception the most run-down, formless, un-interesting place I have ever come across in Germany, and is best quickly forgotten. But the lock is magnificent, its great towers in pink and grey and white having a real style about them. What is more, it allows visitors to come and peer down upon the ships, Bundesrepublican and Peoplesrepublican, Czech and – on this particular afternoon – British.

The Geesthacht barrage was not built for navigation, but to help the flow of electricity. The dam forms a lake of river water above it, and in the night when other power stations are spinning merrily in distant parts of the country but the demand for electricity is low, giant electric pumps at Geesthacht suck the Elbe into their mouths and drive the water up and over the hill-top into a reservoir. Then when day breaks and the domestic load increases, the switches are reversed and the pumps become turbines, the water rushing back to its bed again and producing a useful load of kilowatts as it does so. It is presumably to see this wonder of almost perpetual motion that visitors come to Geesthacht, and also to flee from the town itself into the wooded hills which stretch along the northern bank of the river all the way to Lauenburg, thirteen miles ahead.

The *Thames Commodore* needed only an hour and a half to come in sight of Lauenburg. Beyond the town itself a cut led off on the port hand, running in past a huddle of black-funnelled tugs and empty barges toward the first lock of the Elbe–Trave Canal, whilst the main stream curved away a little to starboard to disappear beneath a gaunt railway bridge of practical girder network. As late as 1878 there was no railway bridge over the Elbe below Wittenberge, although railways existed in the states on either side, but in the early 1860s Hanover concluded a treaty with the Berlin–Hamburg railway and another line, by which a branch was built from Lüneburg to the Elbe opposite Lauenburg, and another to Lauenburg itself. This latter place was at that time within the Danish dominions, and it was partly the unwillingness of the Danish crown to build a bridge into Hanoverian territory which caused the two terminals to be linked instead by a train ferry, a paddle-wheeler equipped with sets of railway tracks and with separate cabins for the three classes of passengers, who had to dismount from their carriages. The ferry was a double-ended ship, and she made the crossing in about ten minutes, most of her energy being of course used to stem the considerable current. At either shore there were ramps of rails up which the coaches and trucks were hauled by steam windlasses, and in spite of what might seem a cumbrous method of linking the two branch lines the noble vessel *Trajektschiff Hohnstorf-Lauenburg* paddled more than twelve thousand wagons across the river in its first year of working. However, the demand was even greater, and the disruption of railway schedules whenever ice came down the river led the railway companies eventually to build a bridge instead. By this time the territory on either shore was Prussian, which made the task somewhat easier.

A traveller once described Lauenburg as being 'worth a change of horses'. To the boatman it is certainly worth a night at the piles by the entrance lock of the Elbe–Trave Canal, because Lauenburg has a real charm of its own. For at least six centuries it has been a point of transhipment and loading, of customs and staple, the home of bargemen and shipping agents and fishers. Its bright red brick-and-timber houses are clustered close along the shore so that the place has an appearance of glowing against the background of the woods of beech and chestnut which pour down the hill-side to the narrow strip of flat land on which it is built. Some of these houses are old enough to have the ray design carved on their eaves as an unconscious memory of the sun-worship which long ago was so widespread in the lands around the Baltic shores, and on one side of the street each upper storey projects further over the roadway of smooth worn stones, as though wishing to whisper to the houses across the way which have turned their backs upon them. They have done this for a good reason – they are more concerned with facing the river, from which their owners used to obtain their living. In fact the view of Lauenburg from the Elbe is even now that of a medieval town of shippers, and it is not difficult to guess that the one house which thrusts itself rudely in front of the rest and pushes right into the water was once the customs-house where tolls were levied on every passing vessel. At one end of the street a pleasant garden has seats where the retired tug-skippers and ships' captains can sit and watch the vessels in the river, whilst behind them is a fine modern bronze, the *Schreier*, or Caller. It shows a young ship's hand standing with one foot on a bollard, his hand raised megaphone-wise as he shouts to the passing ships.

'What is he supposed to be shouting?' I asked, turning to the old men on the seat. 'Cargoes? Information about the depth? Instructions for the tug-captain?'

'He isn't shouting anything particular,' one of the elderly ship-men said, placing his hands on the top of his stick. 'He's just shouting. There are always lads like that at any port. When they see a ship they yell to it. Sometimes it's wishing them a good journey, or perhaps it may be something ribald, a jest in Platt-deutsch. But wherever there's ships there's criers, so here we've got one in bronze in case the supply should ever run out.'

One of the workers in the Lauenburg shipyard had recently made a series of models of the port at various times in its history, and so provided Lauenburg with a shipping museum of quite exceptional interest. It has a model of the rail-ferry, another of the chain-ship and even a section of the original Elbe chain, but it also boasts a miniature lock of the old Stecknitz Canal, and a salt boat of the late fourteenth century waiting to pass through it. For it was here, at Lauenburg, that this oldest of all watershed canals reached the river, a waterway which was built because of the saltlessness of Scandinavia.

The Baltic yielded great catches of herrings, which were in even greater demand before the Reformation than they were later, but the northern countries had no salt in which to preserve them. It is said that the salt trading which soon became so important was begun by a medieval pig which fell through a hole in the earth at Lüneburg, thus revealing the immense resources of brine under the ground. The Lüneburgers were quick to exploit the salt, and eventually the local production was between 20 and 30 thousand tons annually, from 54 evaporating-houses. This salt was then conveyed to Lübeck for export to Russia and Scandinavia in vessels which returned with herrings in the same barrels which had held the salt.

From Lüneburg the salt was carried down the River Ilmenau to the Elbe, then upstream to Lauenburg where a small and winding brook, the Delvenau, joined the river on its right bank. The boats were hauled up this stream as far as possible and then the cargo was unloaded and carried by cart across the divide to where it could be laded again into other boats on the small river Stecknitz, which flowed into the Trave above Lübeck, or carried over to the Ratzeburg lake which emptied by the river Wakenitz into the

Trave at the edge of the city. Lübeck's riches were partly founded upon this salt trade, and it was in the interests of the merchants of that queen of Hanseatic cities that the final link for through transport by water should be made. Thus the Stecknitz Canal was built, a waterway opened to traffic in 1398 and the forerunner of the more modern Elbe–Trave Canal, into the entrance of which the *Thames Commodore* chugged her way on a sunny evening in late August.

Berthing in a pleasant corner beyond the lock we walked back into the town later in the evening to find a glass of wine in an inn which once had served the rough men who plodded along the Elbe bank, dragging the barges yard by yard up the river on the long haul to Bohemia. Indrei was looking at our regional map of Germany and he noticed just outside the town and beyond the Elbe–Trave Canal a point near the river bank which was marked as the Palmschleuse, 'Europe's oldest lock, 1724'. Sharing with me an insatiable curiosity and a fanaticism for canals he suggested that we should try to find it. The only other customer in the inn was a lorry-driver who at once volunteered to take us there in his truck, but as we noticed that he could not easily rise to his feet and remain upright we declined as gracefully as we could. The walk, we said, would do us good. So between hiccups and belches he gave us some rather blurred directions, and we set off. The rest of the crew decided that as it was now nearly half-past-eleven they would be quite content with the mile of starlit walk back to our berth above the lock. But Indrei and I were not to be put off, and climbing over the fences at either side of the railway track which once had led to the ferry terminal we came to a road which led in the direction of the alleged most ancient lock in Europe.

However we had not gone far when we came upon a sign beside the road: 'Zonengrenze 400 m.'. We quickened our step, passed the 200-metre mark, and soon reached the point where the road passed through the barrier of the Bundesrepublik to disappear into the night and the unknown. Somewhere, across 600 yards of dark and silent no-man's-land – though in fact it was West German pasture meadows – lay the mysterious and fenced-in People's Democracy.

At the customs post we stopped. Cars bound for Berlin were arriving, one every few minutes, all of them West German. Two bearded students who had been tramping in Ireland leaned against the wall of the customs shed, waiting for a lift, but the Berlin couples were travelling in their Volkswagens, the back seats full of luggage and treasures brought back from holidays in the western world, and they had no room for hitch-hikers. But the young men were not surprised, nor were they worried. They had often hitched to and from Berlin before. One might have to wait hours for a lift, they said.

At the barrier a passport man checked the identities of travellers. He was very handsome in his discreet blue uniform, very gallant, charming to all comers – especially so, I thought, so that the contrast between East and West could be emphasised. The green-uniformed frontier man was just as kindly and smiling, and both men wished their customers a safe journey over the 287-kilometre stretch of road to the one-time capital city, a route along which there could be no stopping except at one or two resting parks supervised by the *Vopos*, no deviation into a side road without risk of a shot in the back.

They asked us how we liked Holstein. It was an interesting land, I said, quite different from the southern Germany I knew so much better. If it had any fault, it was just that it lacked vineyards. Holstein's river was the Elbe, not the Moselle.

The passport man called across to his fellow officer. 'What do they drink over there?' He nodded his head towards the darkness of the Zone.

'No idea. Do they drink at all?'

'Must do. Bad beer probably.'

'Or turnip juice.'

'You can never tell, with them.' He laughed.

'No. And what they eat is anybody's guess.'

It was like discussing the feeding habits of some rare creature such as a Yeti, known by repute and by its tracks, but never actually seen. I felt a curious desire to ask if the East Germans had four legs, or perhaps six.

In the distance a glow of light swept behind the bushes across the meadows. It was a searchlight. The guards of the People's Republic were checking that nobody was daring to approach the fence.

'Probably heard a rabbit,' muttered the customs officer. 'Nothing much else gets through, these days.'

We walked back toward Lauenburg by the lower road, so that we could see in the faint moonlight the trim stone basin of the Palmschleuse, rebuilt two centuries earlier as a circular pen with the double-headed eagle of Lübeck and the leaping horse of Hanover cut in the masonry on opposite sides, for those two governments had united to renovate and enlarge the ancient course of the narrow and winding Stecknitz waterway. The gates of the lock itself had gone, but the water of the Delvenau brook flowed clear and rippling through the pen and it was not difficult to imagine the salt-shippers of earlier centuries hauling their craft

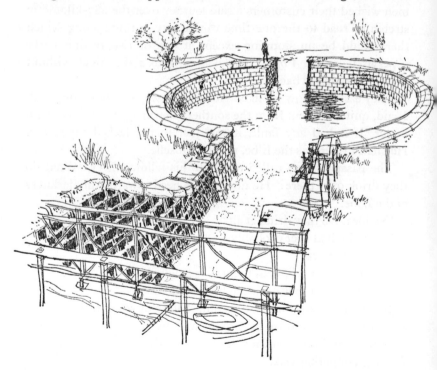

Lauenburg – the old Palmschleuse lock

into this first of the locks which lay between the Elbe and the Baltic port of Lübeck.

Over in Lauenburg a clock chimed midnight, and we left the lock to walk past the one-time house of lock-keeper Palm and head back for the modern canal and our mooring.

We had almost reached the canal bridge when we came to a place where two trees stood at the roadside. As we drew level a pair of figures stepped out of the shadows. One of them shone a light in Indrei's face, then in mine, to dazzle us. I had already noticed that he wore an officer's uniform and that he held a revolver nonchalantly in his other hand, so I did not protest. His companion was a young country lad with a reddish face and a grass-green tunic and breeches. He had a walkie-talkie, and he was holding the microphone at the ready so that if we should attack them their dying call for assistance would bring the vengeance of the Bundesrepublik swiftly upon us.

The officer looked me up and down with his lamp.

'Where do you come from?'

'Down there,' I said, pointing behind us.

'I know that. What were you doing?'

'Looking at the lock.'

'Hm. It is rather unusual to visit a lock at midnight.'

'But this is a rather unusual kind of lock,' I said.

'How is that?' The officer still held us in his beam, flashing it on Indrei, then back to me.

Because both Indrei and I could speak German it had not yet occurred to either of the men that we were foreigners. Of course it would not have taken us long to convince these two watchers of the night that we were not East German spies slipping quietly round the side of the Western frontier post, for we had only to invite them back to the *Thames Commodore* to show them any papers they wished to see. But I have always thought officials are much better met with a challenge which will take their minds off the suspicions of the moment.

'How is that?' I repeated. 'Because it is said to be the oldest lock in Europe. But I do not believe it. That lock cannot be the oldest in Europe.'

I knew that the original Stecknitz Canal locks must indeed have been the first in Europe, dating from long before the time of Leonardo da Vinci, who is usually held up as the inventor of the device. But this was of much later date, and its gracefully curving stonework was typical of the early eighteenth century.

'It cannot be the oldest,' I said again. 'That is nonsense.'

'It is true,' said the officer.

'Certainly,' added the radio-operator. 'Everyone knows it is the oldest lock in Europe.'

'But on the map it says "built in 1724",' I protested. 'On the Canal du Midi there are more than fifty locks still in use which were built forty years earlier than that. I have been through them.'

Local pride was now properly aroused. The officer switched off his light and began to extol to these two mad midnight visitors the wonders of the Stecknitz Canal and the Palmschleuse. Then, with all suspicion gone, our conversation turned to the zone and its psychotic fencing.

'North Vietnam versus South Vietnam,' said the youngster. 'North Korea against South Korea. West Germany against East Germany. How long will it go on?'

'Heaven knows,' I said 'But I wish we could actually see the frontier defences.'

The officer considered. 'Come back in the morning and walk down to the customs post. Somebody there might be willing to go with you. It's worth a try. Goodnight.'

And so the next morning Indrei and I returned to the West German barrier. Ten hours had elapsed, but the two bearded students back from Ireland were still hopefully thumbing each rare car that came to the frontier. The officials in the hut were too busy to waste time on a couple of English eccentrics, but in the customs hall itself we came upon an elderly officer in green uniform who was very willing to go with us. In his company we set off along the road, talking of boats, and canals, and of the officer's own vanished homeland in East Prussia, in the 'Third Germany'.

We had not walked half a mile when we came round a slight bend to where the Delvenau brook passed under the roadway in a culvert. It was a meandering little watercourse overhung with

Lauenburg – the Iron Curtain

willow, its banks flecked with loosestrife. Once it had been the winding course by which the Stecknitz boatmen had hauled their cargoes to Lübeck, and later with the coming of the new Elbe–Trave Canal it had declined into a peaceful old age as a mellow stream of fish and reed-warblers. Then had come 1945, which vested upon the Delvenau the responsibility of being the frontier – 'the line between Europe and Asia', as a Lauenburg shopkeeper later remarked to us. Now it was backed by a curious kind of rural desert, green and uncultivated, an area in which the larks

nested and the warblers would sing in springtime as though the
tangle of underbrush had been planted for their convenience and
the barbed wire put there by some society for the protection
of migrant birds. For the barbed-wire fences were there right
enough, a spidery tangle under the ever watchful eyes of snipers
who scanned the bank of the Delvenau not for snipe but for
moving humans. Further back lay the ploughed strip to show tell-
tale footprints, and behind all these defences the line of watch-
towers inherited from concentration camps, and the smooth
dug-outs topped with concrete, where young men with ready
trigger-fingers waited for anyone so foolish as to try to escape
from the People's Paradise.

Over the culvert a white line was painted from side to side of
the roadway. Beyond it a smart notice board proclaimed that the
land was the *Deutsche Demokratische Republik*. Several hundred
yards ahead a raised outlook post reached by a flight of steps gave
the guards a final chance to shoot through the head from a high
vantage point any motorist who had been lucky enough to crash
the barrier further back.

'Don't go too close,' the East Prussian officer warned us. 'Step
over the line, and if they don't like you that's that. They're very
ready with their shooting, you know.' He retired to the side of the
road to stand casually behind a bush.

Indrei and I stood in the road, two feet short of the line, and
surveyed the extraordinary scene of posts and wire and wasteland.
In the distance we noticed a figure climb down from the watch post
and focus upon us a pair of enormous field-glasses. He stared and
stared, motionless. I took out my own binoculars and stared back,
as unwavering as himself.

After a while the man called up to the box, and his companion
came down to join him. This second young man was dressed in the
same jack-booted uniform redolent of the S.S. I had known thirty
years earlier, and he had a sub-machine-gun casually slung over
his shoulder. The first guard passed him the field-glasses; I passed
mine to Indrei, and the staring match continued. The first guard
took our portrait with a telescopic lens. I put my telephoto in
position and took a picture of him.

At length their curiosity could be held in check no longer, and slinging a gun and binoculars and the camera with the telescopic lens over their arms they began to saunter casually along the road, as though out for a summer stroll. They came to a halt a yard the other side of the white line, looking a trifle sheepish. They were young lads, country fellows, one pink-faced like a farmer's boy, the other darker but handsome. Their boots shone in the sunshine and their insignia sparkled.

'Good morning,' I said. 'How are things?'

'Not bad,' said the handsome one. He was still trying to figure out what these two curious customers in shorts could be doing there.

'Lovely day,' said Indrei. It was hard to think of anything to say.

'Yes. A good week-end.'

'Last week was terrible. Rain, and wind.'

'Yes,' said our East Prussian companion from beside his bush. He spoke definitely to us and not to the guards. 'Rain and wind, it's been like that everywhere.'

'Everywhere,' the pink-faced lad confirmed.

'Not much doing today,' I said. 'Very few cars.' Not one had passed us, as it happened.

'There are usually more in the afternoon,' said the one with the machine-gun.

'Yes, in the afternoon,' said the East Prussian, lighting a small cigar.

'That's a nice camera you've got,' I said to the darker lad. 'A fine telephoto lens, too.'

'Yes. It's a Zeiss.'

'Hm. Don't you wish it were your own?'

He laughed. 'Yes. It must have cost a lot of money.'

'I've got a Zeiss too,' I said. 'Only I haven't such a super lens as that. Look, it's a Contina. Can I take your picture?'

The young men looked at each other, a little embarrassed, then stood and smiled.

'Right there, by the notice,' I said. 'It's been newly painted, I see. Did you do it?'

'No. There are painters for the notices.'

'Well, it looks very nice. You go and stand by it. There, that's fine.'

We took their pictures, and they seemed pleased.

'Come to London, and I'll pose for you,' I said. Not that it was necessary, for Indrei and I had already been recorded in black and white with the mighty Zeiss lens before the two men left their tower.

Eventually the guards strolled away, and so did we.

'I can't understand it,' said our elderly companion from the Western post as he walked up the road beside us. 'I've never, never known such a thing. Always they stay far away, right out of sight or in that cabin, and they never come down to the frontier, to within feet of us. Nor do they ever speak to anyone. I wouldn't have dreamed they would come over, just because you stared at them. And then to stand there talking and posing for their photographs, when they must know that every movement they make is watched from the look-outs and the bunkers further back, and a rifle with telescopic sights was probably trained upon each of them.'

'But they're simple lads,' I said. 'Just like any others. They could be country boys from Holstein, England, Scotland, anywhere.'

'Yes,' he said in a grand-paternal way. 'One must not hold it against them that they are guards. They have to be. Elsewhere, in Bonn or London, they would be growing their hair down to their shoulders instead of guarding barbed-wire fences. Do you realise that they have never known anything different? That fence went up when they were in their cradles, perhaps before they were born. To them, that is the way a frontier is. That is the only kind of frontier they have ever seen.'

We came up to the customs post. An officer invited us inside.

'Well? What do you think?'

'I think it's sad,' I said. 'Sad that this stupid fence exists, sad that politicians can behave the way they do, sad that those simple young men must actually think it quite normal to live behind wire and shoot at anybody who wants to try and live elsewhere.'

'Of course. But just step in here.'

Inside the customs station was a small theatre, very much like a miniature cinema of an advertising agency. There was a projector for slides, too, so that highly educational lectures could be given to groups of official visitors from other countries who could not understand what all this frontier business was about. There was a supply of booklets about the 'People's Right to Self-Determination' as laid down in the United Nations Declaration, with plenty of examples of the cynical way in which this was interpreted in countries within the Russian orbit.

Everyone has the right to life, liberty and security of the person.

Everyone has the right to freedom of movement and residence within the borders of each State.

Everyone has the right to leave any country, including his own, and return to his country.

Or, in the case of the People's Democracy, the right to stay put or be shot, for at least one-hundred-and-fifty murders had been committed along the line of the fence, perpetrated by just such genial young frontier guards as had stood chatting with us in the road – for their instructions were to shoot at sight anybody encountered in the dark within 500 metres of the border, and by daytime anyone in uniform attempting to flee. Civilians were supposed to be shouted at before mowing them down. Cash rewards and gold watches were given for wounding or killing. It was not surprising that membership of the Frontier Force appealed to exactly that element of the people who would have enjoyed torturing Jews and guarding concentration camps, and in other countries were engaged in protection rackets and similar thuggeries.

'I don't believe those young men would have shot anybody in cold blood,' I said. 'They were just a couple of lads.'

The officer nodded. 'Maybe. But they may have no choice.'

And this was true, for to police such a length of frontier it was necessary to have a border patrol of fifty thousand armed men spread along the 800 miles of fence, and most of them were of course conscripted men. That not all of them were much in sympathy with the extraordinary system under which they had grown up was proved by the fact that more than 1500 of them had themselves fled across the border they were supposed to guard. But if a refugee was seen and fired at without being hit, then a very careful investigation always followed, and if it could be shown that a guard's record on the rifle range was better than the calculated aberration in his actual shooting he would at once be suspected of complicity in the escape, and could face a severe term of imprisonment.

The fence which divides Germany from the Baltic to the Czech frontier must be quite the most extraordinary manifestation of governmental psychosis that the world has ever seen. Originally the Communists took the view that it was better to let dissatisfied people leave the country than to keep them there unwillingly as malcontents who might be a continual source of unrest. But the Soviet Zone eventually became so depleted of men and women with brains, imagination or idealism that the policy had to be changed. Orders were given to fence the country along its entire western boundary, not to keep others out but to prevent the rest of the population from abandoning such a happy land.

So, in May of 1952, the work began. Behind the line rather unwisely agreed by the Allies a 10-metre belt was left as a 'control strip', and behind this came another 30 metres of wasteland, a paradise for birds. Next there was a formidable barbed fence on stout posts, and behind it coils of barbed wire. Then came a broad belt sown with mines which exploded at the slightest pressure – mines which nightly took their toll of such unfortunate deer and wild boar, rabbits and hares as succeeded in penetrating a little way into the defences. Another wire fence, then the famous ploughed strip to show foot-prints, a path for the armed guards, a road for the maintenance men, a ditch to trap vehicles, and finally a belt three miles deep which none might enter without a pass. In this were put the hidden bunkers and gun posts, the searchlight towers and machine-gun stands. Anything such as a house or forest which interfered with the field of fire was razed to the ground, and the whole affair was finished off with trip-wires and alarm-pads, all of which would occasionally be set off by such terrified wild animals as might still be left.

Like any other country Germany had of course possessed a

system of communications over its length and breadth. With the coming of the fence these links had also mostly to be severed. A few roads and railways remained and the only two main waterway crossings were left intact, one on the Mittelland Canal west of Magdeburg and the other on the Elbe at the point where it ceased to be a frontier between the eastern and western worlds, but twenty-four railway connections were dynamited or just torn up and barricaded, and hundreds of roads were blocked with concrete traps and a maze of wire, or made impassable by blowing up bridges. And just in case any foolish yachtsman should have the idea that he might sail away across the Baltic, the shore was patrolled by a special anti-refugee coastguard service which would open fire without warning on any pleasure boat which was considered to have strayed more than one cable from the land – an arrangement which makes yachting eastward of Lübeck a rather dangerous undertaking.

That all this must have a numbing and demoralising effect upon the inhabitants is obvious. In the People's Paradise there is no hope for a man except to plough on in misery, paying lip service to his rulers and waiting for his sixty-fifth birthday, that glorious occasion when he will at last be graciously accorded the 'right' to pay one brief visit each year to friends or relations in the Bundesrepublik.

Meanwhile the relief organisations in the land outside the fence keep stressing that one must never, never forget that 'they', the Zone-dwellers, are relatives, friends, Germans under oppression. One must never cease to visit them, ring them up (for this curiously enough is still possible), send them birthday cards and presents, take advantage of the chance to send flowers through florists in the Zone, do anything to prevent them feeling forgotten, abandoned to their fate in the prison cage the Communists have built around them.

We left the frontier and walked back to the canal, ready to resume a voyage in waters where nobody would shoot at the *Thames Commodore*. Beyond the bank the watch-towers stood remote in the wilderness of their separate fields of fire. Young men were no doubt standing there on their raised platforms, sweeping

the area of the Stecknitz Canal with their long-range glasses, and
perhaps letting their glance linger wistfully on the little blue ship
as it skirted the forbidden land and headed for the next lock at
Witzeeze, an hour or more away.

VI

The canal for salt – navigation by Tap Day – the truth about storks – the inn by the flash-lock – Thames Commodore *discovers Mölln – the doctor from Bologna – the potter's wife bewitched – Till's walking staff – the world's comics*

THE Elbe–Trave Canal in which the *Thames Commodore* lay waiting patiently for us to finish with east–west courtesies so that she might get moving, has a very respectable pedigree. In its original form of the Stecknitz Canal it was the oldest watershed canal in the world, not by a short head but by centuries. And this earlier waterway owed its existence to the enterprise of the Free Imperial city of Lübeck.

The city of Lübeck was one of the earliest pioneers of inland navigation, and already in 1188 the council succeeded in obtaining from the hand of the Emperor Frederick I special rights over such small local rivers as could carry the barges of the period. One of these streams was the river Stecknitz, by which the waters of the Möllner See ran out to Lübeck and the sea. What inland craft the Lübeckers were using at that time may never be known, but they must have been boats small enough to thread the windings of the stream when laden with cargoes loaded at Mölln, and particularly with the loads of salt from Lüneburg. Soon after this time the Imperial privileges began to wane and Lübeck could not be sure of special favours for its trading. However, the city was by now extremely powerful economically, and it owed its wealth almost entirely to its water-borne trade by sea and by inland shipping. It was in a position to make its own demands, and the representatives of the energetic Lübeckers went off to negotiate trade on their own terms in London and Visby, and in every land from Spain to Norway and Russia. For four centuries Lübeck was to be the leader in that powerful confederation of trading cities, the Hanseatic League.

The trade in salt continually increased, and in 1335 the Lübeckers introduced a new kind of river barge in which the salt could be loose loaded at Mölln – an early forerunner of the modern motor-barge designed for a bulk cargo of cement or flour. Presumably these vessels had a greater draught than the earlier ships, for a flash-lock was installed at the outlet of the Möllner See and a copy of the lock regulations is extant. These laid down that whenever there was enough salt in the Mölln warehouses to load two dozen barges the lock-keeper was to keep his sluices open long enough to provide a good depth all the way to Lübeck.

The men of Lübeck found water transport so economical that they determined before long to extend the waterway to the Delvenau and so to the Elbe. If somehow the Möllner See could be linked to the Delvenau, and the two mill weirs bypassed, there would in fact be a continuous barge-route for salt all the way from Lüneburg to Lübeck. The first essential was to secure permission for a canal which would not be within their own territory, but with the sum of 3000 good and solid Lübeck marks the burghers of the Hanseatic City persuaded the Duke of Saxony to allow the Delvenau to be made navigable and the connecting link to be built. The Stecknitz and the Delvenau were separated by a divide only seven miles broad, and though in medieval times this was a considerable distance over which to cut a shipping route with shovel and basket the engineers decided that it could be done. They were also confident that they could master the difference in level between the two streams, and after making the cut from the Möllner See to the Delvenau brook they supplied it with two locks at the edge of the Mölln itself. These 'box locks', the 'Haneburger Stowkasten' as the shippers called them in the Middle Ages, could each contain ten salt barges about 35 feet in length. They were the first canal pound locks in the world.

The Delvenau was shallow, and it fell more than 40 feet in its course to Lauenburg, but these difficulties were overcome. Eight 'flashes' were provided, single sluice-gates which broke the river up into a number of steps. The system of navigation was particularly ingenious, for it consisted in manipulating the average flow of the river so that it was reduced and increased on alternate days. Behind each sluice-gate the water would build up for a whole day, and then on the Zapfeltag or Tap Day the staunches were opened and the downgoing ships went gliding on their way, whilst the upcoming craft were bank-hauled by six or eight men against the increased current. Sometimes a ship failed to make the next staunch before the supply of water had run away and the level fell to leave the craft stranded. It then had to wait for the next Zapfeltag two days later before it could proceed.

The Stecknitz and Delvenau brooks both had water enough for the river staunches and flash weirs to be worked, but the seven-mile length of summit canal had no outside supply. However, the engineers ingeniously cut the course through a sandy hillside, and water seeped continually out of the banks into the waterway. After two or three days, according to whether the recent weather had been wet or dry, there would be plenty of water to fill the locks, and the boats which had accumulated in the pens would then be passed down or up.

Lübeck's initiative naturally encouraged the various landowners along the waterway to demand tolls every time a barge passed through their territory, but the city managed in return to keep a monopoly in carrying the salt, and even the Lauenburgers were not permitted to do more than carry firewood on the Delvenau. The whole organisation was in the hands of the small but powerful Guild of Salters, who saw to the construction of the necessary barges and employed the crews. Soon they were shipping other goods as well, and as the importance of the waterway continually increased the Salters developed into a Guild of Shippers whilst the crew members also became united in their own professional organisation, the association of *Stecknitzfahrer*. Originally this was a religious confraternity, but at the Reformation it concerned itself more and more with earthly things and soon established a closed shop.

One of the regulations of the *Stecknitzfahrer* was that every Stecknitz shipper had to operate with barges in convoys of three, for only in this way could the high cost of bank-hauling crews be covered. The villages close to the bank of the navigation were obliged to provide men for towage, and they originally did so very willingly in order to receive payment in solid Lübeck marks; but later, as agricultural conditions improved, the same service came to be regarded as a burden. However, the *Stecknitzfahrer* had the right to demand men for the tow-rope, and they did so. Without bank-hauling the whole system would have broken down, whereas a constant supply of towing-navvies enabled the ships to cross the country between Lübeck and the Elbe in about two weeks – in seven or eight Tap Days, that is.

Although the waterway supplied Lübeck with much of its grain and firewood, the prosperity of the Stecknitz Canal was most closely tied to the trade in Lüneburg salt, an industry which gave as much opportunity for commercial scheming as any mining undertaking of modern times. The Lüneburgers had a complete monopoly of salt production within easy reach of Scandinavia, and they naturally had a tendency to put up the price as often as they could. The Stecknitz-shippers and the Skåne-shippers who forwarded the salt from Lübeck endeavoured to resist the rises in price, and the Lübeck Council tried to force the Lüneburgers to quote annually a total price for their entire production. Lüneburg declined to do so, but was brought to her knees after a few years of trading boycott, and thus a joint monopoly was established, if only upon a foundation of mutual distrust and rivalry. As for the shippers, they supported Lübeck in its attempts to keep down the price, but they backed Lüneburg over the monopoly, at the same time keeping an eye open lest the threats from their own city should force Lüneburg to do a deal with Hamburg and route the entire production down the Elbe instead of through the Stecknitz.

With the monopoly established, the canal shippers persuaded the Lübeck Council to incorporate them as a City Company and pass a decree which forbade 'others' to buy, build, or operate canal boats. Five merchants whose trade was injured by this move rose in protest, and they were sufficiently forceful for the Council quickly to add another declaration which ruled that 'others' meant only outsiders in the sense that they were dishonest traders, or whose actions led to an increase in price. But now the gown-makers and others joined in the dispute, and the final result was that the attempt to introduce a closed shop on the canal failed. The trade in salt was to be free for all, within the bounds of Lübeck territory.

Salt was also imported from Scotland, but a city edict of 1670 declared that as it was generally recognised to be greatly inferior in purity and goodness to the produce of Lüneburg, it must therefore be packed in a different size and shape of barrel in order that there might be no confusion. Any merchant found selling Scottish salt in Lüneburg barrels would have the load confiscated and would be fined one hundred thalers. Any merchant wishing to demean himself so far as to sell Scottish salt at all would have to pack it in special narrow casks.

In 1663 the Swedish government made representations to the City of Lübeck, requesting that the Stecknitz Canal should be enlarged so that Swedish ships might sail direct from Stockholm to Hamburg. However, the Lübeckers had no wish to increase the trade of their rival and neighbour on the Elbe unless some advantage for themselves could be seen, and they proposed that in return the Swedes should give Lübeck shippers equal rights with their own in all the Swedish ports.

The proposals did not suit all the colleges of shippers equally well, but the *Rigafahrer* were certainly in favour. They saw the possibility of carrying to Hamburg the products of the Eastern Baltic such as flax and hemp and grain. They urged the Council to deepen and straighten the canal, they demanded a towpath with relays of horses to replace manpower, and they urged the building of larger canal barges which would carry several times as much as the old Stecknitz boats of shallow draught.

The Council employed engineers to draw up a scheme for enlarging the waterway. Seven locks were to be cut out, the others enlarged and deepened so that a four-foot channel could be maintained throughout the waterway. All sharp bends were to be eliminated and the line of the canal drawn as far as possible *in lineam rectam*. Passing-bays were to be built out, every quarter- or half-mile along the canal, and the bank was to be broad and firm enough for tow-horses. Everything was to be done in such a way that goods shipped in Lübeck could be carried safely, dry, and without transhipment, to Hamburg and beyond. However, before the work could be put in hand the fickle Swedes joined with France in an attack upon the north German states and Lübeck was not at all inclined to spend good money on a scheme to benefit their enemies. The proposals were dropped, and the canal remained as it was.

If the Lübeckers had a monopoly on the canal, the shippers of Lauenburg had their own grip firmly on the Elbe and managed to establish a sole right of carriage on that river for all cargoes arriving by the canal. As Lauenburg ships could not carry on the canal and Lübeck vessels might not run on the Elbe, the result was that everything had to be transhipped at Lauenburg's quay. This was a wasteful if very common system in the Middle Ages, but the Lauenburgers managed to maintain their staple right until 1843, when the monopoly was at last declared to be against the spirit of the Congress of Vienna, which had laid down certain safeguards for freedom of navigation on the main European rivers.

The Stecknitz Canal – the *Steckenfahrt* as the medieval shippers called it – carried the salt ships for more than five centuries. Opened in 1398 it was not finally abandoned until its larger successor the Elbe–Trave Canal was ready for use in 1900. It had a particular burst of activity in 1803 when the blockade of the Elbe caused much of the trade of Hamburg to be transferred to Lübeck, but only three years later Napoleon blockaded the whole continent in an effort to ruin British trade, and this brought shipping in all the northern ports temporarily to a standstill. The canal was for a few years used mostly by ducks.

Apart from the enlargement scheme frustrated by the treachery of the Swedes, other attempts were made to plan the rebuilding of the waterway, and various governments and engineers in turn produced a succession of schemes. If all of them came to nothing this was because of the political intricacies of that part of Europe. And of course there were economic jealousies, too. It so happened that from 1816 to 1865 Lauenburg belonged to Denmark, and nothing could be done to improve the canal without the consent of the Danish crown. Already in 1784 the Danes had constructed the Eider Canal (forerunner of the Kiel Canal) from the Baltic to the Elbe, and they had no wish to see the trade of their own water-way drawn off to an enlarged Stecknitz Canal on which they would not even be allowed to use their own ships.

The boldest of all the schemes for reconstructing the Stecknitz waterway was put forward under Napoleon, whose rule extended over the area between 1811 and 1813. Always a waterway enthus-iast, Napoleon decided to construct the 'Canal de la Seine à la Baltique', the northern end of which was to be formed by enlarging the Stecknitz Canal. However, Napoleon was driven out before the works could begin, and what would have proved to be a most attractive waterway for modern boating enthusiasts in Paris and Scandinavia was never built.

The modern Elbe–Trave Canal has only seven locks, and it was towards the second of them at Witzeeze that the *Thames Commodore* chugged ahead when she left Lauenburg on the Sunday morning. For an hour the Delvenau brook lay close to starboard, with every now and then a bright-painted post set among the scrub willow of its further bank to remind the birds and rabbits that this was the

D.D.R., the People's Republic. Watch-towers looked down from the rising ground beyond, and the barbed wire stretched unobtrusively almost to the brook itself. Through the glasses we could see into the village of Zweedorf, which had the misfortune to be a quarter of a mile on the wrong side of the fence, as far separated from its neighbour Dalldorf as if it were in another continent. Two more miles and the lights of Witzeeze lock shone green and red to show that the chamber was emptying to receive us, then double green as the gates opened and the *Thames Commodore* moved in and made fast.

Behind the lock a track led across the fields to the Dükkerschleuse Inn. The Dükker lock itself was once one of the flashes built by the Lübeckers to hold up the water of the Delvenau until Tap Day, and it may well be that a lock-keeper named Dükker gave his name to it just as Schleusenmeister Palm had left his in the Palmschleuse where Indrei and I had our midnight encounter with the watchmen of the Bundesrepublik. It seemed a reasonable time of day for a glass of wine, so we stopped beyond the canal lock and walked over to the inn. On the way we started a deer. It was a fallow-deer and a female, and I hoped she would never be foolish enough to explore beyond the course of the Delvenau and have her legs torn off by the explosion of a People's Democratic land-mine. Poking about in one of the ditches was a pair of storks. They watched us warily as they searched for juicy frogs.

Storks are of course no ordinary birds. They are much more than a mere larger relative of the heron, and although everyone knows that early in September they circle up and up, higher and higher, and eventually disappear, nobody knows where they go. Or perhaps I should say none used to know where, for the problem was eventually solved, not by the zoologists with their ringing techniques and their absurd theory that the birds fly away to Africa, but by a boatman of Holstein.

It happened that a pair of storks nested regularly on his house, a fact of which he was proud, for the good luck a stork would bring was worth all the pile of fish skeletons and excrement scattered over the roof-top. One year he noticed that one of the birds had broken its leg, probably having caught it in a trap when out

In Holstein

frogging. Being a kindly man – as most boatmen are – he took the bird indoors and nursed it carefully until the leg was set strong again, and the stork could return to a normal life.

It was years later that this good man was on a voyage somewhere in the German Bight when he dropped anchor to wait for a favourable wind or tide, and when he came to raise the hook again he found it was fouled. As this was before the days of submarine cables he probably supposed that the anchor had become entangled in a wreck, and as he had no wish to lose the anchor itself he decided to take a deep breath and climb quickly down the chain to find the obstruction. Much to his astonishment he discovered that the fluke was fast in the steeple of a sunken church – probably, he assumed, that of one of the villages long since overwhelmed by storm floods.

He freed the anchor, but being curious to look at the place more closely he descended lower and – as he could hold his breath for a very long time indeed – at last came into a busy and prosperous town, the people of which received him kindly and without any great show of astonishment. One elderly man hurried to greet him as an old friend, and asked him for all the latest news about his own village and home in Holstein.

The skipper was not a little surprised, and the old man had to explain that he was the stork whose leg had been healed, and the boatman had by chance stumbled upon the solution to that age-old problem of what became of the birds through the long, cold months of a northern winter. Metamorphosed into submarine humans they lived at the bottom of the sea.

The next creature we met along the lane was a dog, a sleek young Alsatian bitch. She was extremely good-mannered and stood up very straight to show off her glossy coat and her handsome triangular blouse of white cloth on which was the word *Zoll* in black. Taking with her a pleasant young man with a cycle and a walkie-talkie, her job was to sniff out those who filtered into the Bundesrepublik by night and to ask them what they meant by it. She looked at us with just a trace of suspicion in her dark eyes, but when I patted her and told her we had come all the way from London by boat she wagged her tail and decided that we must be harmless enough. She was a beautiful creature, and I was sorry that the complexities of the Communist mind debarred her from making the acquaintance of possible boy-friends among the Alsatians of Neu Zweedorf, a few hundred yards away behind the wire.

The Dükkerschleuse Inn, half farm and part hostelry, was as remote a place as one could ever find in Germany. A typical Holstein farmhouse, its interior was all of wood painted in blues and reds after the fashion of houses in Jutland and the Danish isles. The walls of the living-room were hung with pictures of the heroes of two generations earlier, men with high military collars, glaring with steely eyes over their fiercely waxed moustaches. Von Mackensen was there, and Ludendorff, and poor stupid old Hindenburg who was later to be used by the Nazis as a sort of inarticulate father-figure.

There was Little Willie, too, his entire family ranged in size as though they were produced on a running band; and a composite illustration or table with all the most notable Austrian and

Prussian warriors of 1914, among them the great Admiral von Tirpitz with his two long beards, a sort of bifurcated Darwin. For fifty years those figures had peered down from the fading photographs in the plated frames, and when one of the guests who was having a meal at the inn volunteered to tell me all about them I was interested to discover that he really knew less of these characters than I did myself. He was even unaware that the seventh child of a seventh child had been allowed – in order to boost the birthrate – to kiss Hindenburg and be patted on the head by the great *Generalfeldmarschall* himself, a somewhat frightening experience which must have led to psychoses in which the patients woke up screaming as the great walrus whiskers engulfed them in an iron-bristled embrace.

The landlord was an ex-mayor of the village of Witzeeze beyond the canal. Few people in Germany lived closer to the Soviet Zone than he did, for the frontier ran just at the back of the house. Presumably the building had once served for Lock-keeper Dükker, for the remains of the lock were there in the garden, set in a small cut which bypassed a tight meander of the Delvenau. A footbridge crossed the lock, which was little broader than the seven-foot pen of an English narrow canal.

But the bridge led nowhere. It ended in a barrier with a notice, '*Halt! Zonengrenze!*'

We leaned on the red-and-white bar, looking out across the stillness of the silent wilderness beyond.

'You see that meadow?' The landlord pointed to the pasture which lay between the lock and the Delvenau. 'That was mine. I lost it through the tidy-mindedness of an English major.'

It seemed that like the surveyors Mason and Dixon who marked out their famous line across America, this major was given the task of setting up the boundary which was to express the optimistic hopes of the Yalta Agreement. The frontier was to follow the Delvenau, but when the Englishman arrived behind the inn to push his stakes into the ground and his pins into his map he decided to save time and markers and pins by drawing his line in such a way that it nipped off the curving bend of the stream, leaving the bank at one point and rejoining it a hundred yards or more further along. The landlord had protested, but in vain. One acre of his meadow went to the Soviet Zone, but as it was inaccessible from the other side of the Delvenau it had remained ever since as an isolated little island of People's Republic which no eastern cow could reach and where no western cow might dare to graze. It was now overgrown with scrub, and at least the patch provided a safe nesting ground and sanctuary for the little birds of the sedge and bushes.

At Witzeeze the canal reaches its summit level in a watershed pound thirty kilometres long. Two hours up the cut from Dükkerschleuse it runs through the Möllner See, across which the railway company once built an embankment to carry the Lübeck line. So high is the solid embankment that nothing can be seen beyond it, but steaming slowly across the deep water we searched among the trees of the opposite shore and eventually found an opening between two willows at the foot of the railway bank. Some way ahead was a foot-bridge, and finding that the *Thames Commodore* could squeeze beneath it we let her move slowly forward with nearly a foot of water beneath her keel until the channel turned a right angle. Poling her stern round we set her nose into a culvert arch and burrowed cautiously under the railway. There was more water here, and soon we emerged between the weeping willows of an inlet of the Stadtsee. Another half-minute and we found ourselves in a broad and beautiful lake.

The view across the water was as splendid as it was unexpected. Surrounded by a curve of the little houses of the burghers, the square-towered brick cathedral of Mölln stood in a cluster of trees on its own private hill, set in the centre of what once had been an island. Lit by the golden sun of a late August afternoon the town lay mirrored and inverted in the still water of bluish-green. We dropped anchor in the deep, and amused ourselves in swimming until the little trip-boat had vacated the landing-stage for another week. Then we moved in to the jetty, causing the good people of Mölln to wonder how on earth such a boat could conceivably have penetrated their broad and secluded moat.

I had read somewhere that there was an unusual tombstone in that curious cathedral set on the hill, a stone which had in it a square hole now stopped up with a piece of brick. Buried beneath

Mölln

the slab was a local girl of such vicious character that she murdered her own mother. This did not prevent her receiving proper burial in the cathedral when she shortly afterwards sickened and died, but she had only been a few days dead when the hand which had done the evil deed pierced the heavy slab and projected into the nave. Orders were given to attack the hand with a whip, and when the lashes fell upon it the limb prudently withdrew into the tomb – but only to appear again on the following morning. At last the church authorities became impatient in dealing with such an obstinate phenomenon, and one day they replaced the whip by the sword of the town executioner. He rushed upon the tomb, severed the hand below the wrist, and blocked up the hole with a brick.

The hand, I had read, was long preserved in the cathedral as a curiosity.

I asked the verger to show me the stone, but he could not. He had not even heard the tale before, and wondered that none had ever mentioned it to him. In fact the same story can be found in Hamburg, Bremen and other places of northern Germany, so there is no particular reason to associate it with Mölln. However, this peaceful little place certainly had its own municipal executioner, and as he was perhaps a man whom others instinctively avoided he was provided with a special seat of his own which folded down from the wall at the front of the nave. Here he could sit, alone and untouchable, and with an excellent view across the pews to the packed rows of his possible future customers.

Mölln's cathedral has treasures of every kind, and among them are some medieval frescoes showing pilgrims visiting St James for his blessing. Very amiable he stands there, the shell sign hung round his neck and each hand resting on the hat of a traveller bound for Compostella. Beside him is the patron of the church, and as Mölln was the main intermediate point on the Stecknitz Canal the patron is St Nicholas, the friend of bargees. No little boys in pickle tubs lie at his feet, but below him is the scene aboard the trading ship bound for Myra when he miraculously materialised to take the tiller in a storm.

The painting shows in detail the build and rig of a contemporary (thirteenth-century) trading ship, a Mecklenburg 'Kogge'. The worthy bishop, wearing a cowl, is cheerfully holding the tiller amid humpy waves while three of his companions have their hands raised in prayer and a fourth is being sick over the side. Below the surface two of the fishes present are peeping upwards to see what is going on. After all, it was not every day that Nicholas of Myra came steering through their water.

Another drawing shows St Michael weighing the souls, impeded by a nasty little devil who is upsetting the balance by holding down the pan on the hellward side of middle virtue; and a painting on the pillar at the end of the nave shows that the conscientious bellman of Mölln could not even pause for a brief lunch-break, so perpetual was his tolling of the summons to worship or the knell of the departed. He seems to have been a man of inventive turn of mind, for he worked the rope of one bell with his hand and the other by a noose tied round his foot. This meant that he had to stand on one leg, but having one hand free he was able to raise to his lips a mug of good refreshing ale without even watching to see what his other limbs were doing.

If the presence of St Nicholas underlines the connection of Mölln with the medieval bargemen, the cathedral has another link with the canal. A magnificent fourteenth-century seven-branched candlestick, wrought in bronze, was the property of an abbey not far away when thieves broke in and stole it. Perhaps they were surprised in their flight, but whatever the reason may have been the candlestick was dropped into the Stecknitz Canal, where it lay in the mud. Eventually, in 1610, a Stecknitz barge grounded on the obstruction, and the candlestick was grappled and raised. The guild of Stecknitz canal-boatmen had it refurbished and burnished, and they presented it to the church at Mölln, where it still adorns the private pew which was always reserved for the members of their association.

Against the outside of the cathedral is the tombstone of Mölln's celebrated practical joker whose pranks, legendary or real, infuriated the citizens from one end of Germany to the other. His favourite gambit was to apprentice himself to some worthy tradesman and do exactly what he was told. For instance, a baker into whose employ he had needled himself might tell the honest apprentice to put all the loaves in the oven. This he would do – and burn them to cinders. Or if told by a joiner to stick the table-tops together he would do precisely that. And when the shoemaker left him alone with the order to cut out as many shoes as he could, he snipped all the leather into miniature footwear so that the number would be greater.

Soon, however, he graduated to more cunning pieces of buffoonery, by which he could also make some honest (or at least not too dishonest) money. One of his best tricks was played upon the council of Nürnberg, and it was a device which must appeal to many a modern doctor overburdened by the supply of hypochondriacs through the National Health Service.

It was at the time of the later crusades, when the soldiers returning from the Middle East frequently brought with them fevers and other strange sicknesses for which at that time no cure was known. These, together with the usual collection of the halt and maimed and chronic sick so filled the hospital at Nürnberg that there was no room for new cases to be taken in, and the council were considering the provision of a new hospital wing.

Hearing of this, the joker of Mölln presented himself in the guise of 'Doctor Tillius', an eminent doctor trained in the famed medical school of Bologna. Having secured an audience with the council he undertook to cure the whole collection of patients for an agreed and handsome fee. Prudently the council stipulated that they would pay when they saw the results, but the doctor was not worried. An eminent physician such as himself could hardly expect mere laymen to believe that his cures could be so effective, he said.

So the new doctor went his round of the wards and whispered to each patient separately that in order to cure them it would be necessary to take one of their number, kill him, pound him up, and give the concoction to the rest to drink. This, he said, was an infallible cure. However, he was averse to killing any patient unnecessarily, even in the interest of the others, and so he had decided to select the weakest of the inmates. Shortly he would stand at the end of the ward in the company of the hospital superintendent, and would shout 'All those who are not sick, leave the premises'. The last man out would of course be the weakest, and he was only giving the others fair warning so that there should be no mistake.

So, in the course of time, he brought the superintendent to the ward. 'All those not sick, away,' he called. And to the astonishment of the official every single patient tumbled out of his bed and raced for the door – even those who had been there for ten years already, and others who limped on crutches or could hardly drag their bodies along. They fell over each other in their hurry to escape, and within a few minutes the ward was empty. The superintendent was amazed to find that all his charges were suddenly healthy, and grateful to the doctor for having cleared the hospital so quickly.

Delighted with the results, the council paid the physician from Bologna his fat fee. He took it and left Nürnberg immediately. And this was only prudent, for on the morrow every one of the patients was back again at the hospital, queuing for the strange medicine which the physician had promised them the day before.

The name of this ingenious hoaxer was, of course, Till Eulenspiegel, whose merry pranks set many another city by the ears. The earliest known account of his ongoings is found in a book printed in 1515, *Ein Kurtzweilig lesen von Dyl Ulenspiegel geboren uss dem land zu Brunsswik*, but no doubt this was only an anthology of comic tales of earlier date which had become woven around a possibly real individual who had a peculiar but often attractive sense of humour. Till was not a Möllner, but as the title suggests he came from the area of Brunswick. Born at Kneitlingen, he had entertaining adventures right from the day of his christening, for the party which followed his baptism was so hilarious that the nurse staggered as she was crossing a plank over a stream on the way home, and fell in. Saved just in time from being smothered in the mud, baby Till was carried triumphantly home to Kneitlingen, black as a nigger. A good bath soon brought his pink skin to light again, and as he had now been dipped three times in one afternoon all were sure that his life would be no ordinary one. And so it was to prove.

After many years of moving from one employment and one town to another, usually with great rapidity in order to escape the hue and cry raised by the irate victim of his latest trick, Till was fortunate enough to be taken into the employment of the Bishop of Bremen, who for a while kept him as a jester. The bishop was a worthy man, and amongst other things he was very distressed by the problem of magic and witchcraft. Till assured him that the subject was nonsense, but the bishop was not inclined to agree.

Till was one day walking over the market square when he noticed a woman with a stall of crockery. She looked miserably sad, and when she explained that she could not sell her wares and so had no money to take home to her sick husband and their family of small children, the warm-hearted Till was sorry for her. Having just received his wages he was comparatively well off, and pulling out the money he asked her if she would take the thirty gold crowns for the entire load of crockery on her stall.

The woman could hardly believe her good fortune, and she accepted. She was also very willing to agree to a ruse which he whispered in her ear. He then gave her the money and walked away.

Later that day Till came strolling across the market again, this time in the company of the Bishop of Bremen.

'You know your concern for the evil of witchcraft, your reverence,' Till said. 'I can prove to you that any fool can do such things. Even myself. For instance, look at that woman with her stall of crockery. She is calm enough, is she not? But if I were merely to wish it, she would in an instant be made insane.'

The bishop shook his head. No, the evil art was something infinitely more serious, a secret work involving the devil, he said. Till, simple soul that he was, could not conceivably bewitch a poor woman and rob her of her sanity just by wishing it.

'What do you bet, your reverence? Shall we say thirty gold crowns?'

This seemed easy money to the bishop, who at once agreed. The wager was made, and hardly had the two men shaken hands upon it when the woman leapt from her seat, picked up a piece of timber, and attacking her display of earthenware with insane ferocity she slashed and smashed at it until not a piece remained.

So Till received his thirty crowns, exactly the amount he had given to the poor woman. The bishop was somewhat reassured about witchcraft when Till explained that the woman had agreed to attack her crockery the moment he put his hand to the tassel of his cap. Being a kindly man the bishop himself challenged all his guests at dinner that night to wager an ox apiece that they could explain the woman's sudden fit of demonic possession correctly, and of the twelve oxen he won in this way he presented the best animal to Eulenspiegel and ordered the remainder to be sold and the proceeds taken to the wife of the sick potter, so that her family should never want again.

One of the tales about Eulenspiegel mentions a curious connection with England. Till had been employed for a while by a smith, and as usual the time soon came when he had to depart as quickly as he could. As was his habit, he left his trade mark chalked upon the door – an owl (*Eule*) and a mirror (*Spiegel*). The worthy smith whom he had duped was rather slow in the intellect, and as he did not understand what the drawing meant he called to a priest who happened to be walking down the street and asked him if he could decipher the curious hieroglyphics.

The priest looked at the door, and laughed. 'Easily,' he said. 'It means "Eulenspiegel was here".' And as he happened to be an admirer of Till's comical streak he struck a bargain with the smith that he might have the door in return for a new one to be commissioned at the joiner's.

'After his death the door was inherited by one person after another,' the story continues. 'Finally it was discovered by a rich Englishman, who bought it for a high price and took it with him to his land across the sea. Any man who wishes may still see it if he but make the journey to Oxford, where the door is to be discovered among much other honourable jumble in the museum of the university.' I have never met an Oxford man who can testify to having seen it, but perhaps in the course of six centuries the accumulation of jumble has become such that it is buried under the pile. Or perhaps one should take Eulenspiegel in the way that thesis writers have done and regard him as existing only in a psychological sense.

Certainly Till's biography is confusing. I have said that he was born in Kneitlingen, in the fourteenth century. However, this is only one of his many birthplaces, and a few months after we had sailed from Mölln I happened to cruise down the little canal which leads from the oval lock in Bruges towards its vanished sea entrance in the inlet of the Zwijn, long since sanded over. The canal is still navigable to Damme, and there they are proud to relate how Til Uylenspiegl was born there, and they know precisely where his companion Lamme Goedzak lived – a fellow who does not appear in the German version. A few days later I visited that wonderful puppet theatre in an alley off the Petite Rue des Bouchers in Brussels, and the dolls delighted me with an evening of knock-about action in which Til and Lamme were flooring the soldiers of the Spanish Inquisition, towards the end of the sixteenth century. But one must expect a few mild inconsistencies or Tillisms in the life of such a joker. Maybe he really was born in the sixteenth century and died in the fourteenth, just to confuse historians.

Personally I like to think of Till as real. Besides he was certainly buried at Mölln, and I cannot easily conceive of a purely psychological death and burial – at least, not in the way it happened on that particular occasion. Poor Till was ailing fast when he arrived one evening at Mölln. Seeking out the apothecary he begged to be taken in and treated with physic; and as the apothecary himself had a tendency to humour he readily agreed and gave Eulenspiegel a medicine which in fact was an extra strong dose of a purgative.

In the early hours of the morning the purgative began to do what was expected of it and Eulenspiegel was seized with an urgent need to leave the room immediately, only to find that the humorous apothecary had carefully barred and locked the doors so that escape to what was presumably an outside earth closet was impossible. Thereupon, Till went into the dispensary and made emergency use of the flask from which the purgative had come.

'I have no money,' he explained. 'This is where the medicine came from, and this is where it is now returning. Thus the good apothecary needs no payment, for he has lost nothing.'

The apothecary was not pleased with his customer, and as soon as it was light he had him conveyed to the Hospital of the Holy Ghost, not far from the cathedral.

'All my life I have prayed that the Holy Spirit may enter me,' Till declared as they carried him in. 'But he has always preferred to stay outside. Now it is my turn to enter him.'

Till continued to decline, and some days later he formally drew up his will. One-third of his estate was to be divided among his good friends Klaus the joiner, Gottlieb the night-watchman, Kunz the executioner and Lieb the tiler. A second portion was to reward the council of Mölln for taking him in, and the third he left to the priest and the cathedral dignitaries with the request that his body should be buried in holy ground and suitable masses sung for the benefit of his soul. After four weeks the massive iron-bound chest which contained all his worldly wealth was to be opened and the legacy divided out as he had written.

And so he died. The tradesmen and ecclesiastics and the burghers of Mölln attended his solemn funeral to initiate their four weeks of waiting. At last the day came, and when the chest was opened it was found to contain precisely what any who knew Till's circumstances and his pleasant kinky humour might have expected – a hundredweight or two of cobblestones.

Exactly as Till had no doubt imagined, the councillors immediately suspected that the priest who was alone with him for his confession had taken the opportunity to remove the gold and replace it with stones. The chapter was convinced that the council had stolen the riches during the four weeks in which they had had custody of the chest itself. As for the four tradesmen friends, they were sure that one or other of the authorities had tricked them. For months or perhaps years a sullen mutual suspicion descended over the little community of Mölln.

A certain degree of corroborative evidence of this story is still to be found in Mölln, where the iron-bound chest properly supplied with a new load of stones is to be seen in the little house which serves as a museum and which faces across the cobbles to the pleasant bronze of Eulenspiegel, sitting easily and with carelessly crossed legs on top of the drinking fountain. He is wearing a smock and hose, and a fourteenth-century jester's cap with two long tassels, and his right thumb is held up in a casual gesture which suggests that he is cheerful and carefree – as no doubt he was, whether in fiction or fact.

As he lay dying in the Hospital of the Holy Ghost, Till asked that his staff, his sole trusty companion on all his travels as he fled from one wrathful employer to the next, should be planted in the ground above his grave. If it remained dry and dead, that would be an indication that he was remaining below the datum line, but if he went to heaven the stick would take root and sprout. This in fact it did, and the staff eventually became a mighty lime-tree standing close against the cathedral wall. Any apprentices or journeymen who passed through Mölln would drive a tack or pin into the trunk, for this was supposed to be an infallible protection against toothache and other ills. Over the years the great lime-tree began itself to sicken, perhaps from an overdose of rusty nails and copper. Children still played round the trunk, but when enthusiastic Dutch soldiery climbed it and disported themselves among its branches, the poor old tree collapsed.

Till's tomb had of course originally been beneath it, but now the slab was taken up and placed on the outside wall of the cathedral close by. And there it still is, behind a grill and safe from the attentions of those who might like to deface it. Eulenspiegel is wearing hose, a curious coat ending in tasselled points, and a round hat with a feather. His arms are raised so that he can hold up his trade mark for all to see – an owl in one hand, a mirror in the other.

> *Dissen stein soll niemand erhaben*
> *Hie stat Ulenspiegel begraben*
> *Anno domini MCCCL jahr.*

So ran the original inscription on his tombstone.

> *This stone shall none remove*
> *Here stands Eulenspiegel buried 1350 A.D.*

Not *lies* buried, be it noted, but *stands* buried. When he had been placed in the coffin and all was ready for the short journey to the burial ground outside the cathedral the mourners were suddenly interrupted. Apparently the byre had not been securely fastened, for a herd of pigs rushed into the room and overturned the furniture and even the bier. Only when the livestock had been driven out and order restored did the bearers notice that the coffin had been put back upside down, so that poor Till was lying face downwards.

'Never mind,' joked the foreman of the party. 'That fool will decide for himself which way up he wants to be buried.'

So the procession wound up the sloping path to the burying ground. At the graveside the usual service was read, and just as the coffin was being lowered into the grave the sling at the foot end parted. With a thump the coffin landed upright.

'That fool will decide for himself.' The men left the coffin as it

was and filled in the grave, not forgetting to plant his staff as Till
had wished.

In fact a skull, believed to be that of the great joker, was excavated from under the lime tree in 1950, the occasion of the sexcentenary of his death, and it is now proudly exhibited in Mölln.
But a far more attractive memorial is the bronze figure sitting over
the fountain, and the fund of stories which has come down from
the Middle Ages to show that humour has not greatly changed
in the centuries between.

Set into the churchyard wall beside the figure of Till himself is
a bronze plaque bearing the head of an Honorary Freeman of
Mölln, George Bernard Shaw. Through all the time we were
lying at the jetty in the lake I asked the park sweeper, the milk-
man, the waitress in the Ratskeller, the draper, the baker's wife,
the girl in the bookshop, and the clerk in the post office the same
question.

'Please tell me why George Bernard Shaw was made an Honorary Freeman. What connection had he with Mölln?'

Usually I had to pronounce his name Bairnhard Sharve to be
understood at all, but then the answer would come. Not at once,
but after a suitable period of thought, of reflection that it really
would not do to have Sharve large as life, cheerfully beaming from
his plaque, and not be able to tell this over-inquisitive boatman
something at least reasonably credible.

'He lived here for a while,' said one.

I did not believe it, and went on enquiring.

'Shaw? Ah . . . let me think, now. Yes. The action of one of his
plays is set in the town.' The man who volunteered this piece of
information looked at me with the wide and honest eyes of a
modern Eulenspiegel, so I did not argue.

'I see,' I said. And I asked another.

'Sharve? Why, he was the world's authority on Eulenspiegel and
wrote his biography.' I stared at this girl incredulously and she
blushed guiltily.

Next I asked a schoolgirl. If Shaw was a freeman, presumably
they would read him in the upper strata of the *Gymnasium*.

'Shaw?' She was mystified.

'Yes. The man on the plaque up near the Rathaus. Just beside Till.'

'I have heard that the town was occupied by an English garrison in 1945,' she said. 'I expect he was the general in command.' She did not blush at all as she handed me this one. Obviously the place bred Eulenspiegels of both sexes.

It was a girl in the draper's who first confessed that she had no idea why Shaw was a freeman. 'But you could ask the archivist,' she added. 'He must know. He's ever so learned, and old, and surrounded with books and things. You'll find him in the Hospital of the Holy Ghost.'

Very much to my surprise the Hospital of the Holy Ghost was indeed still there, even if it had lost a wing since Till died beneath its roof six centuries ago – if he did. I knocked on the door and discovered that there really was a town archivist. Just as the girl had said, he was ever so learned, and old, and surrounded with books and things. He was delighted to help.

'Well it was like this. In 1950 the sixth centenary of Eulenspiegel's death came round, and the council decided to make an occasion of it. There was a play put on in the evenings, up there by the Rathaus, and there were festivities of all sorts. It was Eulenspiegel year, you know. One can't have a sexcentenary every year; only about once in six hundred, really. So it was a great spree, as you can imagine.' He chuckled at the recollection.

'Of course this Eulenspiegel – as you know – was a great joker, whether he existed or not. And at the time of the festival we had a mayor who was – how shall I put it? A bit of an Eulenspiegel himself, if you know what I mean. More than a bit, actually. He was a real Eulenspiegel and liked his quota of fun. So he thought it would be nice to invite the two greatest living jesters to the opening of the play. They would be welcome to come as guests of the town and stay here all through the festivities. One of them was Bernard Shaw.'

'And did he come?' I asked.

'No. Unfortunately he was ill at the time. But he wrote a very nice note to thank the mayor, and obviously he was really sorry to miss the occasion. So the council decided to make him an Honorary

Freeman of Mölln instead, and I think he was delighted. He would be a very appropriate choice, don't you think?'

'Very,' I said.

'If you ask at the museum you can see his reply to the invitation.'

Shaw's note proved of course to be a postcard, written in green ink. It said that Shaw considered it 'a delight and honour to be ranked with one of the greatest storytellers of all time, Tyl Ulenspiegel,' and regretted that the writer was too ill to attend the celebrations. But the reverse side was even more interesting. The mayor had written the invitation on notepaper which bore a circular seal with the town arms supported by a pair of owls. Round the edge was the inscription: *Amt des Bürgermeisters von Mölln i. Lbg.*' Shaw was always a man to save time in correspondence, and so to address the card he had simply clipped off the heading and pasted it on the front.

The address of Mölln i. Lbg., without even an identifying country, had no doubt puzzled the sorter in Welwyn, but not for long. 'Luxembourg' was added in pencil, and to Luxembourg the card had first been sent. The Luxembourgers had probably turned up the name of Mölln in the directory, for they had expanded the *Lbg* to its full meaning of Lauenburg, and sent the card on its way again.

'It was a pity Shaw was ill,' said the archivist sadly.

'Yes,' I said. Then, 'By the way, you said the two greatest living comics were invited. Who was the second?'

The archivist sniggered again and peered over his glasses. 'You may guess. Then you can see if you're right. Upstairs in the top floor of the museum you will find a sketch of all three, done by a local man. You'll see – Shaw on one side, Till in the middle, and this . . . er . . . other fellow, too.'

'And did he come?'

'No. I'm afraid he never even answered.'

On my way to the museum I turned over the possibilities in my mind. Nineteen-fifty – that was some time ago. If I had had the responsibility of selection, who might I have selected as the partner for Shaw, with all the world to choose from? Groucho Marx? I

was not sure how well he would be known in Germany. Stan
Laurel? Harold Lloyd? Somebody rather more literary would
have been the town's choice, I thought. A man to match Shaw, but
different. I wondered if the councillors of Mölln read James
Thurber. Even if not, Thurber would have had a wide appeal for
visitors. But could one imagine Thurber not even acknowledging
such an invitation?

The museum was shut, but the woman custodian lived nearby.
'I can't leave the house,' she called down, vigorously shaking a
mop from an upper window. 'I can't open the museum just for one
visitor. It says in the rules that it will only be opened for three or
more.'

Enough of these Eulenspiegel inhabitants, I thought to myself.
I walked down a side alley and saw two visitors looking in at the
window of a small crafts shop. The man was large, and he had so
many pieces of optical equipment hung on straps round his neck
that I knew he must be an American.

'Beautiful little town,' I said as I came up.

'Sure. Say, you speak English? You know where we can get a
good meal?'

'Yes,' I said. 'I'll tell you. But before you go there I think you
ought to see the museum. It's fascinating.'

'Guess we should,' said his wife, not entirely convinced.

'It's only just around the corner. And from there I can show you
where the Ratskeller is,' I said.

'O.K.,' said the husband. The pair followed me round to the
square, and soon the man was rattling powerfully at the door of the
museum.

'I guess it's closed,' he said. It seemed a reasonable guess.

I pointed at the notice. 'When closed, apply to the custodian,' I
said. 'Look, it's that house only two doors away.'

The big man strode up to the little medieval house and banged
on the door. The top window flew open, and the heads of the mop
and the woman appeared again.

'Mooseum,' said the man.

'That's right,' said his wife.

'There are three of us,' I added.

The woman hesitated, then shut the window. Soon she came out bringing the key of the museum with her.

Inside I ran quickly upstairs to look for the picture. And there it was, a hilarious sketch of the three greatest comics in the world. In the centre was the cheerful face of the medieval Till Eulenspiegel. Smiling to either side of him, the two moderns. George Bernard Shaw, and Josef Stalin.

VII

The giants of Krummesse – Lübeck, city of spires – the fossil man – Queen of the Hansa – Roggenbuk's fate – Shipmen's Hall – the eskimo of the Skagerrak – city of Buddenbrooks – Thames Commodore *discovers the Ilmenau – Lüneburg, city of salt – the Russians to the rescue*

DONNERSCHLEUSE – the first lock beyond Mölln has a splendid name. It is very much like any other lock in the depths of the country, and if it is indeed Thunder Lock I failed to find out why. Yet there is something nordic about the area and maybe this was a place where Thor was particularly fond of hurling his hammer and making the thunderclaps which in lands further south were continually fabricated by Jove. Certainly the northern pantheon has left its traces over the landscape. Odin's own magical horse Sleipnir rears on the gable ends of the farms, and the awful serpent of Midgard can occasionally be found wriggling a well-camouflaged way through the carvings on the main timbers.

If the Elbe–Trave Canal is flanked mainly by pastures and copses of fir, this is just because towns are scarce. Only the smallest of villages are to be found along its line, and of these Krummesse is probably the largest, the broad and foursquare timbered tower of its ancient church standing solidly on the hill above its lock. It is a very nordic building, this church, and it hints of the days long ago when the first missionaries came to Holstein. They had much to contend with, particularly as the inhabitants seem to have included numbers of giants, some of whom were evidently regular church-goers. In fact the church was designed for them and the door built to appropriate dimensions; and just in case twentieth-century man should not be disposed to believe it the villagers can still point to the outline of the original arch, which once extended twelve feet above the present top of the doorway.

Of course Holstein was always well stocked with strange beings, whether they were larger or smaller than standard humanity. I cannot remember ever having myself encountered the fairy folk of the north, but one of the more curious events recorded of Krummesse is the occasion when a farmer and his wife happened one night to be walking past a *Hünengrab* – or Hun's Grave – outside the village. These ancient stones have of course no connection with the Huns, but are burial mounds and tombs from the Bronze Age. They are supposed, however, to be favourite haunts of the Little People, and on this occasion the couple were surprised to see crossing the track just ahead of them a long procession of individuals whom they described as being no higher than a chair-leg and led by a little fellow riding a tiny horse and wearing a tall pointed hat.

Were I to see such a collection of gnomes, I am not at all sure what I would say or do; but the couple declared in unison, 'All good spirits praise the Lord'. The effect of this was not to make the Little People vanish. Their leader swelled and swelled until he was a giant, then he ordered the whole troop to turn back, and they marched off into the side of the hill.

Two miles above Lübeck the canal runs to its end in the river Trave. Below the junction a pair of brawny fishermen in rubber aprons stood in a boat which was moored to stakes in the bank in such a way that it remained set across the stream. Slowly they were hauling hand over hand to pull in a net which they had laid in the Trave. It was a very long net indeed, and even when we were turning the next bend they had still not reached the bag.

I wondered what they could catch in that river, clean but a little peaty. Could it conceivably be salmon? Further down, Lübeck and Travemünde would certainly pollute the estuary a little, but not enough to keep out a really determined salmon. Besides, the Trave was once such a salmon river that a Duke of Holstein gave the wealthy city his fishing rights, and errand boys became so sated with the pinkish fish-meat that at one time it was inserted as an article in their contract of employment that they would not have to accept salmon for dinner more than twice every week. This, I think, would be a very reasonable stipulation even in times of relative scarcity. I like salmon, but once a week is enough.

The first sight of Lübeck is unexpectedly peaceful. The more horrid suburbs of this city of a quarter-of-a-million people are hidden away to the sides, and Lübeck itself sits tightly compact on an island formed by the old course of the Trave and the newer course of the shipping channel, which cuts boldly through a hill and is spanned by fine bridges of the period – for the canal was built at the height of the iron age, and its works are supplied with every conceivable rivet and twirl and knob that casting and forging could provide. The edge of this island is fringed with tall willows and limes and elms, and of the city itself only the splendid spires rise above the foliage. The impression is of a place of mystery but also of great pride, for the spires of St Mary's and St Peter's, the cathedral and St James's are amongst the greatest and finest in the world. The towers are brick, very straight and erect, very severely gothic, each one of them topped with its tall green needle-cap of copper, and only St Peter runs to the luxury of four little corner turrets just to show that the Lübeckers could also make small spires if they put their minds to it.

Lübeck's square church towers rising from its island hill have long been famous, and ever since the Middle Ages the city has been renowned not only as the driving force in the Hanseatic League but also as the City of the Seven Golden Spires – seven, because two of the five churches raised in the twelfth and thirteenth centuries – St Mary's and the cathedral – are twin-spired. To one of these pairs is attached the tale of a family tragedy.

It was in the days of Duke Henry the Lion and to mark his return from a crusade that the two slim steeples were set upon the top of the new cathedral towers, and this astounding piece of twelfth-century engineering is said to have been undertaken by two steeple-makers who were father and son. Each set to work upon one of the steeples, and it soon became clear that the spire put up by the son was altogether more beautiful than that of his father. As the steeples rose, the Lübeckers not only noticed the difference between the two, but remarked upon it.

A feature of Lübeck's cathedral is that the gap between the two towers is bridged by a pair of beams which fly over the width of the roof of the nave. Perhaps they were put there to make the towers more stable, but the father steeple-builder had another idea. Hearing the comparisons between his own work and that of his son he began to seethe with jealousy, and yet he managed to conceal his feelings so that his son would not suspect. Then one day when he was up on the tower and discussing with the workmen how the building was progressing, he remarked casually to his son that he had laid down his adze on one of the span beams.

'Be a good lad and climb out of the window and get it for me,' he said.

The son did so. He saw the adze at the further side of the gap and set out to walk the beam and fetch it. Half way over he was overcome with giddiness – a particularly dangerous ailment for a steeple-maker, one might think – and fell to his death on the cathedral roof, far below. As a result the father became the sole master of the work and completed both the towers himself, but it is said that the one of them has always needed repair and attention whereas the other, designed by his son, has ever stayed firm and straight.

In fact both towers lean, and considering their weight and age this is not altogether surprising, even if the Lübeckers can account for the matter differently. Before Henry the Lion went off to the crusades he set aside the ground for the cathedral, and he chose the site because of a curious incident. Every morning he used to see a stag of considerable age come to drink at a spring close to his own residence, and when one day he noticed something sparkling around the animal's neck he gave orders to his men to catch the creature. This they eventually did, and Duke Henry was surprised to see that a golden cross was growing between the antlers and a gold chain hung from the neck of the stag. So unusual was this adornment that the Duke examined it and discovered an engraved plate which told that Charlemagne himself had provided the gold chain four hundred years earlier. On that occasion, when the stag was relatively young, Charlemagne had chased the animal and cornered it, and he was just about to let fly his arrow when the stag

knelt with its fore-legs and shuffled forward in obeisance, finally
nuzzling at his hand. This most exceptional and polite behaviour
caused the great Emperor of the Holy Roman Empire to reward
the animal with a golden necklace.

Henry the Lion was intrigued by the inscription, but he also
felt that a stag which four centuries earlier had grovelled before
Charlemagne must surely have been sent to him as a sign. It
occurred to him that the place where the animal habitually drank
was to be earmarked for holy purposes and so he immediately set
it aside as the site of the cathedral. This, of course, was more pious
than practical. Ground from which a spring flows is unlikely to be
the most suitable place on which to erect such a massive building.
Sure enough, through the centuries there has been some sub-
sidence and the towers have gradually developed a slight lean.
That at least is the tale in Lübeck, but when I asked what became
of the quatercentenarian stag and Charlemagne's golden chain,
none seemed to know.

The cathedral has other tales also, such as the one which tells of
a wealthy merchant at the end of the fifteenth century, a man so
concerned with his business that the idea never crossed his mind
that one day he might have to die. The first occasion when Death
appeared as a reality was when it claimed the merchant's wife, after
which it paid him a visit in his counting-house and asked him
politely whether he did not wish to go the same way – for in
those days Death was gentlemanly indeed, never dictatorial and
bullying nor capriciously coronary, but invariably courteous and
considerate.

The merchant said Thank you, but no. He would rather go on
living. Later his friends died one by one, and his own grown-up
children also. On each occasion Death knocked at the door,
repeated the question and then departed. At length the man was
quite alone, but he still did not tire of living. On the contrary, he
prayed to the Almighty that he might be spared, even if he
became fossilised through age. And so he lived, older and more
wizened and faded, until at last he was a wambling old shade of a
man, bereft of his senses. People avoided him, the children teased
him, and now at last he began to wish his life at an end.

Yet his old acquaintance Death never came. The unhappy man asked people if they had seen him about, and somebody told him that at midnight Death habitually took a stroll round the inside of the cathedral, presumably to look at the tombstones he had helped to provide. So the old man repaired to the cathedral, only to discover that it was locked and there was none to open for him at that time of night. He whined and wept but all in vain. He was forced to remain outside.

So things went on, the insane and bent old fellow scrabbling each night at the closed door of the cathedral, until it happened that some roof repairs were to be put in hand and the tiler had come with his men and put the ladders up on the roof, ready for work to start in the morning. That same night the poor old merchant began to haul himself up from rung to rung, wheezing and groaning as he climbed towards the ridge of the roof, from where he thought he might perhaps see into the nave and catch a glimpse of Death, and even have a chance to call to him. Yet he was now so feeble and short of breath that he did not manage to climb higher than the edge of the roof. Feeling faint he squatted in a corner, and there the next morning he was found. But already his limbs had begun to stiffen in the unwonted posture, and to bring him down to the ground was impossible. It was almost as though he were frozen to the roof. Fortunately the fellow ate little, and for many years he subsisted on a single communion wafer which the kindly sexton carried to him every New Year's Eve. At last Death came on his rounds, but it was the sexton he took away. The wizened merchant was left.

A new sexton was appointed, but he had heard nothing of the old man on the roof and had no idea that he should provide a communion wafer on New Year's Eve. It was many years before there was any need to inspect the roof again, so the man remained undiscovered until at last some workmen were sent up to examine the tiles. They found him, completely turned to stone. And there he is supposed to have remained ever since, but none that I asked in Lübeck were sure whether he was still there or if a bomb had mercifully ended his enforced fossilisation and reduced him to rubble on the terrible night in 1942 when much of Lübeck's glory was destroyed for ever and, like St Paul's in London, the twin spires of the cathedral flickered in the glare of the flames.

The engineers who laid out the canal had an eye for beauty. First comes the fleeting glimpse down the Trave itself and then the stately progress along the park and beneath the trees and bridge to where the broad water of the canal harbour mirrors the imposing form of the Burgtor, which for five centuries has straddled what was once the only landward connection of Lübeck. Beyond the bridge the cargo vessels lie at the quays and the river Trave winds its final eleven miles of course to Travemünde, from where the Baltic ferries race across the sea to Denmark and Sweden. But turning the point of the island the boatman can pull in at the broad quay which is still flanked by red brick warehouses and chandlery stores and seamen's inns which were there in the days of the Hanseatic League.

For Lübeck was the Queen of the Hansa. Already in the thirteenth century the seven cities of the Wends formed strong trading links with each other and then with the lands to the east and west. It was Lübeck's mayor, Alexander von Soltwedel, who succeeded in beating off the marauding Scandinavians and consolidating the community of trading interests to form the famous Hansa, an association of trading cities pledged to sweep the seas and the land routes free of danger and to unite their forces for mutual protection. More than one-hundred-and-twenty cities and city-states sent delegates to the first meeting of the League in Lübeck, where the order of precedence and rules were established. The council also set up four main trading posts, in Bruges, London, Novgorod and Notodden – this last being later removed to a safer position at Bergen.

No trace of the London office survives – at least not in the physical sense. The Hanseatic merchants had their warehouses approximately on the site of Cannon Street station, for in those days the river Thames was broader and the line of Upper Thames Street was more or less the waterfront. Even today the area of the Vintry Ward and Queenhithe has much the appearance of an old quarter of Hamburg or Lübeck, and the furs which are carried by lighter to the warehouses still remind one of the men of the Hansa, the

Easterlings' as the English merchants called them, for did they not hail from the Baltic, the Eastern Sea?

Gone are the Easterlings, but the solid reliability of their money and their merchant bankers has remained through one devaluation after another. In Cockney fashion the beginning of the word has been dropped, but *Sterling* is still the word for our currency and an adjective for reliability. At least, so it seems, but another school of antiquaries prefers to derive it from the four starlings on coins of Edward the Confessor – an ingenious theory indeed when one remembers that the birds were martlets, and what a Londoner understood by the word 'starling' was not a bird at all but a piled foundation for an arch of Old London Bridge. Besides, this book is about a voyage into Hanseatic lands, so obviously I must be adamant and stick to the Easterling interpretation.

How well the German traders stood in their relation to the City of London is shown by the ancient trust that was given to them to be responsible for the upkeep of the Bishopsgate, the gateway which spanned the roadway which led from Old London Bridge to the north of England. Up to the reign of Elizabeth I these men alone shared with the citizens of London the defence of the gate and the maintenance of a watch, from which it is clear that they must have been trusted very much more fully than other foreigners. From the year 1282 the Hansa merchants also had the right to elect an alderman of their own.

Lübeck itself is of course older than the Hansa, but before the time of Henry the Lion its past vanishes in the mists of legends such as the tale of Roggenbuk, a strange water-spirit that seems to have been something of a hybrid between merman and dragon, a being that fed exclusively upon humans, who flung themselves into the sea when they heard the alluring strains of the music which flowed from his harp, which happened to be constructed of dead men's bones. All in all, Roggenbuk was a decidedly dangerous sort of character, and the shippers who traded to the Trave became so discouraged when their best sailors leaped overboard to their fate that they preferred to sail to other ports. However, a sensible old woman agreed to attempt to negotiate between the inhabitants and the water-spirit, and she reached a useful compromise. Roggenbuk would have to do with one victim a year, but to make up for this economy the one chosen would be a beautiful virgin, decked out with flowers. For the monster, it seems, was not aesthetically insensitive.

It was also agreed that Roggenbuk would play on his harp until he had made the girl insensible, and then he could emerge from the water and take her away. The populace would have peace for the rest of the year, provided they did nothing to irritate him.

This arrangement worked well enough for many years, but eventually a young man decided that the time had come to call a halt. He undertook to rid the country of Roggenbuk, if he were given a house and pension in return. He was dashing and handsome, he rode a white horse and carried a lance from which fluttered a pennant with a cross. It will not astonish the reader to discover that he was none other than the ubiquitous St George, who was one of the most experienced dragon-slayers and maiden-freers of all time.

St George stood by the bound maiden and waited, chatting to her reassuringly. As there was yet no sign of the beast he delivered a brief resumé of Christian doctrine and baptised the girl. He had barely finished when the sea appeared to boil as Roggenbuk wallowed towards the land and wriggled up the beach. The monster opened its mouth wide enough to gulp down both victims at once, and this gave St George his chance. While the maiden fainted from fright he pushed his lance right down the creature's throat. With a terrible groan Roggenbuk expired.

St George waited till the girl had recovered, then he told her that he took the greatest exception to the way in which the people dealt with the sick, for it was the custom in those parts to keep the place healthy by beating to death with clubs any who had a disease or infirmity. This, he said, must stop. The girl was to take his reward of house and pension and use it to establish a hospital. Then, without even giving her a kiss, he rode away, swift as the wind.

When the rest of the people arrived on the scene – having kept at a safe distance to avoid the effects of Roggenbuk's harp melodies – they unbound the girl, did as she told them, and established the infirmary at Travemünde. They also towed out to sea the corpse of the monster. It sank, and became turned into a rock which since that time has wrecked many a good ship, and which still bears the name of Roggenbuk.

Presumably Lübeck itself was not at that time in existence. It is said to have been established in that fateful year 1066, which brought not only the final sack of Haithabu and the Norman conquest of England, but a revolt by the Wends against the Holy Roman Empire. These Baltic men slew their own King Gottschalk and chose as their ruler Kruto, a chief from the isle of Rügen.

Kruto decided to build a fortress commanding the Trave, and in the corner between that river and the Wakenitz he established a fortified city named Buku. One year he sailed away on a marauding expedition, and this gave Gottschalk's son an opportunity to call upon the help of his allies the Saxons, and invest the place. Buku was not well sited to withstand a siege, especially when the access to the sea was blocked by Saxon ships, and soon there was a scarcity of provisions. The city was saved by an enterprising fisherman named Luba, who loaded into his boat all the fresh bread and meat and vegetables on which he could lay his hands and then rowed down the river.

The Saxons stopped him. Who was he? Where was he going, and why? Luba said he was sorry if he was doing anything wrong, but he was on his way to the markets at various places downstream, where he hoped to dispose of his produce at better prices than he could obtain in Buku. According to this tale, a variant on the familiar ruse of stuffing the final piglet with grain and dropping it from the battlements, the besiegers were so impressed that they doubted their ability to hold out long enough to starve the city into surrender, and they immediately sailed away. Luba was rewarded by having the city renamed after him and winning for the Guild of Fishermen the privilege that they alone might land live fish from the river and sell them in the market. This monopoly persisted unchallenged for more than six hundred years, until the fishers of Travemünde successfully overthrew it by offering live cod for sale, fish which lived in salt water and so could not validly be regarded as fish from the river.

Those who knew Lübeck before the destruction of 1942 will

shake their heads and say that the city gives but a shadowy hint of its former glory, that the once lovely Queen of the Hansa has been reduced by the results of that disaster to a mere crippled crone. Maybe, but any boatman who was not familiar with the city more than a quarter of a century ago must surely find it one of the loveliest of all the northern cities of Europe. Even today the noble buildings of the great merchants convey something of the enormous power and serene confidence of men who were quite prepared to tell foreign rulers what they could do with themselves – and if necessary to send a fleet to help them do it. Even in our own century this doggedness survives, and without it the great brick towers of the gothic north could never have risen again, nor that fantastic town hall been rebuilt, a palatial building with flying buttresses and minarets and everything that the widely travelled Hansa captains had seen on their voyages.

Beyond the swing-bridge at the end of the canal we turned sharp to port to select a berth with what we thought would be the best view of the city of spires. The *Thames Commodore* always pitches camp in this way if she can, and finding a broad quay opposite a row of business-like little houses of chandlers and captains and shipping agents she drew in and made fast. It was only when I found a street map that I discovered this basin to be the Hansahafen, where for centuries the ships of the wealthy merchants of the league had lain. Across the roadway a number of intriguing streets and alleys led back from the waterfront, climbing to the backbone of the city itself. Sometimes their gables leaned so far over to gossip with those across the roadway that brick arches had been inserted overhead to prevent their falling into each other's arms. One such alley was the Engelgrube, which had nothing to do with angels. It was a case of *non angeli sed angli*, for at the foot of the street was the quay where the ships of the English trade would lie to load and unload, and where by a pleasant coincidence the *Thames Commodore* had helped herself to as pleasant a berth as her forerunners centuries before. At the upper end of this passage and propped by a trio of flying arches on its open side, was one of the most remarkable institutions in Europe, the *Schiffergesellschaft*, or hall of the Honourable Company of Shipmen.

Lübeck – The Schiffergesellschaft

The house of the *Schiffergesellschaft* is a typical building of the southern Baltic, plain and rather severe with its four-stepped gable in red brick topped by a golden ship voyaging under full sail as a weather vane. The house was bought by the guild in 1535, and somebody later knocked out the gothic doorway and replaced it by an elegant rococo entrance. Above the door there is another sailing ship, this time a painted one, and to either side in kinky old-style German lettering the verses which are found on the dedication page of this book. Standing to the sides of the steps and several feet in front of the building are set two tall flat slabs, somewhat like tombstones. These have painted tops which show a water-joust in progress, and across them they carry the legend *Allen zu gefallen . . . ist unmöglich.* One cannot please everybody – for what is a fair wind for one voyager will be a contrary wind for another.

These slabs are called *Beischläge*, and others can be found in Lübeck. They were the outer pew ends of seats which stretched to the wall of the house itself and which could be tipped up out of the way. A pair outside the entrance to the town hall once served as a court of petty sessions where citizens might bring their charges against each other, and there was also a pleasant custom that any bridegroom from one of the patrician families of this Hansa city was obliged to go there for one week before his wedding and stand by the seat for an hour, decked out in his best suit. During that time any citizen might lodge a complaint against his character or integrity, and if it were upheld the young man was banished from the city and might not renew his addresses to his beloved until he had satisfied any claims against himself.

Inside the house one steps down into as extraordinary a restaurant as can be found anywhere; and curiously enough the *Schiffergesellschaft* has served the double function of livery hall and public eating place from its earliest days. The walls are painted with age-darkened pictures of Old Testament scenes – the flood, with a very seaworthy ark, Lot's daughters making their father drunk enough to set about a bit of incest, Solomon and the disputed maternity case, and others. Magnificent model ships hang from the ceiling, and beneath them the hall itself is laid out with three long

rows of tables, for all the world like an Oxbridge dining-hall. Here
one may eat and drink among the clerks and typists from offices
in the city, who take their lunch sitting in the same elegant pew-
like seats where the shipmen themselves would once take their
meals when, at the height of winter, the Trave was frozen over or
the Baltic itself icebound. The pew ends are carved with the arms
of the various companies or divisions of the guild, and one can
identify those of the Riga shippers, the Bergen shippers and the
Reval shippers. There were other divisions of the guild, whose
pews have gone, such as the Novgorod and Skåne voyagers. And no
doubt the Stecknitz boatmen used to look in for an evening of wine
and gossip when the ice made the locks of their salt route unusable.

At the end of the hall is the raised 'confessional', so called
because it is hidden away behind a fretted screen. Here the wardens
and court of assistants would sit, spying out over the others in the
body of the hall, and when the bell was struck within this sanctum
all had to hearken. The word of the court went as unchallenged as
did the order of a captain on his ship, but as those who resisted it
could not very well be keel-hauled under the building there was a
blackboard on which their names were written so that they might
be subjected to the general scorn and contempt of their fellows and
the public. At first a name would be added in chalk, but if the man
still proved unwilling to accept the ruling of the court of the guild
the chalk was rubbed out and the name replaced in paint. And
there the board still hangs, although two centuries have passed
since the city forbade the use of such a sensible device in any
house of meeting. The inscription in a somewhat ancient and
perhaps Wendish form of German says that the undermentioned
have gone against the brotherhood of the Hansa, and as they are
unwilling to do without question as they are told their names are
written up and will stay there until they have done the bidding of
the company. Meanwhile they are not to be served with beer.

The hall has many strange relics brought back by the skippers
of Hanseatic Lübeck, and among them is an eskimo kayak
recovered in 1607 in the Skagerrak. Carried far from Greenland
by wind and current the poor paddler died of starvation or thirst
and drifted, upright and dead in his seat, until at last a Lübeck

F

captain sighted the strange object and lifted it aboard his ship. The eskimo was by then reduced to a skeleton within his own dried and shrivelled skin and a suit of furs, and he was left in position when the sad relic was first displayed in the hall of the Shipmen's Company. Only in quite recent times did people come to think that this was in any way improper and so replace the bones by a wooden model which could not upset the susceptibilities of even the most delicate of those who might drop in for dinner.

Immediately opposite the *Schiffergesellschaft* stands one of Lübeck's great churches, which is of course dedicated to St Nicholas, the steersman-bishop of Myra who became Santa Claus to the landlubber and patron saint to the sailor and bargee. Within it lies a particularly poignant memorial, for there is a chapel in which are commemorated notable losses of Lübeck ships across the ages, and lying on the flagstones is one of the holed and battered lifeboats of the ill-fated *Pamir*, lost in a hurricane with almost all of the young cadets aboard her. St Mary's has another sad relic, for within the great church the bells still lie mute on the floor, broken and half melted by the heat of the conflagration of 1942.

Yet Lübeck's memories are not all tragic, and one cannot chug along its quays and see the gables of the rich merchant families without recalling that this is the city of Thomas Mann and the Buddenbrooks. By good fortune the splendid façade of Buddenbrook House survived the air-raids, as did many other patrician houses, and to remind one that Thomas Mann won the Nobel Prize for literature for that great novel, the Swedish citation of 1922 hangs on the wall at the foot of the stairs in what is now the Volksbank. Perhaps the quotation from the Buddenbrook ethic carved over one of the doorways in the bank is as appropriate for a modern finance house as it was for a merchant family: 'Do only such business by day as will permit you to sleep at night with an undisturbed conscience' – a reasonable enough maxim for a man, whatever his trade.

Even more famous than Lübeck's spires is the massive gateway of the Holstentor, set across the road which approaches the Trave and the inner defences of the island city from the direction of Hamburg, and immediately beside it is a group of handsome warehouses, tall and severe and braced together with iron cramps. They are as fine as any in Amsterdam and in fact they are the salt stores to which the men of the Stecknitz Canal-boatmen's Guild hauled the barges with the produce of Lüneburg. They formed a buffer depot to take up the strain of the fluctuations in supply and demand, and their size and commanding position on the bank of the Trave hint at what an important trade this must once have been before salt imported cheaply from other lands brought about a decline.

Although Lübeck was a leading port of the Hansa, the river Trave below the city was much too shallow to take the larger sea-going vessels fully laden, and so a system of lighterage was developed not unlike that which still operates in the Port of London today. (A lighter is of course a craft which serves to lighten a ship by off-loading some of its cargo, and in German the name is similar – *Leichter*.) The various colleges of shippers – the Riga, Skåne, Bergen, Novgorod-shippers and others – each main-tained at Travemünde a floating pontoon or barge which served as a control centre for lighterage. Here part of the cargo of an in-coming vessel would be taken off into small craft and then the ship would proceed upstream to Herrenwik, where a further lightening was necessary. At last the ship would arrive in Lübeck, followed by a flotilla of barges carrying the bulk of its cargo. Some of these craft had lug-sails, but the smaller ones were bank-hauled from the towpath or even poled up the river, much as similar boats are still moved in China today.

At this time there was no feasible means of enlarging or deepen-ing a navigable channel, but by 1541 a dredger was working in Lübeck harbour. This was a 'mud-mill', a Danzig invention, and it proved successful at least in holding further silting at bay. The cost of maintaining this machine and also of improving the piling and unloading facilities at Travemünde was paid for by a levy of 'pile-money' charged upon every ship entering the port from the sea. And these vessels were many indeed, for Lübeck was the centre of the Baltic trade.

At Lübeck the *Thames Commodore*'s Hanseatic run had reached its outer limit. Ahead, the Trave merged into the waters of the

Baltic which she had only left a few days before at Holtenau. To the west the forest lakeland of Holstein lay inviting but un-approachable by water, to the east the sailor's paradise of the Mecklenburg lakes was shut away, imprisoned by the psychopathic minefields and barbed wire of the People's Republic. But having negotiated the northern part of the old salt route she had a wish to thrust her nose into the southern part of the medieval water high-way, and as soon as our young companions had climbed the quay ladder and dispersed on their own private travels my wife and I set off again to retrace the canal through Mölln to Lauenburg and the broad and rather capricious stream of the river Elbe. We were bound for the river Ilmenau, the course of which I had discovered on a map.

Below Geesthacht barrage the tide in the Elbe was low. Navigat-ing according to the boards on the bank, supplemented by my own imagination and the *Thames Commodore*'s inclinations, we steered down the river between the shoals with anything from a quarter of a fathom to five fathoms below her broad belly. But a foot or two of water is as good as fifty unless one is travelling at speed, and we had no trouble in finding a course between the shingle banks and the groynes. We had to keep our eyes fixed on the surface of the river to watch for tell-tale swirls and patches of flat water, but that did not greatly matter. There was no view to be had, and over the high banks we never saw more than a church spire, a power pylon, or some of the higher television aerials in the villages behind the dikes. An hour below Geesthacht an unlikely looking creek devoid of water cut through the dike on the port side and we knew it could only be the Ilmenau. We waited in the entrance for an hour, by which time the flood tide had filled the muddy ditch with nearly six feet of water and was running up strongly. The time had come to start up the river to the great Salt City of former times.

The lower Ilmenau is not beautiful. After a brief wriggle it straightens out into an uninspiring canal cut, long and almost straight and very much like a 'drain' of the English fenland. The names of strange hamlets came back to me, places we had visited thirty years earlier in the course of a voyage through the Middle Level, names such as Welches Dam, Hundred-Foot Engine,

Popham's Eau. The Ilmenau tideway had something of the same improbable bleakness about it, and yet there was a difference. In the Fenland one could usually make out a village somewhere in the distance, but here there was only the wide sky heavy with late summer clouds, and the black murky water creeping along the channel in reluctant obedience to the orders of the moon. So lethargic was the flood that the *Thames Commodore* caught up with its leading edge and had to slow, creeping step by step behind it. Two hours had passed before she turned into the short final straight, at the end of which was the weir of Fahrenholz. A few rather run-down barges were loading potash beside an overgrown railway yard which had become a cemetery for rusty old loco-motives that had long since wheezed their last.

The moment we came in sight of the lock I knew we had come to just such a waterway as the *Thames Commodore* would enjoy. The open sea and the large rivers have their own fascination, but there is nothing quite so attractive as a small and forgotten river navigation, where the machinery is ancient but just workable and the course itself was laid out by nature when she was in no par-ticular hurry. Men may have added the locks to improve her handiwork, and a river authority have established the little lock-houses with their rose gardens, happy places for the recluse, though maybe a little lonely for the keepers and their families in the gales and floods of winter. But a winding, pastoral river is surely a fore-taste of paradise.

Fahrenholz lock was about the size of a lock on a 'broad' canal in Britain. Weed was growing in the walls and water spouted through the mitres and round the heel posts, but it was in fair order just the same. In fact the river Ilmenau still had some com-mercial traffic, several barges of timber running up it every day to just below Lüneburg, and when the water had raised us to the upper level we found two of them waiting to lock through and hurry down to the Elbe while the canal was full and deep. Easing our way past them we began to navigate a pretty and winding stream of swans and ducks and meadow flowers, a river not unlike the Thames in its uppermost reaches.

Another lock at Wittorf, and half a mile beyond it the river was spanned by a pretty bascule bridge straight out of van Gogh. The lock-keeper was racing up through the village on his bicycle to open it for us, but a country bus reached it ahead of him. There must have been some doubt as to its reliability, for the bus stopped at the approach and the passengers all climbed out to walk across the span on their own feet. Some of the women seemed to share the bus company's doubts, for they carefully took their shopping baskets and parcels out of the vehicle before it attempted to cross. At last the driver, alone and intrepid, drove his bus so swiftly at the bridge that it had no time to notice that a vehicle was bearing down on it, and before its ancient timbers had time to do more than utter a few groans and sighs the bus had reached the other side and was ready to take its passengers aboard again. Not that they hurried. It was not every day that a ship from London appeared at Wittorf, and the villagers preferred to wait until the keeper had pulled the chain, the bridge had tilted on end, and we had gone sailing by.

I suspect that the *Thames Commodore* may have been the first ship ever to carry the Red Ensign up the Ilmenau – and by 'red' I mean blue or white also. The aged keeper at the third and final lock said so, and he bustled away to fetch the children from a nearby farm to see such an improbable sight. However, I doubt if his memory went back more than sixty years, and there might well have been a visit by some eccentric boatman in the second half of the nineteenth century. H. M. Doughty went to Lüneburg in the course of his *Our Wherry in Wendish Lands* voyage, and his daughters drew some charming illustrations of a town which eighty years later looks no different. But he did not take the *Gipsy* up the river. The party went by train from Lauenburg.

This last lock is close to Bardowick. In the village beside the river two slim slated steeples cap a pair of squat brick towers, and between them the end of the nave of the cathedral rears up as though looking to see who may be mad enough to navigate the Ilmenau. It is an old cathedral, tired and mellowed, and it now serves only an insignificant village, for in 1189 the citizens of what was then one of the largest towns in the land were unwise enough to rise in insurrection against their lord. But the Duke was more

On the Ilmenau

powerful than they thought. He turned on them, slew the inhabitants, and to encourage his other subjects in loyalty he burned the houses to the ground.

We were now in the final pound, and little by little the depth of water decreased from three feet below our keel to two, then one. The river flowed fleeter, the long manes of weed flicking in the current and the fish darting alarmed to the side at our approach. The bottom was clean and sandy as we crept ever onward past the factories and under the railway, but there was just water enough for us to draw into the old city itself and run the bow gently into the sandbank on the bend above a broad quay with a magnificent row of half-timbered warehouses where once the salt had been stored. An old dockside crane stood rusty; it had not been used for many years. But there was deep water still at Lüneburg's quayside, and as the river shallowed abruptly ahead of us we backed a little and drifted across to make fast in splendid isolation at the deserted quay. We had reached the terminal of the salt trade of the Hansa.

Doughty wrote of Lüneburg that nowhere in all northern Europe was there 'a building which, more than this stately Rathaus, brings back before our modern eyes the special character, the wealth and lordliness of medieval burgherdom. . . . The proud old times have passed away for Lüneburg. Her grim old walls no longer stand round her; her ninety towers no more greet as from tower to tower the other Hansa towns on the many miled Elbe. She is now but a shade, a ghost city; yet, I think that a shade with more semblance of its substance, a ghost more lifelike of a medieval Hansa town, cannot be found in Germany.'

Certainly I doubt if there can be a more beautiful waterfront in all Germany than that of Lüneburg. The splendid façade of the hall of the merchants is in fact barock from the 1960s, for this magnificent building was burned down in 1959, but the reconstruction has been faithfully done. Across the roadway is one of the most remarkable cranes still to be found, a hoist which was already operating in the fourteenth century. No doubt it has been improved since that date, but it still has the original bird-like form with body and neck and upturned bill topped with a weathervane, and it is perched securely on the round base-house on which it could swivel to load the barrels of salt into the craft of the Lüneburg shippers, who would carry the cargoes as far as Lauenburg before transferring them to the Stecknitz boatmen – for neither might carry on the waterway of the other.

Opposite the crane are the tall riverside houses of the Stintmarkt, ochre and pink and green, their timber framing in neat squares and rectangles. These practical merchant dwellings have looked out over the river for several centuries, but if they look elderly rather than decayed that may be because life does not move very fast in Lüneburg.

At the bend of this line of balconied houses an arch leads over the roaring weir-passage of the abbot's mill toward the Am Sande. As for the abbots, they seem still to grind their corn, and as we walked through the passage a lorry was busy pouring an avalanche of grain at the top of a chute which led to the storage cellars. The

Lüneburg quay

husky, rich scent of the wheat blended with that indescribable but romantic scent of a weir to form an aroma such as can only be found at mills. Closing my eyes I could smell Sonning Mill in Berkshire – though that, I believe, is centuries newer than the mill of the Lüneburg abbots.

The city of Lüneburg still manages to breathe and exhale the air of the mercantile prosperity of the Hansa. Its fortunes were founded upon the fifty-four evaporating houses, each with four pans working night and day to produce an output of twenty to thirty thousand tons annually of pure salt which would find its way by the Ilmenau and the Stecknitz Canal to Lübeck, and thence to

Bergen and Novgorod, to Riga and Stockholm, and all other markets beyond the easy reach of the Scots and Spaniards. Great wealth flowed into the town and the salt merchants built the rich houses which still stand, tall and splendid, along either side of the broad Am Sande. If bucket-hoists are no longer used, modern pumping equipment still carries on the work of extracting the salt from below ground and the place has also developed a reputation as a resort where one may take the very salty waters or indulge in the Kneipp cure so beloved of many Germans. One spring is good for the digestive organs, another stimulates the appetite, a third is said to be good for the respiratory tract. What more could one want – unless perhaps a good local wine? Vines, however, do not grow so far northward, and we had to be content with buying in the market a pound or two of several strange species of fungi brought in by country women from the huge expanse of woodland and heather of the Lüneburger Heide.

Contrary to appearances, the Am Sande is not the market. This is in a square of its own, along one side of which is ranged the most famous and best preserved town hall in Germany, with hall upon hall of wonders. Nowadays the market is a peaceful and colourful scene of stalls of butter and eggs and fruit, of poultry and cheese, flowers, edible fungi and bilberries. But the same square was once the scene of an extraordinary incident when, in 1813, the citizens swiftly took to arms and drove out the small garrison which the hard pressed Napoleon had left in possession of the town. The bells rang for freedom, but the news was quickly carried to Bremen, where the French general decided to treat the Lüneburgers to a dose of the familiar French medicine. He sent a force of 3000 men to cross the Lüneburger Heide and shoot down the city gates with cannon. The aldermen and any other prominent citizens were seized, for public execution on the following day at noon. The men were bound, lined up in the square, and a minute or two before noon their eyes were bandaged. The people, held back by a line of exultant troopers, stood round the edge of the market, sobbing. General Morand stood ready to give the signal to the officer of the firing-squad.

Suddenly there was a shout, a cheer, and the sound of shots

from the direction of one of the gates. An order was shouted, and the entire French force rushed away to man the defences. The market was left unguarded, the twenty-seven men in the centre, bound and blindfold, and the crowd pressed back round the edges of the buildings. None could imagine what might be happening.

In fact a force of Cossacks and light troops was at the gates. Hearing of the fate of Lüneburg, three commanders had selected their swiftest contingents and had raced fifty miles within twenty-four hours to rescue the citizens. The Russians pushed into the centre of the square, unbound the men, and so achieved the very first victory in Germany against Napoleon's tyranny. As for General Morand, he was fatally wounded and thrown down outside the gate, where the prisoners passed him, 'weltering in his blood'.

And that was Lüneburg's last skirmish. By some extraordinary chance the Second World War with its bombs and artillery passed it by, and industry and modernisation have been held back outside the city itself so that Lüneburg has been left unharmed and glorious, a memorial to the taste and wealth and grandeur of the hey-day of the Hanseatic League.

VIII

*Admiral aboard – the devil down the hawse-pipe – Alte
Liebe – Otterndorf siel – the Elbe–Weser waterway –
Bederkesa – Bremerhaven – light cargoes, shallow river –
life in the watts – fresh water from the sea – coffee and honey
for the nation*

FROM Lüneburg the *Thames Commodore* set course for London,
but in Hamburg she paused overnight to pick up a new steersman. Wishing to run down from the city in style she had decided
to invite Admiral Engel to join her there for a day on the water, and
at ten o'clock he arrived on board, fresh and happy to be on board
ship again.

Siegfried Engel was not much short of eighty, and he had been
a friend of her predecessor the *Commodore*, which he had steered
for a few miles up the fast-flowing Weser above Minden, six years
earlier. Once the officer in command of the fishery protection
vessels on the high seas, he was the most peaceable of admirals,
and being a very accomplished linguist he spent his years of retire-
ment in a beautiful little house on the Lüneburger Heide, translat-
ing books from French, English or Italian for German publishing
houses. As a seaman he could always catch the spirit and mood of
an event or incident, and his translations were the best I have ever
known. He had translated the *Commodore*'s voyage to the Skagerrak, and in the course of doing so we had become involved in the
Battle of Eckernförde Bay.

In the tale of that first northern voyage I had included an account
of the engagement in 1849, when two Danish warships imprudently
allowed themselves to be driven before the wind into a cul-de-sac
between Kiel and the Schlei. There they were fired upon by
Prussian shore batteries, and as it was impossible to sail out to sea
again the captain's only course was to surrender; but a young
midshipman who preferred death for himself and others to dis-

honour snatched a match and fired the magazine aboard the *Christian VIII*. The ship and most of its crew, as well as the troops on board, were blown sky-high.

That would have been the end of the matter, except that it was the custom in the Germany navy to assign particular glory to the officer responsible for any victory. As the Danish ship had been sunk by a Danish midshipman this was not so simple, but after much discussion it was sensibly decided to award the laurels to the highest ranking officer present in the German squadron which had followed the Danes, but had not actually engaged them. It so happened that on board one of the ships was Queen Victoria's brother-in-law, Ernst of Saxe-Coburg-Gotha, who held a high and non-functional courtesy rank. A medal was accordingly struck, and the Duke was acclaimed as 'Victor of Eckernförde Bay'.

This story, which I had come upon in the University Library at Cambridge, had all the ring of truth about it. The whole incident was Prussian down to the last comma. Siegfried Engel translated it with relish and he was pained when the publishers sent a letter requesting its deletion. It did not reflect well, they evidently thought, upon the Prussian navy. Admiral Engel replied that he had no doubt about the likelihood of the story, and he thought it amusing. He advised the publishers to leave it in.

But the publishers did not agree. Their next move was to refer the matter to the Admiralty of the Bundesrepublik, whose reaction was exactly as one might have expected. They simply said that such a thing could not possibly have happened, and hinted that only a very brave onslaught against overwhelming odds enabled the Prussians to achieve the destruction of the Danish ship. They were decidedly piqued at such a reflection upon their great naval commanders of a century earlier, and made it clear that the publishers must refuse to publish the book at all if it contained such lies. So, regretfully, we had to drop the story from Siegfried Engel's translation.

Now Admiral Engel was himself aboard, as happy as a schoolboy. I took the ship down the town canal and through the locks, and only when we reached the main highway of the Elbe did I hand him the wheel.

'But you are quite wrong in thinking an admiral can steer,' he said, watching anxiously as the bow turned a little, first to one side and then the other. 'I have not been allowed to take the wheel – except by you – for the last sixty years. As soon as one is an officer one has to give up the fun of being at the wheel. You can stand there smartly, issuing orders to the helmsman; but steer – certainly not. That's the way they are in all navies, I expect.'

But soon the skill of sixty years earlier had returned, and the serpentine wake straightened out. Siegfried Engel's eyes never left the water ahead as we sped down on the falling tide past the drydocks to port and Blankenese to starboard, and on toward the widening of the estuary.

There was once an auction at Blankenese at which some unusual lots were put up for sale. It happened that a vessel was wrecked among the hungry sands at the mouth of the Elbe, a ship carrying from Rome a great quantity of casts of antiquities which had been made for the Prussian royal palaces. Soon after the stranding and abandoning of the ship the fishermen of the Elbe made for the wreckage, as fishermen still do to this day, to see what might be acquired. They came upon a number of packing cases, but when they had broken them open and found them to contain nothing more useful than plaster they smashed the casts and threw them into the sea. Fortunately their impatience caused them to give up in disgust, and much of the cargo was later salvaged undamaged and put up for auction in Blankenese. Perhaps waterlogged casts did not appeal to the public, for the entire collection was acquired for less than the actual cost of the raw plaster by an architect, who used the statuary to embellish a splendid house he was building for a wealthy client.

Admiral Engel would perhaps have liked to steer all the way to London but we were anxious not to tire him, and as he had somehow to find his way back to his home in the woods we put in to a harbour some way down the Elbe and dropped him. Then we continued alone toward Otterndorf, just short of Cuxhaven. It was a choppy day and for much of the way the refreshing salty spray was flung over our bow to land with a smack on the windshield, but by tea-time we had the Brunsbüttel locks on the beam and knew that another hour would see us somewhere near the entrance to the Otterndorf siel.

If the mouth of the Elbe is almost invariably a rough place in a boat, I suspect this may be because of what happened on a particular occasion long ago. A good and honest skipper had fallen upon hard times because his old tramp had been written off and he could not raise the money to buy another. He was pacing the waterfront of Hamburg when the devil – who presumably reckoned that the Reeperbahn could look after itself for a few minutes – put on his best city clothes and accosted the man. If it was only a matter of a ship, he said, he would provide one. The skipper could own it permanently, and the only condition was that whenever the vessel returned to the Elbe the skipper would have some job ready at hand for the devil to perform. No doubt he had in mind a nice piece of raping, or sacrilege, or dropping rocks on convents, or maybe just simple wrecking, but he did not specify anything particular. He was, it seemed, easy to please.

So the captain received his coaster, and she was a good one, well found in every respect. He signed on a crew and sailed away with an export cargo, returning some weeks later with a full lading after a most profitable voyage. But with Scharhörn and Neuwerk on the beam he began to be worried. Soon they would be in the Elbe, and he had not given a thought to providing a job for the devil to do.

The skipper's son was at the wheel, and seeing his father pacing up and down and shaking his head he asked the old man what was wrong. The skipper unburdened his conscience, and to his surprise he found that his son took the matter very calmly. The young man told his father to stop worrying and go below; he himself would deal with the matter.

Sure enough, with Cuxhaven close on the starboard bow, who should come flying aboard but the devil. The ship was forging ahead with a strong flood tide and a following sea, and from my own experience in the Elbe I imagine she must have been doing fifteen knots at least.

'Let go the anchor,' the steersman called, with every appearance of alarm. And as the heavy hawser began to race through the pipe he turned to the devil. 'Hold her up,' he said.

And the devil, who knew little about ships and the inadvisability of interfering with the anchor, ran to the bow and obligingly grabbed the end of the hawser. There was a rather squeezed curse of anger as he was dragged clean through the hawse-pipe and down into the water of the Medemrinne channel, somewhat bruised from his adventure. There he has remained ever since, and maybe his infuriated presence below the surface has something to do with the nasty seas a boatman may often experience where the incoming tide swings past the Alte Liebe toward Otterndorf to starboard and Brünsbuttel further ahead to port.

The Alte Liebe is a small lump of headland which forms the outer edge of the harbour of Cuxhaven, where the coast sheers away southward into the area of sands and watts among which the *Dulcibella* just escaped being wrecked by her malicious opponent in *The Riddle of the Sands*. With the glasses I could just make out the signal-tower on the Alte Liebe, a shape familiar from our earlier voyages round that rather formidable corner, but now for the first time I understood the origin of its curious name. On our way down the Elbe that same morning Siegfried Engel had given us the explanation.

The story as he once had heard it was that long ago, when relations between Denmark and Prussia were as bad as they usually were, a Danish sailing-ship was driven aground in a storm, stranding on the beach at the very edge of the harbour of Cuxhaven. She was the *Olivia*, and what became of her crew the Admiral did not know. However, the Cuxhaveners were ready, as people usually are, to show their national animosity, and so they amused themselves by hurling stones at the broken wreck for no better reason than that it was Danish. This habit continued for some time, and no doubt the holiday visitors to Cuxhaven also worked off much of their pent-up hatred and frustrations by throwing stones at the decaying timbers until, little by little, they had built up such a heap of cobbles that it became a shoal, a mound, and eventually a spit of dry land. But with the passing of time the name of the Danish vessel had been misunderstood, and now the *Olivia* was interpreted by the local people – who even now speak that dreadful language known as *platt-deutsch* – as *Oll' Lieve*, 'old love'.

Perhaps it was pedantically-minded cartographers or the officials of the lighthouse authority who decided that the name of the headland must be registered in the proper stage German of the educated classes, for the *Oll' Lieve* became transmuted into the correct and formal *Alte Liebe*. Once this had been done it was open to the locals to imagine all kinds of romantic happenings, and to tell how a sailor bound for far-away countries would leave his old love weeping and waving on the headland until his ship had disappeared into the waters of the German Bight, or how perhaps another returning home would remember the old love he had left behind, the one to whom he had so rashly promised to be true.

The day had begun breezy but pleasant. Now, as if determined to catch us out and break some crockery before we could reach our next canal, the wind freshened, the temperature dropped, and a heavy and threatening cloud came storming up the estuary as though heading directly toward ourselves alone. Such sudden changes in the weather may be the work of depressions and fronts and all the other workaday phenomena of the meteorologist, but if the weather men are notoriously unable to forecast them correctly this might be because they do not understand the malice or evil which may lie behind the causes themselves. Indeed, it is told that once a ship was sailing over these same waters of the German Bight on just such a sunny day as would have sent any forecaster into a sleep of anticyclonic content, when a black cloud very similar to the one which now lay ahead of us appeared as though from nowhere and grew and grew until it threatened to burst as a violent storm. The captain wished to strike sail and let the ship drive, but the ship's cook ran to the cannon and put a charge down the barrel. Striking a flint he pointed the gun at the cloud and fired.

This is, of course, a system of rain-making which has in more modern times been used with good effect in Australia and other thirsty areas, perhaps because the smoke particles from a burst will start condensation and precipitation. Yet it was not rain which fell upon the ship when the missile struck the nimbus, but blood. Good, red, arterial blood, it poured from the sky as a thick haemo-globinous rain, and if this may seem unusual it only serves to underline the brilliance of the cook, who had so rightly guessed that the cloud was hexed, and that the witch was inside it. In fact there were three witches hidden, for no sooner had he shot at the cloud than three women were found dead in their beds, each pierced to the heart. One, most unfortunately, was the captain's wife, but the skipper was not sorry to be rid of her. With such interfering tendencies she was obviously not the sort of woman one would want hanging about the ship.

On this afternoon, however, the cloud disappeared to starboard without our firing a shot, and as we reached the buoy which marked the Otterndorf turn the sun came out again, flooding with golden light the immense sea-dike which kept the Elbe in its proper place. Sweeping up the row of birch branches set along the edge of the channel across the sands we headed out of the estuary and within a few minutes we were in the still water of a curious little creek at the foot of the dike itself. Some fishing-boats lay at the piles and we brought up alongside. We had arrived at the Otterndorf siel.

A siel is an automatic gate at the outlet of a river, very similar to those on the lodes of the Cambridgeshire fens, the idea being that the gates will only open when the water on the inside is higher than that on the outside. Siels have for centuries been the only barrier between the storm floods and the villages behind the dikes, and to found them properly was a very important matter, on which the lives of the people might well depend. So it was the custom – though not, I am glad to say, in the days of the efficient *Wasser-und Schiffahrtsamt* – to keep at bay all the evil forces which might disturb the foundations, or the dike footings, by offering them the life of an innocent child. The villagers would select an infant, place it in an empty barrel or a little cradle, hand it a biscuit or some other sweetmeat to keep it happy and gurgling, and then bury the container at the foot of the masonry. Not that this unpleasant habit was confined to the dike-men of the German Bight. It is said that the first London Bridge was made secure in just the same way.

Otterndorf's siel is a curious place. In fact there are two siels there, one at the end of the canal and another close to it where the river Medem runs down from the little town itself to join the Elbe. Small barges can run up the Medem to Otterndorf – as they can up a number of other siel-guarded creeks along the shores of the Elbe – so there must of course be a gate for them to pass through.

Between the two waterways there is hidden away one of the most attractive little inns imaginable. That there should be customers enough to support an inn behind such a remote part of the sea-wall is surprising, but perhaps the establishment thrives on the reputation of its cooking. Surrounded by its own trees of apple and pear blossom the *Zur Schleuse* (or Lock Inn) gets its supplies of fish direct from the Otterndorf fishermen whose ships lie just over the bank, and I know no better place for a fried sole. Yet the inn is fortunate to be there at all, for when the flood of 1962 rushed into the Elbe to inundate Hamburg the water was then sixteen feet above the level of the spring tides and stood far higher than the tops of the chimneys of the Gasthaus zur Schleuse at the foot of the bank. However, the dike held, and the landlady assured us that she never really worried about inundation. She felt safe enough behind the flood bank, she said. She felt secure anywhere, provided she was not aboard a ship. Boats, the sea, tides, she hated them all.

Surprised, I asked her why, and discovered that this was something implanted with unfortunate suddenness during her childhood.

'It was on a coal steamer,' she said. 'She was the *Anna*. We were steaming down the Elbe, when suddenly a storm came up from nowhere. That may surprise you.'

I assured her nothing surprised us about the German Bight. A storm could develop in minutes, whatever the weathermen might forecast. On our outward trip we had passed round the Mellum, I added.

'Ah, then you understand. Well, I was only five at the time, and we were sailing down the estuary when all of a sudden the storm swept down on the ship and threw her about like a cork. Before anyone could grab hold of me I had been flung down the steel ladder-way into the engine-room. I fell into the engine.'

They had had to graft pieces into one arm and a leg, and she must have been a lucky girl to have escaped alive. Altogether I could not blame her if in later years she had not become a great enthusiast for boats.

I do not know whether the canal siel at Otterndorf was built over the stifled cries of an infant, but certainly it is a rather forbidding place. The flood dike of the Elbe must be forty feet high, and it is pierced by a bricked tunnel which has two massive mitre-gates at its outer end to act as a non-return valve and hold out the sea when the estuary water is higher than that of the canal – which for more than half the tide is the case. At the inner end there is another pair of gates, so that together the two pairs form a lock which is entirely underground beneath the dike, shut away from all but such dim light as filters in over the top of the inner gates. Behind these is another pair with the mitre facing the opposite way, to prevent the whole length of the canal from emptying when the tide falls away outside.

The canal is used by barges up to 100 feet in length, which is a little under the size of the locks at Bederkesa and Bremerhaven. But the lock at Otterndorf is only half as long, and so the barges have to run straight through the siel when the water level is such that the gates at both ends can be opened at the same time. Anyone who has tried opening lock-gates against a head of even four inches of water will know how difficult it is; but the gates of the siel have stout windlasses and cables, and as soon as he can turn the spokes the keeper will open up to let the water stream in. A few minutes later the flow will stop, and then the canal will begin to stream swiftly out. During the brief period that the gates at both ends can be kept open any waiting barges have to run through the hole. There is not a moment to be lost, so the siel opening is always an occasion for shouting, and swearing at the ship's boy, and sending someone to run down the bank and hammer furiously on the side of any barge where the skipper is asleep.

Usually there will only be two or three craft to be passed at one tide, but the Otterndorf siel-keeper told me that once when ships had been delayed up at Hamburg by a storm he had seventeen barges on one tide, all waiting to bore under the dike. With the help of some of the men and a block and tackle he hauled the gate open against a head of several inches of water, and on the strong current the ships began to stream through the tunnel. All seventeen had passed before the inner gates had to be let go, to swing together with a clap just behind the rudder of the last in line.

The *Thames Commodore* found two barges waiting to go in, but the keeper invited her to go ahead of them and use the lock, instead of waiting for level water. There was just room for her, but I kept her engines running gently ahead to hold her nose against the gates so that she would not wash back and crush her dinghy. Then the doors of her prison were swung to, and she lay panting in the dark with the walls curving in closely over her flanks. The keeper lifted only one paddle to make sure that we should not be crushed against the roof, and we crouched on the catwalk on either side to hold her in the centre. It reminded me of the ship's first voyage, when she had stuck fast between the walls and ceiling of the Islington tunnel on the Regent's Canal, but at least the Otterndorf tunnel was only fifty feet in length and not half a mile. Once we had been lowered almost to the canal level I stopped the engines so that the keeper could open the outer gates, and we saw ahead of us the canal itself with a trio of barges waiting their chance to run through. We moved out into the Hadelner Canal, the first link in a chain of curious little waterways which I had always wanted to visit.

Eleven years earlier we had been unable to use this inland route because the water-police at Bremerhaven warned us that the siel gates at Otterndorf were being repaired and could not be opened. Two years after that we had run up to that same lock from the outer side, only to find that the whole waterway was closed for reconstruction. Now at last the century-old canals of the moorland had been dug out and embanked and smartened up to form the Elbe–Weser Schiffahrtsweg, a very useful link which cut off the worst corner of the German Bight so that a yacht might at last travel from the Baltic to the Mediterranean without once venturing out to sea. Yet the canal had not been rebuilt just to please the *Thames Commodore* and a few other watery cranks. It was designed as a channel for the barges which traded from Holstein through to Bremerhaven and the Weser, and as these were rather small craft of very modest height the headroom under the bridges was

set too low for many yachts and only just high enough for ourselves.

I doubt if a ship higher than the *Thames Commodore* could have
passed that way at all, for even with her windshield stripped she
only just slipped under the Hadelner bridges, and two of them she
had to pass going forwards but full speed astern at the same time.
This somewhat Irish method of progression was due to a peculi-
arity of her construction, for when the windshield had been dismantled the highest point of the vessel was then the hydraulic
engine controls. These happened to be made so that the levers
were at their highest when set in the dead slow position. They
could be pulled back to reduce the ship's height by five inches, but
then they were set at 'Full Speed Astern' – which was not the most
useful position when trying to go slowly ahead. But a ship as wise
as the *Thames Commodore* knew as much about the laws of
momentum as she did of the speed limit on the canal she was
navigating, and so she would run straight at the lowest of the
Hadelner bridges and suddenly go 'Full Speed Astern' on the
engines when nearly half her length was already under the span.
Her weight would carry her through and out the other side, and
then I could push her controls back again to the 'Slow' position.
In this way she cleared all the bridges by at least two inches, and if
this may seem little it was enough for her. Like her predecessor she
believed in close navigation, and the tighter the fit of a canal the
more she enjoyed it.

The Hadelner Canal ran just inside the dike for a mile or more,
then turned and headed due south across the farming country of
the Hadelnerland, running past one deep-eaved farm after another
and under a succession of country bridges set lower than those on
the rest of the waterway. For the first two hours from the bank of
the Elbe we had to keep the windshield dismantled, and we
noticed that the rare barges we met had had to turn their wheel-
houses inside out to avoid having them knocked right off. At
length we came to the point beyond which all the bridges had been
raised – not very much, but just sufficiently to clear the *Thames
Commodore*'s windshield. We reconstructed the upper works and
proceeded cautiously to where this canal of the northern marshes

ran into the river Aue, a minor stream which meandered placidly among the meadows for a mile or two before curving suddenly through a cutting to emerge at the very edge of a clear blue lake which stretched far across from the little town of Bederkesa and was bordered by a forest of tall, dark, resinous fir-trees. The scent of the trees drifted over the water, small sail-boats were tacking across the lake, and children sweated and strained in pedalos or splashed about in rubber canoes. We would have liked to take the *Thames Commodore* into the mere to drop anchor for a night of gentle rocking on the wavelets of the lake, but the old salts sitting on the seats along the canal shook their heads, telling us that even her modest draught was too great for the bar at the entrance.

Bederkesa itself is a small resort – and that is all there is to say about it. When Doughty first carried the Red Ensign through the Bederkesa–Geeste canal in 1890 he found it a very picturesque place, with old half-timbered buildings dropped down without any regard for symmetry or angle, their huge doorways open for the wains. At the same time 'the place had a dolorous look of poverty. Dirt and neglect pervaded everything. No gardens – not even flowers in the windows. Manure heaps festered at their provident proprietors' front doors,' he wrote. Now, in a century of hygiene, the muck-heaps have gone and so has the poverty. Indeed, there is little left from the old days, and the houses Doughty admired must either have crumbled away or fallen before the sword of the sanitary inspector. Bederkesa is just a place with a butcher and baker, newsagent and post office, and perhaps an inn or two, a handy shopping point for the boatman but little more.

Yet Doughty found this canal 'as a river of Paradise, after that mother of dead cats the Ems–Jade canal'. And he was right. The waterway has a curious charm of its own, perhaps because each section of it is so different from the rest. Just beyond Bederkesa is the toll house, and after that the Bederkesa–Geeste canal runs ahead as a long straight cut, a channel so narrow that it has three passing places where craft may meet. Then come the upper reaches of the river Geeste itself, but the whole tract of moorland is so deserted that only once in all the eighteen miles of patient passage to the lock at the edge of Bremerhaven did we see a small

Bremerhaven – the River Geeste

farmhouse by the bank, a pretty building of red brick with low eaves, and crossed ridge boards set at either end, cut in the shape of Odin's horse. Then for mile after mile there was not a house to be seen and when at last we came to a copse which sheltered a gaunt brick building such as one might find on the Lancashire moors the place proved to be empty, tilted slightly back on its heels and the hinges creaking as the faded door swung in the wind. It was, as my wife remarked, a splendid place for a murder. Even more, I thought, for some dark event of Brontë passion and tragic love.

Beyond this solitary house the Geeste led on undisturbed, wandering ahead without a cow or a tractor on the marshy land to either side. A few gulls dabbled in the peat and curlews flew up to look at us. Sandpipers trilled and danced ahead in short dashes from one curtsy to the next, but we never saw signs of human habitation again until the factory chimneys and pylons of Bremerhaven broke the skyline ahead and the Geeste waterway ran to its end in the barrage and lock at the head of three miles of wriggling tidal creek. Had we been only two minutes later the level would have been too high for us to pass under the guillotine gate, but now we could be locked out into tidal waterways again, ready to surge down to the great port on the tide, which still was rising.

The tidal Geeste twists and turns through Bremerhaven as though it was pre-cut to a particular length which could only be fitted into the available space by coiling it up. We chugged along its windings on the rising water and soon passed a shipyard where men were busy painting a deep-sea trawler and refitting a lightship. Ten minutes later we passed beside another lightship which was being refitted, and near to it men were slapping the orange under-coat on a new ship, a trawler. It was only when I saw the name of the light vessel that I realised it was the one we had already seen, but from the other side, a mile or more further back.

Down in the town and near the main bridges we sought out a pleasant berth along one of the few available quaysides, and sat back in comfort. After a while the water had fallen several feet and my wife commented on the quantities of gulls which wheeled and turned over the ship, dropping close over our side to fish in the water. The sight was an unusual one, and being partly Scottish she began to think that they indicated some dreadful portent. And this suspicion was not entirely unfounded. Following the hint conveyed by my nose I went on deck and discovered that we had made fast over Bremerhaven's cloaca maxima. The falling tide revealed a gaping cavity several feet in diameter from which issued a soup compounded of unspeakable ingredients, a fine supper for gulls but hardly a suitable fluid for the *Thames Commodore* to berth in. With our hands over our mouths and noses we swiftly let go and ran to the port entrance to turn toward the lock and enter the Fischereihaven.

Rain, rain, and more rain, a storm blowing in from the north carried a heavy load of sodden clouds on its back, and all through the night the water fell so continuously that the ever-watchful customs officers of the Bundesrepublik made only two visits to the *Thames Commodore*. The second young man to stand dripping on our deck in his smart green uniform promised to come back about midnight with some papers, but either he must have thought better of being soaked a second time, or else we slept so soundly that his knocking did not wake us.

Early in the morning the sky cleared, and the deep-sea trawlers in the Fischereihaven sparkled in their wet, rust-flecked paint, green and black, red, blue and white. Already their loads of fish had been auctioned, and the trays of halibut and ling, tiger-fish and mullet and sole were being rushed away by fork-lifts to the fish express. Men in waders were hosing down the quarter-mile of auction hall, and a consommé of thawing ice, blood, scales and squashed fish trickled over the quayside. Not that many such tasty remnants actually reached the water, for the keen-eyed seagulls were ever ready to swoop and snatch them from the quay before they could reach the edge. It made a pleasant daily change from the sewage.

By the entrance lock to the fishery harbour we found ranged a collection of small tramps and coasters, some of them old and rusty, others smart and modern and well found. All of them were laden, and they were obviously just lying waiting. As these vessels were all privateers and time was money to their skippers it was not difficult to guess that the score or more which had put in to the port had done so because a bout of violent weather was expected to descend at any moment upon the German Bight, as it so often does. Our own course lay up the river Weser and we should be safe enough from the worst that even a gale could do, but as the *Thames Commodore* still had a few hours to wait until the powerful tide was running up to Bremen, there was time enough to walk over the quay behind the signal station and visit the old warehouses which contain the excellent and very modern shipping museum.

In spite of its name this museum is not just a display of shipping. Certainly it has such an intriguing item as a model of a fishery protection vessel of the sixteenth century, a direct forerunner of the ships over which our Elbe steersman Siegfried Engel had held command, but it is an Institute of Oceanography, and so its exhibits reflect the important work done by research men concerned with the many problems of the sea. One of these is the vast and ever-shifting area of watts.

A watt is by definition an area left bare at low water and covered by the flood tide, and though in some sense this applies to the whole of the coast, in a tidal sea area the watts as such are really those

large flat areas such as the sands over which motorists drive at low
water from Cuxhaven to the isle of Neuwerk several miles from the
shore – not infrequently misjudging the time of low tide or the
hardness of the surface, to judge by the immense number of
wrecks in the area which turn out not to be fishing-boat hulls but
the rusted carcases of imprudent Volkswagens.

Bremerhaven lies in an area famous for its sands and watts, and a
watt has a particular fauna of its own. At low water the watt is
exposed. It will be dry and in summer it may be extremely hot,
whereas in winter it can be frozen. Rain will reduce the salinity of
the water still held in it, strong sunshine and wind may concentrate
its shallow pools almost to the point of crystallisation. Yet at high
water the watt has a comparatively uniform temperature. These
changes will of course occur twice daily, and such variety is more
than most creatures can stand. But down beneath the surface there
is much greater uniformity, and it is there that the watt-livers have
their dwellings, the worms and molluscs which retire during the
ebb but feed by tubes and filters when the water has returned to
bring a suspension of microscopic creatures and Bremerhaven
sewage for their daily nourishment. Only the dead shells lie on the
surface, and their abundance is an indication of the great density
of population below the surface. In former times carts would go
out and load these shells by the million to take them to kilns where
they were burned for lime, but nowadays they are used instead to
provide an addition to poultry meal. The crab fishermen used to
go out with dog-sledges, driving over the watts like men displaced
from the frozen north, but this intriguing mode of fishery has also
vanished. Times have changed, and one of the watts which once
was rich in seals has now become dangerous even for the buried
worms, the NATO air forces using it as a bombing target. All the
same it seems preferable that the bombs should be dropped on the
inoffensive invertebrates which inhabit the watts, than on thickly
populated cities.

Another concern of the Institute is with the ever-growing problem of freshwater supply. Resources are dwindling, consumption
continually rising, and ironically enough 71 per cent of the surface
of the earth is covered with water. The only trouble is that this

water is very salty. If the salt could easily be removed, all the problems of water economy would be solved.

There are several possible ways of obtaining fresh water from the sea, the oldest being by distillation. This is of course nature's own system, for all our fresh water comes ultimately from rain which falls out of condensed clouds of water vapour evaporated from the surface of the sea by sun and wind. It is possible to cover pans of salt water with sloping glass roofs on which the evaporated moisture will condense, running down into guttering. Such a device will daily produce about one gallon for every five square yards of glazing, and if this might be a help to a man on a desert island who had been prudent enough to have taken a crate of glass with him, it involves too much space to be a commercial proposition for a whole community.

Distillation can of course be done with external heating where fuel is particularly cheap. Kuwait has unlimited oil to burn, and so it produces its drinking water by distillation. Curaçao also uses forced distillation, and so does the neighbouring island of Aruba. Another system in use at Abidjan allows warm surface water to evaporate and condense on pipes filled with cold sea water from below the thermocline – that curious temperature frontier known to bathers when they momentarily put down a foot into an almost freezing layer beneath the warm water of the surface.

Others have produced fresh water from the sea by freezing – the salt being locked out of the crystals of ice – and as this process uses less energy than distillation it will probably become more widely used in lands such as Israel, where rain-water is always short. In California and South Africa electrodialysis is used, but no method has yet been found which will enable man to take the water out of the sea and leave the salt behind, without paying. And as humans much prefer to get something for nothing, research still continues.

By mid-morning the tide was ready to carry us up the river, and a strong wind had decided to help it – a wind which was the advance guard of the blow which the tramps and coasters were expecting. We took the *Thames Commodore* up to the lock and went into the pen in company with a pair of powerful trawlers bound for Iceland. While the water level in a lock falls away there is always opportunity to sit and dream, and on this occasion I found myself wondering whether the ingenious persons who devise school examination papers had ever thought of setting the question, 'Distinguish between Bremen and Bremerhaven and describe the connection, if any, between them'. I am sure I could never have answered such a problem until I had first been to the Weser by boat, and I very much doubt if I could even have distinguished between the various great rivers which empty into the German Bight. Yet Bremerhaven's origin is unusual. The town did not grow up gradually. It was custom-built.

Like Hamburg, Bremen was always a place of traders and sailors. Long ago its ships were ranging to Iceland and Spain, and in 1189 the men of Bremen were engaged in the Third Crusade, along with the nobles and cut-throats of other lands. The captains of the Lübeck and Bremen ships used their sails to establish a field hospital, and it was from this humble beginning that the proud and famous Germanic Order of Knights was founded.

In the fourteenth century Bremen joined the Hanseatic League, and throughout Hanseatic times the city continued to flourish. But two factors were to combine to influence its future. Ships were being built continually larger and of deeper draught, whilst the long tidal channel up to the city was becoming ever more obstructed by silt and shoals. The vessels which traded to Bremen could not lie very deep in the water and so they tended to load cargoes which were bulky but light, and which would fill a ship without much increase in its draught when laden. Thus it came about that the port developed as the main European centre for two particular imports, tobacco and American cotton, both of which are even now the staple of Bremen's trade.

However, in the 1820s Bremen had an imaginative mayor, Johann Smid. One night when he was unable to sleep he was pondering as usual the future of his city, convinced that Bremen's trade was much too vulnerable if linked so closely to ever lighter cargoes and a continually shoaling river. There must be a break with the past. And that night he had the sudden inspiration of building an entirely new port, moving the docks right down to the estuary. He would build a new harbour for Bremen – in fact, a new

Bremer Haven. He at once set about buying a tract of marshy land from the state of Hanover, and there he established the new port in an area where there would always be sufficient water.

So Bremerhaven came into being, and handled all but the smaller ships until the engineer Ludwig Francius, convinced that the city could not for ever do all its business through a port forty miles distant, took the Weser in hand and had the upper part of the estuary corrected with training walls and the whole length dredged. This removal of obstacles increased the tidal range in Bremen itself from a mere eight inches to ten feet, and ships of 20 foot draught could now reach the city on the tide instead of those only drawing eight feet of water. Today the river can take 30 foot of draught.

The channel down the Weser had long been marked and the buoyage continued right out to the Frisian Islands, where it has for centuries ended in a buoy bearing the sign of the silver key of Bremen. The marking was of course a costly operation, and in the fifteenth century the City Council handed over the duty to the Chamber of Commerce, who were allowed to make a levy on ships using the channel, very much as Trinity House will take annual Light Dues off vessels from the *Thames Commodore* to ocean liners. But from the way in which the marking was done one can see that in winter the port must have been almost at a standstill. The buoying and sounding boat left the city on the feast of St Peter (22 February), by which day the ice was expected to have broken up. On 11 November marks were taken up again until the following year.

Since Francius took the river in hand the two ports have both been active, with Bremerhaven handling about one-third of the total trade and nowadays dealing with the transatlantic liners, the largest of the cargo vessels, and the mighty tankers. However, Bremen itself is the major port of the two and a run up the river on the tide is a wonderful experience. Short of the city the tideway is no larger than the Thames up at Hammersmith, and down this channel the cargo liners cautiously edge their way in stately procession. Greek and Panamanian, British and Japanese, American and Italian, they tower above the sandy beaches and tip the sailing dinghies to rock on their wash. When at last Bremen comes into view one can look along one tidal basin after another and see the shipping ranged so thickly beneath the cranes that there would not seem to be room for a row-boat.

And still the trace of history is there in the light cargoes. Ships bring cotton from more than forty different lands. Wool arrives from Australia and New Zealand, the Argentine and Uruguay. Tobacco pours into the port from America and the West Indies, Brazil and Indonesia to the tune of about sixty thousand tons a year – and a ton of tobacco is worth a deal of money, even before the tax men have put on their impost of excise.

But there are other cargoes – timber and rice, tropical fruits and grain, wine and coffee. More than thirty great coffee mills grind away in the city, and on average each of them roasts enough for two-thirds of a million cups daily. The delicious scent of grinding and roasting hangs in the air, and when they sniff it the government men will no doubt smile greedily. The coffee tax will bring them a million marks today, a million marks every day of the year.

A stranger import is honey. The West Germans are great honey-sucklers and they consume about two pounds per head in a year. This means that fifty thousand tons of honey must be available, and in spite of the batteries of hives which are so familiar a feature of the German landscape the native apiarists can only provide a fifth of what is needed. The rest must come from overseas, from lands where people are more addicted to other foods. Mexico, Australia and the Argentine ship most of the honey to Bremen, where white-coated scientists in the Institute for Honey Research test it, measure its viscosity, try new blends and combinations, and for all I know return home in the evening sighing for a good stout piece of bread and jam.

But the big ships cannot pass the city bridges, and so the waterfront of the Tiefer in the town centre is reserved for trip boats, barges and the *Thames Commodore*. And surprisingly pleasant it is, for whereas Hamburg is a vast and bustling mass of rather indifferent architecture Bremen is a compact city still confined within its medieval boundary. Perhaps Roland is in some way responsible, for he is said to be the guardian of Bremen's freedom, a freedom which has always been mainly mercantile and political but may perhaps also include immunity from the replanners who can so easily destroy the essence of any city that is known to them only from surveyors' plans and office files, by imposing a deadly and mummifying uniformity over the whole.

IX

*The hen and chicks of Bremen – Roland the brave – the
Countess and the cripple – wines of the Ratskeller – chimes
of Neander – steam on the Weser – Verden, city of horses –
the Middle Weser*

BREMEN'S origin was very different from that of its dependency
of Bremerhaven, and the Bremeners say that long, long ago –
and probably still just in the B.C. era – the people who lived far up
the Weser in the land of hills and forests were attacked by their
neighbours, as most people were. Some of them reached the river
bank and put out into the stream in boats or on a raft, drifting
onward until the woods gave way to marshes and the marshes at
last to a wild country of heath and dunes without so much as a
tree. The one good thing about their situation was that the river
appeared to be full of fish, even if the water had now developed a
peculiar habit of rising and falling twice daily through a range of
several feet – $11\frac{1}{2}$ feet, to be precise. So the refugees were not
entirely without food, and yet the land to either side looked bleak
and inhospitable. They were doubtful about selecting it as their
new country, particularly as the local spirits had failed to give them
a sign as to whether they should do so or not.

However, they put in to the shore to look more closely. At least
they had no human competitors in the area, and that in itself was
an advantage. They were still undecided when one of them noticed
a hen and chickens strutting through the heathery undergrowth.
What kind of a hen it can have been I am not sure, but maybe it
was a blackhen, or even a grouse. One of the party suddenly
realised that this could only be a sign from the spirits or gods of
the area which, being interpreted, meant that if there were food
and shelter for a hen and her chicks so also there would be food and
shelter for the women and their children. In this conviction the
newcomers pitched their camp and set up their first buildings of

G

logs, presumably taken from timber floating down the Weser. Thus was Bremen founded, on a low sandy hill beside the river. Since then it has grown considerably but it has not forgotten the hen which started it all. In gratitude its portrait has been carved over one of the arches of Bremen's famous town hall.

The town hall has a row of cloistered arches beneath which sit the gaffers, looking out upon the square. Round the corner is a fine modern bronze of the four animals, donkey and dog, cat and cock, which became the Bremen town musicians. On one side of the

Bremen – the City Hall and Roland

square a building carries a slogan reminding the Germans of the
West never to forget 'those who carry the burden of our separation',
the unhappy remnant behind the wire of the People's Republic. In
front of the old men stands the huge figure of the guardian Roland,
that same hero who is said to have died broken-hearted at the
window of the Rolandsbogen above the island of Nonnenwerth
in the Rhine, where he had sat day by day, year after year, to
watch for the figure of his unattainable beloved as she filed across
the court to the chapel. Originally there was a wooden column in
the market, carved with a statue of Roland, and this was a symbol
of free trading. But the medieval authority of the episcopate did not
altogether approve of freedom in any shape or form, and when in
the fourteenth century they put down a popular revolt they used
the occasion to teach the people a lesson. Their beloved Roland
was burned in front of their eyes.

The Bremeners learned their lesson, but not in the way intended.
Some forty years later they erected a new Roland, this time of
incombustible material and of gigantic size. He was no longer
to symbolise mere free trading in the market, but the freedom
of the city itself under the conduct of its citizens. As for the
cathedral, it maintained a separate existence like a miniature
Vatican. Falling to the Swedes in the Thirty Years War it was
later seized by Denmark, which prudently sold it to Hanover. Thus
it came under British protection, and Freiherr von Knigge, the
'Great British' officer in command of its tiny garrison is buried
there.

The Roland of Bremen is perhaps the most famous statue in
Germany. He is also larger than any other of the pre-Hohenzollern
period, and he is obviously a thoroughly pleasant fellow. This
Roland is a young man, and even if he has spikes on his knees
and holds his great broadsword against his shoulder one feels
that he would not hurt a fly. He smiles, which few great warriors
do, and his smile is not one of superiority. If I had been
Hildegund I might easily have fallen in love with him and
retired to a nunnery when the reports of his death at the battle
of Roncevaux reached me – even if they were later to prove greatly
exaggerated.

At the feet of this Roland grovels a curious little cripple, a figure almost as sacred as Bremen's hen and chicks. He has no connection with Roland himself, but was just put there so that he would never be forgotten. For to him, Bremen owed its medieval boundary even if that has now long been overstepped. He should properly be wearing beggar's clothes of the eleventh century, for it was in the year 1032 that the city fathers called upon their neighbour the Countess of Lesum to beg some more of her land for their increasing population. It so happened that the widowed Countess was childless, and as she was generous by nature she was continually watched over by the Duke of Saxony, her somewhat avaricious brother-in-law to whom the whole estate would pass at her death. He did not stoop to poisoning her, but he did all he could to prevent her spending an unnecessary groat.

The Countess listened to the deputation from Bremen, and deciding that she had more land than she needed for herself she at once offered the fathers as much as a man could walk round in an hour.

'Why not give them as much as a man can circuit in a whole day?' The Duke's remark was meant sarcastically, but the Countess nodded.

'If you wish it,' she said. And she confirmed to the city fathers this greatly increased offer.

The aldermen being perhaps a trifle doddery, or maybe thinking that they could find in the city a swifter walker than themselves, they invited the Countess to accompany them into Bremen to find a man who would walk round the boundary of her gracious gift. And of course the miserly inheritor went with them.

On their way they came to a cripple, begging beside the road. 'There's a good man,' said the Duke quickly. 'Hey, there, my good fellow. Get up and help these good gentlemen by pacing out the edge of their land.'

Not even the kindly Countess could intervene. The Duke had chosen the man, and that was that. Yet as the Duke went on to explain the matter the good Bremener with the paralysed legs began to itch and heave, and flinging himself on the ground he performed a land-bound crawl with his arms, dragging his body along so fast that the official party had the greatest difficulty in keeping up with him. By evening he had traced the circle, and Countess and councillors were jubilant. As for the Duke of Saxony, his future prospects were considerably reduced.

In fact he inherited nothing, for the good Countess Emma lived for forty years after her husband's death, and knowing very well what sort of a brother-in-law she had she increased her endowments to the church and gave away almost everything she had. She actually outlived the Duke, and thus her estate and tithe passed to the Emperor Conrad, whose wife was quick to come posting to Bremen to receive what she expected to be a fortune in land and riches but proved to be little more than the title. The Duke of Saxony's son Dethmar then inherited all that could be saved from the church foundations, but he made the foolish mistake of sending armed men to hold up and rob the Emperor Henry, who was on his way to Lesum. After a bitter fight the robbers were beaten and one of them peached on Duke Dethmar. Outraged at such a true accusation, the Duke swore he would prove his innocence in trial by duel. Here again he was unfortunate, for the man selected to challenge him in single combat ran him through and killed him.

I had not expected to like Bremen. The docks and river – yes. But the city itself had had little appeal from the moment I saw a travel film designed to sell the place to American tourists. As a result I had come to think of it as a mass of night clubs and expensive restaurants and jewellers, and though I do not grudge jewellers their money or caterers the dollars they can extract from overseas visitors who believe that in Heaven the only things on the menu will be Chicken Maryland or a guaranteed nine-ounce T-bone steak, and if I even wish rabbit-club proprietors nothing more than might be supplied by a course of deep analysis, the fact remains that there is a great gulf between the world as lived from a small boat and that which is served trussed and dressed and oven-ready to the expected visitor. And this is what I had forgotten. There may well be places in Bremen, as in every city of commerce, where middle-aged men can lick their chops and eat their steaks whilst tired girls try to look cheerful on staging placed at just the right height to arouse interest, but the true Bremen is that of the

Hanseatic League, the bustling port of tobacco and cotton and honey, and the little semicircle of ancient city set at the side of the Weser where the barges lie in rows along the piles in the Tiefer. And within this enclave where the age-old Bremen has risen from its ashes there is gaiety and character, tradition and beauty, and that feeling of stolid enduring which one senses in so many cities of Europe where nothing is ever pulled down by planners but endures until fire, war, or the sheer tiredness of old age crumbles it to the ground.

Besides, even Stepney is beautiful when experienced from a boat, and the first steps ashore are an adventure. One feels like a Marco Polo in miniature, or like a Hanseatic merchant putting into a strange port where he can be sure that just because he has come peacefully by water he will be sure of a welcome. And Bremen is much better than Stepney, for if there is a town hall in that borough I am sure it is not sited over a stock of half-a-million bottles of wine.

Heine might well have been a small-boat man. Certainly he portrayed exactly the feelings of the captain of the *Thames Commodore* in the opening lines of one of his poems.

> *Happy is he who is safely in harbour,*
> *Leaving behind him the sea and its tempests*
> *And now may sit peacefully glowing with warmth*
> *In that good City Cellar of Bremen.*

Bremen's Ratskeller is famous. It is more than five-and-a-half centuries old, and the people of the city still repair to it in the evening to take a meal or a bottle of wine in the womb-like security of the vaults beneath the city hall. Not that the cellar itself is particularly uterine, for there is an immense variety of German wines to be had. The city fathers of Bremen have always taken their wine seriously, and though many of the original tuns have had to give way to more accommodation the nave and transepts of the main vaulted hall still contain four splendid casks. Two date from the 1620s, the others are a century older, and the largest would hold nearly forty thousand bottles of some specially selected vintage.

Along one side runs a row of small boxes or boudoirs where one may have a private and intimate party. No doubt the burghers still discuss matters of trade and shipping in these alcoves, but no amorous intrigues are allowed. A rule of the house forbids the doors to be closed unless the party consists of at least three members. Wine, certainly; song in moderation; but women only at arm's length.

Vast quantities of wine are stored in the cellars which extend beyond the hall itself, and one of them contains the cask of Rüdesheimer 1653, once a highly praised vintage but a wine now only served on very special occasions and in quantities small enough not to make the very important drinking personage pull too long a face – for there is a limit to the extent that hock improves with keeping. There is the Apostle cellar too, with its dozen great casks named after the Twelve, and containing other scarcely drinkable wines of the eighteenth century. Indeed the fluid within these old stagers is by now become an exceedingly concentrated and astringent acid bearing no obvious relation to wine at all.

The very vintage and veteran Rüdesheimer is, fortunately, not for sale; for if it were merely priced on the principle of taking the price per glass in 1654 and adding compound interest across the three intervening centuries the figure would run out at more than £4000 a glass. But the range of wines on the current list is formidable enough and some of them cost more than £20 a bottle and are presumably only demanded by men who are hoping to put through deals of the greatest importance and can charge a flagon or two to the firm's expenses account. The more modest wines are cheap and excellent, for the cellarers of the Ratskeller know as much about wine as any. Besides, the stock is continually turning over, and every year new purchases will be made, the cellar-master travelling to the Rhine and Moselle and other growing areas, perhaps tasting several hundred in a matter of hours before he buys a cask of this or a tun of that. During the season he will purchase about 75 thousand gallons, enough to replace the amount the Bremeners will consume out of their cellared hoard in the coming year.

Six centuries ago Bremen was already appointing a pair of wine councillors. Their post was highly honoured but the work was demanding, for it was the business of these men to supervise the whole of the wine trade in the city. They were unpaid, but as a minor perquisite each was allowed forty gallons of Rhine wine annually, and four bottles on each of the score or more of official feast-days. But if a specially desirable new vintage was to be purchased in such large quantities that the city could not provide the funds, the wine councillors were expected to put up the money themselves until such time as the amount could be paid off.

Many of those who used to spend their evenings in Bremen's Ratskeller, sipping a bottle of this good wine, another of that, a glass or two of a third and perhaps a fourth, fifth and sixth as well, would find themselves singled out as targets for the attack of the Saake. This individual was described as a '*tückisches Scheusal*', a malicious creature of horror one might say, which had the peculiar habit of hiding in doorways or round alley corners, waiting for a lift home. Invisible except for a pair of eyes which shone very much like the candles at a house door, the Saake would spring out unheard and unseen, stare its victim in the face to halt him, then leap upon his shoulders. Though without form and void the Saake was extremely heavy and the effort of carrying him would make a man sweat, mumble incoherently, and stagger until at last his legs gave way. Sometimes a citizen might fall off a quay into the Weser, but more often he collapsed senseless and awoke hours later to find a watchman or constable standing over him and shining a light in his face. Usually these officers would think that they had come upon a drunk, but the victim would quickly reassure them. No, no, it was the terrible Saake that had got him, and now that he had recovered he would like to return to the Ratskeller for just one more glass of wine to give him the courage to thread the dangerous and spook-ridden alleys on his way home to his beloved wife. One more glass. Or perhaps two. Maybe three.

The Bremeners were always realists, and their conviction that trading deals were best conducted over a glass of mellowed wine was such that they made the custom almost mandatory. Indeed, the council once passed a resolution that if two men could not bring a negotiation to an agreed conclusion they were to be locked in one of the cellars until they did so. During their incarceration they could order as much wine as they liked, but they very rightly had to pay for it.

The city also had a system of concluding agreements with others by drinking the visiting representatives under the table, a principle which still survives in international diplomacy in our own day. However, it is sad to relate that Bremen actually cheated, for when visiting ambassadors or trade attachés were known to be particularly redoubtable drinkers the council was not above importing from elsewhere men who could drink deeply and still stay upright in their chairs.

Deep in the cool vaults of the Ratskeller one is insulated from the sound of the traffic above. One may also be quite unaware that Bremen has its bells, among the more curious peals being the one consisting of thirty bells in Meissen porcelain which hang in the open above the curious thoroughfare of the Böttcherstrasse, an alley of intriguing architectural virtuosity built by Ludwig Roselius, a wealthy coffee merchant of the twentieth century. These bells tinkle three times daily to ring out sea-shanties and songs of the Weser, and ten little scenes appear one after the other, each showing a pioneer of ocean navigation by sea or by air. The Meissen chimes have a curiously refined and fairy-tea-party sound about them and naturally their sound does not carry very far – for the bells must not be struck so violently that they will shatter. But the carillon of the more orthodox bells of the Kaufmannskirche send their sombre call thundering over the roofs of the little sleeping houses of the Schnoor, the old quarter of the city now become a colony of artists and craftsmen, to wake the men on the barges upon the river. It was just nine in the morning when we flicked off the lines to continue our journey upstream, and the bells were sounding off with the ancient chorale to which Neander's great hymn is sung, *Lobe den Herrn* – Praise to the Lord, the Almighty, the King of Creation. And this they did every day.

I have always liked Neander's splendid hymn and its tremendous music. Perhaps it is the forgotten biologist in me that re-awakens in response, for if the young visionary Joachim Neander lived long enough in Bremen to be remembered in its bells, to me he is always a man with a curious prehistoric connection. Besides, he is an excellent example of how easily the academic can be misled. Even the simplest of palaeontologists is likely to know that *Tal* or *Thal* means a valley, and if the Rheintal is the Rhine Valley and the Neckartal the Neckar Valley what could be easier than to show one's erudition by telling a class of keen, note-writing university students that of course our latest ancestor *Homo neanderthalensis* was so-called because his remains were found in a cave on the banks of the river Neander? I remember dutifully writing down this piece of information as an undergraduate and I have seen the same in biology books of the highest reputation. However, the fact remains that Neander was not a river but a hymn-writer, a composer of powerful chorales.

If Neander was active in Bremen, he is perhaps even more closely connected with the gorge of that little woodland brook the Düssel, on the lower reaches of which was built the village or *Dorf* which today has become one of the most flourishing industrial communities of Western Europe. The tall office blocks of the two tube-making giants, Mannesmann and Phoenix Rheinrohr, rear up into the sky, and few recall the humble Düssel as it slips quietly through the city of half a million to empty into the Rhine. But outside the town is the cliff where the young visionary Joachim Neander would stand, shouting in exultation as the dark anvil-headed cloud of a thunderstorm swept menacingly across the Rhine plain and the vivid cracks of lightning spoke to him of the fiery chariot of the Almighty. Half a year Neander lived in that gorge, his romantic heart open to all the sights and sounds of nature. It was there that he wrote the verses of *Lobe den Herrn*, the splendid song of praise which now tolled to us over the rooftops from the Bremen church where once he had served. No wonder the gorge became known as Neander's Gulch, Neanderthal, and that the name should be transferred to the bones of those simple hominids who had lived in a cave of that same bluff, scores of thousands of years before Mannesmann and Phoenix shares were quoted for public subscription.

At Bremen the boatman crosses the line which separates the lower river from the middle, the Unterweser from the Mittelweser.

Presumably this imaginary division runs across the stream from bank to bank on the line of Bremen lock at the upper edge of the city, for it is there that the tideless water begins. Seven great locks in eighty-five miles lay before us on our way to the Mittelland Canal at Minden, and so slight was the traffic that we had most of them to ourselves. As the whole enterprise was run free of charge I had a curious feeling of guilt that we were using such an immense amount of water at no cost, each time we climbed from one step to another. But the Weser had water enough and to spare, and certainly sufficient to work a number of power stations at the weirs and to cause a stiff current swirling round the ends of the groynes which were added in the 1880s as a first step towards making the river navigable.

These groynes achieved a depth of water of one metre, enough for the small barges of that time and even for the noble passenger vessels of the period. In fact steamers had long been churning and flailing their way up the river, and as early as 1819 the *Herzog von Cambridge*, with an engine built by Boulton and Watt, huffed and puffed herself right up to Hannoversch Münden at the top of the Oberweser, hoisting sail to give an extra push whenever the wind was dead astern, and occasionally throwing a tow-line ashore to a team of horses when she thought nobody was watching.

One of the finest of these first Weser steamers was the *Wittekind*, named after the Saxon chieftain who for years led a defiant resistance against Charlemagne in the woodlands of northern Germany. She was built at Blackwall on the Thames and put in command of a certain Captain Moody, who steamed her straight across the North Sea and through the storm-swept waters of the German Bight in mid-winter – a remarkable feat for a river paddle-wheeler which, on account of the shallows above Hamelin, was built to have a draught of less than 18 inches. A few weeks later this handsome ship set out on her inaugural voyage under her new skipper, Kapitän Sägelken. She was met on her way by a ship bearing a military band, and all the guns on the battlements of Minden were fired in salute as soon as she drew near. Indeed, all who lived within range of the river streamed across the country to shout and cheer on the banks, for a steamer was still a rare sight upon the Weser.

Perhaps it was this enthusiasm which went to the skipper's head, for he seems quickly to have become careless. Before the week was out he had charged the cable of a river ferry so violently that it parted, the cut ends whipping back to the land, killing one unfortunate person who happened to be standing on the bank, and felling a second. Next he ran the ship on a shoal at such speed that her hull was bent out of true, and at another grounding a few days afterwards the bottom was stove in and the ship sank, just after the last of the 200 passengers had managed to scramble ashore with their baggage. After a few more incidents the company wisely dispensed with Sägelken's services, which were becoming too costly.

Compared with the excitements of travelling on the *Wittekind* our own voyage up the Mittelweser was uneventful. The river wound ahead through a countryside of pasture, most of which was hidden behind high banks although the cows would occasionally peer over the ramparts to watch us. Beyond the second lock at Langwedel we turned into the river Aller and headed up towards Verden two miles distant. The banks were so littered with debris that there was no possibility of drawing in to the quay used by medieval shippers, but there happened to be an excellent private harbour belonging to the Water Authority, who extended to the *Thames Commodore* their usual welcome. There we let her draw snugly alongside the ice-breaker *Hai* to be bedded down and wait for six weeks until we should return to make the swift run home to the Thames. The *Hai* (or *Shark*) was four times her size, and when we recalled the rough bumping we had had round the Mellum Plate a few months earlier it was encouraging to discover that the *Hai* had been sent down the estuary to relieve the crew of the light vessel *Weser*, and cutting round that same unpleasant sandbank she had lost the whole of her wheelhouse.

Verden has a curious connection with those famous pirates Claus Störtebeker and Godeke Michels, who terrorised the German Bight at the end of the fourteenth century and whose villainies I have described more fully in *Small Boat to Elsinore*. Michels is believed to have been a Verdener, and perhaps that is why the

Verden on the Aller

two unprincipled sea-robbers and murderers were so strangely patronising as to provide as a strange penance the money for seven great windows in the cathedral at Verden, to portray the seven deadly sins. They also made over the income from some of their properties, and the poor and also the employees of the cathedral chapter of Verden received an annual dole which was originally fixed at six herrings and six bread-rolls apiece. Even today this dole or its equivalent is dutifully paid out before the town hall, but sad to relate the windows have gone. In 1945 some fanatical S.S.-men dynamited the bridge over the Aller in an effort to hold up the pursuing British troops, and they used such an immense quantity of explosive that Verden was partially wrecked and the seven great windows with which the sea-rovers had sought to buy a ticket to heaven were shattered beyond repair.

But Verden is a pleasant town, a country market with the spires and towers of its tired old churches peeping up through the green of the trees which flank the clean, clear Aller. It boasts a stork's nest on a roof in the main street, and as the birds have unfortunately chosen a ladies' hairdressing establishment the shop doorway is protected by a wide board overhead so that a coiffure fresh from the curlers and driers will not immediately be garnished with the half-digested skeleton of a grass-snake vomited from above, or by a liberal shampoo of storky excrement. Naturally, not even a hair-dresser would be so foolish as to try to drive the birds away, for they bring not only heaps of mess but loads of good fortune. To have storks on the roof-ridge is the most classy advertisement possible and the gable itself is thereby made superior even to those near neighbours whose timbers end in the mere carved heads of horses.

These gable steeds are, I think, a relic of Odin's magical mount, the grey horse Sleipnir whose eight legs enabled him to be amphibious and to gallop over the sea as well as by land. But at Verden the head of a horse may have an extra significance, for horses are the local speciality. Further up the Aller is Celle with its state stud-farm. Indeed, the whole of the Hanoverian land is famous for its horses, particularly those of a small local breed which are excellent in show-jumping. Twice every year the town stages jumping and handling shows followed by auctions of bloodstock, and to ensure a high quality only eighty animals are selected for sale out of four hundred possible entrants. These lucky eighty are taken to Verden for a course of several weeks on such matters as how to behave and how not to lose their tempers, and prospective buyers are allowed to examine the school reports of the bright young equines. Show-riders from all over the world flock to Verden to bid for young hopefuls, and after the sales many of the creatures will start on a long journey overseas, either to make names for themselves in the Olympics and other international contests where elegance, obedience and high-horsemanship are sought after, or regrettably to disappear into the limbo of also-rans. For, unlike Sleipnir, they have to make do with only four legs apiece.

In spite of its storks and horses there is something curiously English about Verden, and it was some time before I realised that this familiarity was wrought simply by the royal arms carved over doorways, the lion and unicorn and the crown with the monogram

GvR suggesting that this was not a German town at all but a street in Windsor or Sandringham. For now the *Thames Commodore* had entered Hanoverian territory, and the George the Fifth of the monograms was George the First of England. Indeed, the Hanoverian monarchs had a surprising collection of titles. Verden has a pleasant little museum which contains replicas of various workshops and trading establishments of former times, and in the apothecary's shop I noticed a government proclamation of the eighteenth century hanging on the wall. It began with the modest announcement 'We, George the Second, by the grace of God, King of Great Britain, France and Ireland, Defender of the Faith, Duke of Brunswick and Lüneburg, Hereditary Treasurer of the Holy Roman Empire and Elector of the same, etc.'

I wondered what might possibly be covered by that neat little 'etc.', particularly when the Georges had already managed by some curious sleight of hand or of protocol to include France among their alleged dominions. But the proclamation which followed was also curious, for it shed a sinister light on life in Hanoverian lands two centuries ago. The announcement stated that because people had bought poison from apothecaries and had 'misused it for highly punishable purposes', all poisons were henceforward to be kept in a special locked cupboard, but it did not explain how this would help if the chemists were already willing to dispense arsenic and other villainous concoctions to any who wished to buy them.

We left the *Thames Commodore* on a sunny morning of September, snug in her green pyjama suit of tarpaulin. It was late in October when my wife and I returned for a quick run home to the Thames, and early one morning steered her out of Verden's peaceful harbour to let the current of the swift Aller snatch her and bear her speedily down to the Weser. There we turned left, to head upstream through the remaining five locks which lay between ourselves and Minden, rather more than one autumn day's voyage upstream.

The biography of the Mittelweser is a curious one. As early as the 1660s a canal was cut to join the rivers Oder and Spree, and this completed a through route from the Oder to the Elbe. In the following century other waterways such as the Finow Canal were built in Prussian lands, but somehow the Weser was always left out of any cross-country plans. A large river, it was still untamed in the era of the *Wittekind* and persisted as a stream which could rise dangerously during floods and yet fall a few days later to a level at which one could wade across it at many points. By the time canalising engineers had begun to busy themselves with the idea of converting the Middle and Upper Weser into a main north–south waterway the railway age had arrived, and the energetic proprietors of the smoky old locomotives of the Prussian State Railways were in a position to obstruct and defeat any plans for canalisation by threatening to undercut the shipping rates – just as they had done on the more important Moselle.

However, the notion of a major waterway to link the Rhineland with Berlin was also in the air, and as this would cross the Weser at Minden it would also connect Bremen with the Ruhr. To the German pit owners this was most attractive. Emden's port had thrived on British sea-coal until the Dortmund–Ems Canal was built, but now the sea-going vessels could be filled to the scuppers with good Ruhr coal instead. In contrast, the ports of Bremen and Bremerhaven were still wide open to the colliers of the Tyne and Tees, and as the vast stoke-holds of the new giant liners of the North German Lloyd could swallow a rich quantity of steam-coal the wise magnates did all in their power to push for the Mittelland Canal to be put in hand as quickly as possible.

Yet curiously enough this canal would probably make the Weser unnavigable. The Mittelland Canal would run for hundreds of kilometres almost on a single contour, and west of the Elbe it would cross only one stream of any size, the Middle Weser. A waterway of such length and breadth as the planned canal was certain to need a great supply of water to keep up with the evaporation from the surface and the seepage into its great length of banks. This water could only come from the Weser, and the abstraction of such a quantity from a free-flowing river could reduce the level almost to that of unnavigability. So there was the curious proposition that the act of bringing the ships to the Middle Weser would render that waterway itself almost incapable of carrying them at all.

This difficulty could only be solved by canalising the Weser itself, adding weirs and locks so that the level was kept constant and the rate of flow reduced instead. Twenty-five such barrages were to be built between Hamelin and Bremen, an undertaking so formidable and costly that many more years passed in discussions, delays, and second thoughts. However, in 1905 the Prussians decided to build the Mittelland Canal from Berlin to Hanover, a stretch which did not involve milking the Weser for water and yet would connect an important industrial area with the capital and (by way of the Elbe at Magdeburg) with Hamburg. The Weser, by now somewhat improved by its groynes, was left out of the plans altogether.

The First World War quickly put an end to schemes for extending the waterways, but after the collapse in 1918 Prussia was faced with the demobilisation of millions for whom there was no work, and the government decided to employ many of them in digging the continuation of the Mittelland Canal from Hanover westwards to its present junction with the Dortmund–Ems canal. Inevitably this development was opposed with all the steam the railway directors could engender, but eventually the Mittelland Canal was completed, a fine waterway which leapt the Weser on a long aqueduct at Minden. The water to feed the canal was pumped out of the river to the higher level, and the Middle Weser itself was bled of its own sustenance. Ships sailed over the aqueduct, but on the lower level traffic was almost limited to timber rafts and small half-laden barges.

The fairy godfather who was to restore the fortunes of the Weser was Hitler. Unemployment was high in the early 1930s, and with the encouragement of Bremen and the shipping interests the finance ministry was persuaded to make money available to employ some of the surplus labour in beginning the canalisation, not with twenty-five barrages but with the few larger ones which now exist. New plans were made, and work began on three of the dams. Then came the Second World War, and the Middle Weser works were abandoned.

However, by 1942 when the works were suspended some cuts had already been made and the barrage at Petershagen was half built. These initial works had cost 39 million marks and it seemed foolish to let such an investment run to ruin. When prosperity returned in the 1950s the plans were taken up again, and within ten years the canalisation was complete. The Middle Weser was open to shipping, not just for rafts and small privateers but for the heavy inland craft which could pound along the level of the Mittelland Canal.

I had not expected the Middle Weser to be a spectacular piece of river, so I was not surprised to find that the stream curved to and fro between half-forgotten hamlets and meadows where cows watched the passing boats with a suspicion inherited from their pre-canalisation forebears. Seagulls penetrated as far inland as the broad reaches above the locks – though this was perhaps not so surprising when one considered that they also followed the ferries plying on the Lake of Constance, more than one thousand kilometres up from the mouth of the Rhine. Maybe there would have been storks in the summer, but on this late October day when the *Thames Commodore* plugged up the river from its confluence with the Aller the landscape belonged to herons and peewits, which seemed to have staked a claim to the whole of the pasture-land and the belts of meadow between the banks and the water's edge. Heavy laden the barges would glide past, blue-flagging each other to pass starboard-wise instead of the more usual port-to-port, but the herons would do no more than raise one foot like ladies hesitating before the shop windows of autumn sales.

The morning began with a curious and faint wind, a draught so warm that it might have been the Föhn of the Alps. The sun shone too, but the heat came from the air beneath a clear sky. Slowly the firmament became more opaque, and as it did so the breath of air developed into a fresh breeze, then a strong wind. Continually it increased, without ever pausing unless to send a fierce gust to skim the surface as a harbinger of what was to come. This variable wind was no hazard on such a river, for the lock-cuts had been put between high banks topped with thickets and crowned with a mixed line of birch and poplar, but I was surprised to see that the wavelets of our wake were now becoming whipped by the wind to lose their caps and send a shower of droplets skimming over the water. I had rarely if ever seen this happen on an embanked river,

and as the wind was growing from strength to strength I fetched
up the ventimeter which had been given to the *Thames Commodore*
by one of her young admirers. It was a beautifully simple instru-
ment, and for that reason quite accurate. Turned to the wind it
showed that even below the river banks we could measure force 8,
a formidable strength for such a position. Ah well, I thought, this
is pleasant enough, and it adds variety to the surface of an otherwise not very remarkable river; but I also began to understand why
the herons with their slow flight and huge wing span preferred to
stand among the rushes than fly aloft.

Beyond Dörverden lock we steamed out into another long and
curving reach, and when the course lay straight down wind for
nearly a quarter of a mile I was surprised to find that the waves at the
further end were nearly two feet high, coursing along the river
with a surging sound such as one might hear when lying in bed at a
shingle-beached seaside resort at the receiving end of a storm. We
were outstripping the waves, and as we cut them with our stem
they leapt up in delight and sent their water to jump on the fore-
deck and take a ride aboard us. The ventimeter held to point
astern was now clocking 38 knots with occasional gusts of a higher
figure.

Soon the river ahead of us simply disintegrated. There was still
plenty of water in the bed, but even before our stem cut its tension
the surface was snatched off and flung to the port bank in an
obliterating curtain of water as thick as a snowstorm. Again I tried
the ventimeter, and now its disc soared up the spindle to strike the
roof of the measure and stay there, running off the scale at 56
knots, or force 10 on Admiral Beaufort's useful scale. It was hard
enough for me to remain seated on the steering stool, and in spite
of her weight of steel the *Thames Commodore* leaned over as though
bowing to the spirit of the wind.

The river now curved round to starboard until we faced the
wind, and as we chopped the breaking waves the gale lifted them
to fly right over the saloon and windshield, leaping clear of the
after-deck and dinghy to land hissing in the river astern. It was an
impressive but a beautiful sight, and one I had never met before –
but then I had never been on the water in quite such a gale.

Autumn leaves, yellow and fading, were torn from the trees and went skimming over our heads. A branch of a tree on the left bank sailed through the air like the discarded broomstick of a witch and landed on the other shore. With a soft splash of white and ochre a batch of seagull excrement struck the windshield and spread out like a coloured ink-blot test. I looked up to identify the originating bird, but although I scanned the sky ahead for more than a mile there was no gull to be seen. The lump of dung might have been flying horizontally down the gale for many a mile before it happened to strike us, for the same high wind was in fact uprooting trees, exploding tiled roofs and overturning cars all across the country. Our ventimeter was not designed for such extremes, but the meteorological report next day told us that at times the wind speed had reached 70 knots in the eleventh notch of the Beaufort measure – when, according to the data supplied with the ventimeter 'the air is full of spray; breaking rollers and high wind cause damage to deck fittings', and if we had been on the open sea (which fortunately we were not) we should have been able to see 'the edges of the wave crests blown into froth'. And all this at surface level, not at the 33-foot height above the ground, where the meteorologists took their data because the wind speed there was about one-third higher.

A wind of this strength was certain to cause strange phenomena, even on a river. The few barges we met were being wonderfully washed down by the water we threw at them by breaking the last thread of surface tension which held the river together at all, but the real surprise came when Miriam went below to bring up a tray of coffee. She had hardly reached the galley before she came hurrying on deck to take the wheel. I must go at once to the galley and watch, she said mysteriously.

Handing over, I went below. There in the galley was a miniature Versailles, for in the centre of the sink there came and went a pretty little *jet d'eau*, a fountain which rose up above the edge of the basin and then subsided to await another gust before leaping again. We were nearly beam to the wind, and such was the force of the gale that it could drive the Middle Weser right up our waste-pipe to gambol in the ornamental pool of stainless steel, dancing in the

sheer exuberance of its freedom and entertaining us with its frolics
and with the thought that we were lucky not to be sailing the
storm-tossed waters of the estuary or rounding the bleak, wind-
riven dune and marshland of the Mellum Plate.

X

Thames Commodore homeward bound – night over Dorsten – from Emmerich to Bruges – the springtime of life

THE wind which whipped the top from our wake and blew it as a driving horizontal rain to smack the worried cows about their rumps could not keep up its strength for ever, and before we reached Minden it had blown itself out. Only the fallen trees, felled telegraph wires, and roofs with bare and slateless patches remained to show that the countryside of Lower Saxony which now lay bathed in the quiet golden warmth of a late October sun had only a few hours earlier been almost blown away.

It was six years since I had last been through the deep lock at Minden which covers in one bound of more than forty feet the leap from the Weser below to the Mittelland Canal above, six years since the old *Commodore* had chugged patiently along that contour waterway which skirts the edge of the gentle Wiehengebirge but passes through no place at all. During the interval the canal had been widened along much of its length, but the greater difference was in the shipping. On the earlier occasion we had met or passed only West German craft, with perhaps a rare Dutchman on his way to some improbable destination, but now the iron curtain had been lowered as far as barges were concerned and we were in the company of East Germans and of Poles. Every hour or so we would overhaul another of the broad-beamed ships with the red and white ensign, a barge from Wroclaw or Bydgoscz – places better known to most as Breslau and Bromberg. They led us all the way to Rotterdam, bringing for export the rich grain harvest of the Polish plains.

Not one of these eastern ships had a name of its own. Instead there was a national number painted on the stern and superstructure, for in a people's democracy even a barge must be stripped of its individuality. Babies, I thought, would soon be registered with numerals only. Yet the men who steered the curtain-craft on their way were just as any other barge captains – friendly, unhysterical men who liked to spend the evening over a glass of wine in the *Anker* or the *Schiff*. And they must have been either politically contented with their lot or domestically tied to their homelands, for no great effort was needed to reach political asylum. They were made fast to West German quaysides every night, free to come and go as they wished.

Since first the *Thames Commodore* had taken the water we had planned our disjointed voyages in such a way that when she crossed the Channel her outward run was about the period of the spring equinoctial gales and her departure from France or Belgium toward the Thames usually fell at the time when a genial October was being kicked out of the calendar by a rude and forceful November. On average, these periods are not the smoothest times of the year for a crossing but she liked a frolic and she had never yet been held up by the weather. However, I remembered a rather bumpy crossing we had once had aboard the old *Commodore*, when we left Ramsgate with two bottles of milk and reached Boulogne with half a pound of some of the best cheese I had ever tasted, and I hoped that if we now raced hard for the Channel coast we might reach it before the next storm arrived. Instead of taking the canals slowly, on this occasion we would allow her only the briefest halts to buy bread and diesel fuel. Otherwise she was to keep her mind on the business of getting home. So, with the whole length of the pretty Mittelland Canal behind her in one day, the next evening saw her chugging cautiously in the early dark toward her third huge lock in the Wesel–Datteln Canal, the busy but not unattractive waterway which links the Rhine with the Dortmund–Ems north of the Ruhr. At six next morning she was already bearing down upon Dorsten, just as the first streaks of orange purple announced the translucent dawn of another perfect autumn day of clear, windless skies and warm sunshine.

Dorsten is a place of chemical engineering, and it may be a dismal place in which to live, though doubtless the pay is good.

Nobody would consider it beautiful unless perhaps they happened to glide past its harbour in the early hours of an autumn morning, a delight reserved to the *Thames Commodore* and her companions of Bydgoscz and Wroclaw. Then the long pennant trail of weird smoke from the thin and stately lip-edged chimney cuts a band of dark brown between the stars set in the greens and mauves of the coming dawn, and the sodium lights on their thin curved standards lean over the quays as though their only thought is to produce the deep-piled yard-broad carpet runners of gold to converge upon a passing ship and break into a heaving confusion of broken fiery orange upon the waves thrown out by her stem. Sulking and sleepy, the jib of a powerful crane is at rest, motionless, almost horizontal, the hook dangling free, the cables just visible where they cut the dimness. Below it the ships are still, each with a little white light that watches through the night. The gleaming retorts and tubes of the process plant catch the separate gleams of these little lamps and convert them into horizontal dashes. Beyond, the offices are flooded with the cold bath of mercury vapour light as the chars sweep and polish before the new day begins. There is not a sound from Dorsten, not yet. It lies there in all the improbable beauty of a prospect unknown to the landsman. A momentary glimpse between the harbour walls, down past the ranged tanker-wagons of chemicals waiting their turn to unload, and then it is gone. The rheostat of sunrise turns up the lighting and the first long shadows of morning fall across the Wesel–Datteln Canal. Three more great guillotine locks to the Rhine. By midday we shall be surging over the wash of the hurrying barge fleets of Europe's greatest river.

Emmerich – whenever I see that name on the destination plate of a continental express I wonder what it means to the travellers. Probably no more than an opening of the carriage door, a quick look at the passports, a half-salute as the official moves on down the train. Emmerich as a real place probably has no existence for the traveller by train – and rightly so, for it is a town interested only in shippers and their needs. All day the big transports of the Rhine drop anchor off the waterfront and the launches of the customs men dash perilously between them. Bakers and grocers, clearance agents and fuelling men bob in and out of the moored armada to sell and carry and fetch. Never for a moment is the Rhine at rest, for all through the night new arrivals are chugging to a halt in the broad stream to wait for customs clearance next morning. A stroke on the bell, a shout, a churning of the propeller, and a clatter and splash as another anchor goes down to the good holding ground of the Rhine bed.

The *Thames Commodore* was not inclined to wait for officialdom to stir. Before light she was away, slipping out of the harbour to gallop down to Lobith in the Netherlands and swing in to the jetty, so that we might scramble quickly ashore and push under the door of the German customs office a polite note saying that we had come and gone and wished them good-day. Nodding to a couple of sleepy young Dutch officers we jumped back aboard and headed out into the stream again. Having nothing to detain us any longer in the Netherlands we sped across that country without either going ashore or spending a dubbeltje, and next morning we were chugging up the broad ship canal towards Ghent and the waterway to Bruges.

There is no place quite like Bruges to spend one of the last nights of a voyage. The smell of its water is never forgotten, but the sheer loveliness of the approach from Ghent in the fading light of evening is ample compensation. The canal cuts round the city through the moat, and on the ancient mounded ramparts two of the windmills, survivors from the Middle Ages, still stand as they have done for centuries. In the town itself there is hardly a house which has not some exquisite feature of its own – the trade-sign cut in the brickwork, a brass door-knocker in the shape of a fish, the little hoist protruding from the gable or perhaps a niche in which a saint or virgin whose features have almost disappeared under the repeated whitewash of time will be lit at night with a flickering candle. And down beyond the Béguinage through the door of which the hunted would flee for asylum, the city swans glide on the Lake of Love, wondering why the little trip boats have stopped so early in the season and there are no more visitors with zoom lenses and bread crusts. Not that bread is short, for these swans are a permanent charge on the bakers of the city, who each day must in turn provide the levy of fifty rolls, casting their bread upon the waters to feed the hungry long-necks which their fore-fathers were ordered to keep for ever as a reminder of what they did to Pieter Langhals (or Longneck), the lieutenant of the Emperor Maximilian. Langhals had invented the rack, and the men of Bruges tried it out on him, pulling him apart – a very proper fate one might think if one was not an Emperor in need of such a ruthless assistant.

Bruges at the turn of autumn to winter is lovelier than perhaps at any other time, and if I had to spend a year or two in prison I would hope to be in the gaol of Bruges and hear filtering into the cold solitude of my tight-barred cell those chimes from the belfry tower of the rich woolmen of long ago. But still the voyage is in-complete, the *Thames Commodore* is anxious to reach her home river, and at the first opening of the swing bridge in early morning she must be away.

All across Westphalia, down the Rhine, through the great Dutch delta and across Belgium we basked in the heat of still October days. At night the stars would shine down clear and unabashed from a dark firmament of sky, winking to us through the bare treetops which cast a mesh of lace between them and us. The late moon glistened upon the myriad crystals of the hoar frost upon our cabin roof, promising us another brilliant day to come. It was won-derful cruising weather such as late October can so often provide, and we reached Calais ahead of the storm as I had hoped. But not by enough margin. The first sudden blast struck the Bassin Carnot about forty seconds after our arrival. Soon the wind had increased to gale, then strong gale. Miriam set off for home in the packet boat and I walked down to the pierhead to watch the *Invicta* through my glasses until she passed out of the lee of Cap Gris Nez. I saw her turn a little, and the very first free-running wave from beyond the headland sent up such a shower of water when she struck it that her whole bulk disappeared in the spray. There would not be a big queue for lunch, I thought. Nor would the *Thames Commodore* be leaving on the next tide.

Alone, I settled down to work for a few days at a quayside near the town hall which is such an excellent landmark for mariners. I had always thought the building hideous, but now it began to grow upon me. Turrets, angels, gargoyles, red brick and slate, dormer windows, there was not a fixture or fitting known to builders of the period which the architect had not introduced, and usually in quantity. Yet there was something appealing about its sheer eccentricity, and the same character was continued inside the building also. There were designs illustrating the ejection of the villainous English but there was also an excellent room for marriages, with diaphanous maidens and pastoralia to remind young couples that 'Youth is the springtime of life. Spring is the youth of the year'. And Rodin's Burghers of Calais, cold but brave upon their pedestal among the wind-blown leaves across the courtyard, seemed to bow their heads in agreement. It was winter now, and they were bent and aged.

But the *Thames Commodore* was still in her youth, the springtime of her adventurings. This year had taken her to Sweden, and back through the lands of the Hansa. Another summer was not so far away and as I sat in the docks of Calais I wondered where she would like to go next. The Camargue perhaps, or the lakes of Värmland. Or to Bavaria, where her predecessor had so enjoyed a summer voyage. I was still considering the matter when I realised that the storm was passing. I walked over to the café and phoned my son-in-law to come over on the early morning packet.

For a November morning the sea was reasonably calm. The white horses had collapsed from the sheer exhaustion of four days non-stop racing. The heavy steel lifting bridge at the dock entrance whined and rose slowly to tilt on its heels, the signal flashed green to let us pass out to the fore-harbour. Clear as a pillar of cloud by day we could see Dover Castle beckoning to us as we ran out past the pier-heads of Calais. Two hours and ten minutes later our little ship was passing close beside the familiar red shape of the South Goodwin lightship, the first outlying bastion of her own homeland of England. Soon she was up to the Thames, following where the men of Hamburg and Bremen and Lübeck had carried the flag of the Hansa long ago. It was dark before she reached the City of London, sweeping on the tide to pass the Tower, the fine fortress

which was already guarding the river when the Easterlings
opened their trading depot at the foot of Dowgate and brought to
London some of the spirit of mercantile enterprise and adventure
which still hangs over its quays today.

INDEX OF NAMES

*(For ease of reference people and legendary creatures or beings are
listed in italics)*

Aabenraa, x
Abel, King, 21, 22, 25, 28, 29, 33
Abidjan, 176
Adolf IV, Duke of Holstein, 85–6
Aerø, xi
Alfred the Great, 52
Aller, R., 193, 195, 196
Als, x, xi, 9
Alster, R., 82
Altmark, 89
Amsterdam, 51, 83
Anglia, 9
Anselm, 3
Ansgar, 48, 51, 53
Ardennes, the, 50
Aruba, 176
Audorfersee, 70
Aue, R., 171
Ausonius, 11, 13, 55
Aussig, 90

Baghdad, 39
Baltic, ix, 10
Bardowick, 154–5
Beaufort, Admiral, 200
Bederkesa, 171
Beowulf, 12, 13
Berlin, 197, 198
Bergen, 142, 149, 151, 158
Birka, 39, 48, 51, 52, 53
Blankenese, 82, 162
Bremen, 158, 174, 177, 178–9, 181 ff., 197, 198
Bremen, Bishop of, 125, 126
Bremerhaven, 169, 171, 173, 175, 177–8
Breslau (Wroclaw), 203
Bromberg (Bydgoscz), 203
Bruges, 127, 142, 206–7
Brunsbüttelkoog, 76–7
Brussels, 127
Bülk Point, 59
Busdorf, 38
Byzantium, 39

CANALS:
Alsterfleet, 85
Bederkesa–Geeste, 171
Dortmund–Ems, 198, 204
du Midi, 100
Eider, 115
Elbe–Trave, 89, 113, 115–16, 136
Ems–Jade, 171
Finow, 196
Gieselau, 75
Hadelner, 169, 170–1

Kiel, 14, 39, 40, 59, 67, 70, 75, 77, 115
Mittelland, 107, 192, 198, 204
Regent's, ix, 69, 169
Stecknitz, 95–6, 98, 100–8, 111, 114–15, 123, 149
Wesel–Datteln, 204–5
Zollkand, 85
Cap Gris Nez, 207
Celle, 195
Charlemagne, 50, 139–40
Childers, Erskine, 2, 61
Christopher I, King of Denmark, 33
Conrad, Emperor, 186
Constance, Lake, 199
Cooper, John, 56, 58
Corinth, 47
Corvey, 48, 51
Cuxhaven, 81, 162, 163, 164, 175

Dalldorf, 116
Dannevirke, 41
Danzig, 39
Delvenau, 95, 98, 100–2, 110, 111, 115–16, 119, 120
Dethmar, Duke, 186
Doerflinger, Fred, 70
Donnerschleuse, 136
Dordrecht, 83
Dorestad, 44, 52, 53
Dorsten, 204–5
Dörverden, 200
Doughty, H.M., 154, 156, 171
Dover, 208
Dowgate, 209
Dragomir, Queen (Dagmar), 16
Dükkerschleuse, 116, 120
Düssel, R., 191

Easterlings, 143, 209
Eckernförde Bight, 25
Edward the Confessor, 143
Eider, R., 40, 48, 70, 72, 73, 74
Ekke Nekkepen, x
Elbe, R., 8, 52, 77, 81, 82, 84, 87 ff., 152, 153, 156, 162, 163, 167, 170, 196
Elsinore, x
Engel, Siegfried, 160, 161, 162, 164, 174
Emma, Countess, 186
Emmerich, 205
Ernst of Saxe-Coburg-Gotha, 161
Erik Plough-Penny, 16–21, 29, 54
Eulenspiegel, Till, 124–30

Faaborg, x

Flensburg, 14, 15, 33, 65
Francius, Ludwig, 178
Frederick, the Great, 10, 89
Fyn, x, 15

Geeste, R., 171, 172–3
Geesthacht, 92–3, 152
George, St, 144
Gerhard I, Duke of Holstein, 86
German Bight, 9, 81, 117, 165, 167, 169, 174, 177, 192
Glückstadt, 77, 79
Goedzak, Lamme, 127
Gothenburg, 84
Gottorp, 41
Gottorp, Dukes of, 30
Gottrik, King, 41, 42
Gottschalk, King, 145
Gray, Thomas, 84
Grosse Breite, 13, 22, 23, 46–7
Gudmundsen, Lauge, 18
Gunnar, 46

Haddeby (Haithabu), 20, 27, 33, 38–9, 40, 41, 45, 48–9, 51–4, 65, 81, 145
Haddeby Noor, 42, 47, 54
Hamburg, 52, 69, 77, 79, 82–3, 90, 92, 113, 114, 115, 142, 151, 163, 167, 168, 179
Hamelin, 192, 198
Hanover, 93, 198
Hanoverian monarchs, 196
Hansa, 149, 151
Harald Bluetooth, King, 46
Harald the Hard, King, 53–4
Heine, Heinrich, 187
Henry the Lion, Duke, 138–40
Herrenwik, 151
Hildegund, 184
Hindenburg, General, 118, 119
Hitler, Adolf, 198
Hochdonn, 76
Hollingstedt, 43
Holm, 30–7, 54
Holstein, 32, 72, 97, 116, 136, 152, 169
Holstein, Dukes of, 3, 17, 72, 73
Holtenau, 68, 79, 152
Horich the Elder, King, 48
Horich the Younger, King, 48
Hovi, 48
Hummer, Wessel, 19–20

Ibrahim ibn Ahmed, 51, 56
Ide, Joanna, 56
Ijsselmeer, 81
Ilmenau, R., 95, 152, 154, 157
Isle of Dogs, ix
Itzehoe, 33

Johann I, Duke of Holstein, 86
Jutland, 52

Kappeln, xi, 3, 7–9, 10–11, 14, 25, 54, 55, 57
Kattegat, 39, 52
Kiel, 2, 14, 24, 40, 55, 57, 58, 59, 85, 160
Kiel fiord, 52, 62
Kieler Bucht, xi, 5
Kleine Breite, 22

Kneitlingen, 125
Knigge, Freiherr von, 184
Knight, E. F., 7, 12
Königsburg, 16, 22
Krieseby, 14
Krummesse, 136–7
Kruto, 145
Kuwait, 176

Laboe, 24, 60, 61, 62, 66, 68
Langhals, Pieter, 207
Languedoc, 50
Langwedel, 193
Lauenburg, 77, 93, 98, 99, 112, 114, 115, 133, 152, 154, 156
Leningrad, 69
Lesum, Countess of, 185
Lindaunis, 11, 14, 16
London, 7, 84, 110, 142
Luba, 145
Lübeck, 39, 54, 56, 69, 96, 98, 99, 109–10, 112, 113, 114, 115, 137–8, 142, 145, 149, 150–1, 157, 177
Ludendorff, General, 118
Lüneburg, 93, 110, 151, 153, 155, 156–7, 158, 159
Luxembourg, 133

Mackensen, Field-Marshal von, 118
Mälar lake, 39, 51
Maasholm, 6–7, 11, 30, 32
Madingley, 62
Magdeburg, 90, 107
Maguinness, Juliet, 56
Main, R., 51
Mann, Thomas, 150
Marco Polo, 187
'*Margaret, Black*', 33, 34
Marken, 7
Maximilian, Emperor, 207
Mecklenburg lakes, 152
Medem, R., 167
Mellum, 167, 193
Melnik, 90
Mersey, R., 71
Michels, Godeke, 193
Minden, 192, 197, 198, 203
Missunde, 18–19, 22, 54
Mölln, 110, 120–4, 128, 129, 136, 152
Möllner See, 110, 120
Moody, Captain, 192
Möweninsel, 27
Morand, General, 158–9
Moselle, R., ix, 56, 97, 188, 197
Müllenhoff, Prof., 77
Mynnaesby, 3, 5, 7

Napoleon, 90, 115, 158, 159
Nasser, President, 80
Neander, Joachim, 190–1
Nelson, Lord, 5
Neu Zweedorf, 118
Neuwerk, 163, 175
Nicholas, St, 122, 150
Nore, the, ix
Notodden, 142
Novgorod, 39, 142, 149, 158

Nürnberg, 123–4

Oder, R., 196
Odin, 136, 172, 195
Offa, King, 72–4
Ohthere, 52
Olpenitz, 3
Øresund, 53
Osterrönfeld, 72
Otterndorf, 162, 163, 164, 166–7, 168, 169

Paris, 50
Petershagen, 198
Pompeii, 41
Pontoppidan, Bishop, 49

Råå, 56
Ramsgate, ix
Ratiu, Indrei, 56–7
Rendsburg, 14, 69, 70, 71, 72, 74
Reric, 41
Reval, 149
Reynaud, 50
Rieseby, 14–15
Rhine, R., 49, 86, 89, 90, 188, 205
Riga, 68, 149, 151
Rimbert, 49–50, 51, 52, 53
Rodin, Auguste, 208
Roggenbuk, 143–5
Roland, 179, 184
Roselius, Ludwig, 190
Rotterdam, 82, 163
Rügen, 145
Ruhr, 65, 197, 204
Runcorn, 71

Sägelken, Kapitän, 192
Saxony, Duke of, 111
Scheer, Admiral, 62
Scharhörn, 163
Schlei, R., x, xi, 1–21, 36, 40, 42, 48, 55, 57, 58, 160
Schleimünde, 2, 3, 5, 7, 59
Schleswig, 14, 19, 22, 24, 28–29, 30, 32, 54, 55, 56, 57, 59
Schleswig-Holstein, x, 2
Shaw, George Bernard, 131–5
Sieseby, 13, 14
Sievers, Mars, 72
Skagen, 39–40
Skaggerak, 131–5
Skeaf, 12–13
Skåne, 112, 149, 151
Skaw, 39
Skild, 12–13
Sleipnir, 195

Smid, Johann, 177
Soltwedel, Alexander von, 142
Somme, R., 51
Sønderborg, 65
Sonning Mill, 157
Spree, R., 196
Stade, 81
Stalin, Josef, 135
Störtebeker, Claus, 193
Stör, R., 33
Stockholm, 39, 158
Sundsacker, 11

Teddington, ix
Thames, R., ix, 67, 153, 178, 208
Thor, 136
Thurbar, James, 134
Tiberius, Emperor, 77
Trave, R., 93, 95, 137, 138, 142, 145, 149, 150
Travemünde, 137, 142, 144, 145, 151
Treene, R., 40, 41, 50
Tortosa, 51
Tirpitz, Admiral von, 119

Ulsnis, 15–16
Urk, 7
Utrecht, 44

Valdemar II, King, 16, 85
Van Gogh, Vincent, 155
Venice, 83
Verden, 193, 194, 196
Verdun, 49
Viborg, 52
Visby, 110

Wakenitz, R., 95, 145
Wends, 42, 52, 54, 66, 145
Wermund the Wise, 72–3, 74
Weser, 23
Weser, Burg, 23
Weser, R., 48, 51, 169
Wiehengebirge, 203
'Willie, Little', 118
Willibrord, 48
Windsor, 36
Witmar, 53
Wittenberge, 93
Wittorf, 153, 154
Witzeeze, 108, 116, 119, 120
Wroclaw, 203, 205
Wulfstan, 52

Zweedorf, 116
Zwijn, R., 127